FAITHFUL MAN

FAITHFUL MAN

365
DEVOTIONS
FOR LIVING IN
FAITHLESS TIMES

BARBOUR
PUBLISHING

© 2024 by Barbour Publishing, Inc.

Entries written by Glenn Hascall and Josh Mosey. Editorial assistance by Elijah Adkins.

ISBN 978-1-63609-915-6

Cover Design: Greg Jackson, Thinkpen Design

Published by Barbour Publishing, Inc., 1810 Barbour Drive, Uhrichsville, Ohio 44683,
www.barbourbooks.com

Our mission is to inspire the world with the life-changing message of the Bible.

Member of the
Evangelical Christian
Publishers Association

Printed in China.

FAITHFUL MAN: 365 DEVOTIONS FOR LIVING IN FAITHLESS TIMES

Masculinity has come under fire in recent years, but the world needs Christian men like never before. *Faithful Man: 365 Devotions for Living in Faithless Times* celebrates men, the ones who pray boldly to God, speak truthfully to culture, and serve sacrificially in their families, churches, and communities.

Each entry encourages you to "be the man"—the man who

- stands strong
- runs for the prize
- hears God's call
- captures thoughts
- chooses meekness
- welcomes the impossible
- lives by God's principles
- seeks the kingdom
- and performs dozens of other bold, God-honoring tasks.

You'll be challenged and encouraged to fill your God-given role in your home, your workplace, your community, and your world.

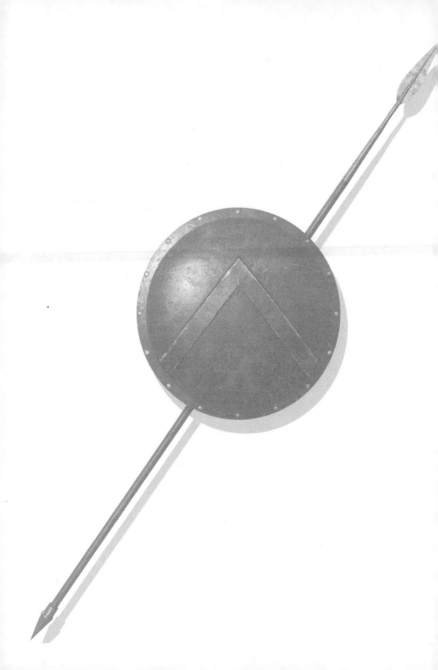

DAY 1

BE THE MAN WHO STEPS UP

Again a message came to me from the LORD: "Son of man, give the people of Israel this message: In the day of my indignation, you will be like a polluted land, a land without rain. Your princes plot conspiracies just as lions stalk their prey. . . . Your priests have violated my instructions and defiled my holy things. . . . Even common people oppress the poor, rob the needy, and deprive foreigners of justice. I looked for someone who might rebuild the wall of righteousness that guards the land. I searched for someone to stand in the gap in the wall so I wouldn't have to destroy the land, but I found no one."

EZEKIEL 22:23–26, 29–30 NLT

God was on a mission to put righteousness back into focus. He knew that the only way things were going to improve would be if He stepped in—all His other candidates had stepped back.

You might think your response would have been different. Perhaps you believe you would have been a courageous man who unwaveringly followed God's leading. That's easier said than done.

Stepping up to follow God means experiencing a lot of "what ifs" and "how abouts." It means intentionally walking away from who you've been and moving toward wherever God is. Stepping up doesn't come naturally: it takes active engagement in training and a willingness to lead others just as you are led by God.

As a Christian, you must realize that standing in the gap is part of your job description—waiting fearfully in the crowd was never an option. You were *designed* to be courageous. But a man of courage will never succeed if he thinks his courage is found in himself.

Your feet were meant to walk with God.

How have you attempted to stand in the gap in the past? What can you do today to help God rebuild your culture's wall of righteousness?

DAY 2

BE THE MAN WHO LIVES BEYOND THE CRUEL

Their lives became full of every kind of wickedness, sin, greed, hate,
envy, murder, quarreling, deception, malicious behavior, and gossip.
ROMANS 1:29 NLT

You could take some time right now to set this book down and read the latest news instead. You could dwell on the tragedies and determine that the state of the world is cruel, disheartening, and. . .well. . .awful.

You could do these things. . .but why would you? After all, the news cycle is pretty predictable. It's just a summary of Romans 1:29—all the stuff that no one wants to see, just in a new package each day.

The more time you spend with this kind of news to the exclusion of God's good news, the more strength is leached from your internal storehouse. When the bad news gets a higher spot on your priority list than the Bible's encouraging words, you'll miss the joyful infusion that only God can give.

You could take a spiritual bath in cruelty, or you could be restored, replenished, and refreshed by good news, which leads to new strength. Even when it seems like the latest inhumanity demands your full attention, you have the choice to live beyond the cruel. To reach beyond wickedness. To survive without the gossip. The choice is simple. . .but often overlooked.

God's Word doesn't pass on faulty intel. It never requires a retraction or alteration. So when your cruel culture seems more menacing than inviting, make the better choice! God's strength is always available—and it's the only way to get by in a Romans 1:29 world.

How can news suppress your inner strength?
Why can God's Word have the opposite effect?

BE THE MAN WHO'S PURPOSEFULLY FAITHFUL

Good planning and hard work lead to prosperity,
but hasty shortcuts lead to poverty.
PROVERBS 21:5 NLT

As a rule, people don't drift toward success. If life is a river, success is always upstream. We won't get there by floating along. We must go against the flow.

The first step to becoming purposefully faithful is knowing what success looks like. Only when we have a destination can we be intentional about getting there.

The world measures success in terms of money, personal accomplishments, and possessions. It measures worth by the number of friends we have on social media and how we look physically. Worldly success compares people to other people. Achieving by the world's standards does require good planning and hard work—but when our lives are over, this world's adoration will be meaningless as we stand before God.

Don't waste time comparing yourself with other people. To see if we are moving toward success, we must compare ourselves to our Creator. Do we value what God values? Do we love as God loves? Do we forgive like God forgives? When people look at us, do they see God clearly?

As with worldly achievements, true biblical success also requires a plan and hard work. Not only will we go against the flow of the world's definition of success, we'll have to fight our own inclinations toward laziness, selfishness, and pride.

Living intentionally means wading upstream, step by step, motivated by God's love within us. It means making time to read God's Word and pray. Then we can move forward with confidence, avoiding the pull of the river's flow on our feet.

There are no shortcuts to becoming a purposefully faithful man . . .only the next step in the right direction.

How intentional are you in Bible reading and prayer? Are there areas in which you are drifting instead of moving upstream?

BE THE MAN WHO REMEMBERS WHAT HE'S LEARNED

My son, do not forget my teaching, but keep my commands in your heart, for they will prolong your life many years and bring you peace and prosperity. Let love and faithfulness never leave you; bind them around your neck, write them on the tablet of your heart. Then you will win favor and a good name in the sight of God and man.

PROVERBS 3:1–4 NIV

Education must be important. Otherwise, why would we spend twelve of our formative childhood years attending school? After learning to read, write, and find the value of *x*, we now use most of those skills daily. However, while a scholastic education is important, our spiritual education is even more so.

Peace, prosperity, love, and faithfulness; these things rarely result from traditional education. Instead, we learn them as we spend time with the source of all peace, prosperity, and love. And as we experience God's faithfulness to us, we learn to be faithful to Him.

What does this spiritual education look like? Sometimes, lessons stick the most when God allows us to make mistakes. Getting ourselves into a mess helps us recognize our need for Him. Fortunately, there's a safer way to learn: by reading and memorizing God's Word, applying it in our daily lives, spending time in prayer, praising God, and bringing our needs before Him.

It's never too late for a faithful man to begin his education. When it comes to spiritual matters, we're always in our formative years. And when we learn the lessons of holiness, we'll have success with both God and man.

How seriously are you taking your spiritual education?
What lesson might God be teaching you at this moment?

DAY 5

BE THE MAN WHO ADMITS WEAKNESS

"Pardon me, my lord," Gideon replied, "but how can I save Israel?
My clan is the weakest in Manasseh, and I am the least in my family."
JUDGES 6:15 NIV

When Gideon explained to God that he was the weakest in an already weak family, God essentially told him, "I know. But you don't need your strength when you have Mine!"

God's messenger angels addressed Gideon as a "mighty warrior." That's why Gideon insisted that there must've been a mistake. But God doesn't make mistakes. Gideon would need to come to terms with the fact that his personal self-assessment was no longer the truth.

Judges 6–7 goes on to describe what God did with this "weak" man. When Gideon raised thirty-two thousand soldiers to defeat a national enemy, God said that this was too many. So He started thinning the pack. If any soldier was afraid, God gave him permission to leave.

Ten thousand remained. But to God, this was *still* too many. If Gideon went to war with ten thousand men, people might overlook the fact that God was the true deliverer.

In the end, only three hundred men remained—an army with zero chance for success unless God stepped in. And He did.

By admitting weakness, Gideon made a great decision. By avoiding the false idea that God helps those who help themselves, he became eligible for God's assistance.

The strength you need won't just bubble up from some internal artesian well. True strength comes solely from God. Stop looking for it elsewhere.

Why is it important for God to display His strength in your weakness?
How can you let God know He is welcome to work through you?

BE THE MAN WHO WEARS GOD'S ARMOR

Therefore, put on every piece of God's armor so you will be able to resist the enemy in the time of evil. Then after the battle you will still be standing firm.
EPHESIANS 6:13 NLT

There is an unseen battle raging all around us. It affects the choices we make, the way we see the world, and how we treat others. Ephesians 6:12 (NLT) says, "For we are not fighting against flesh-and-blood enemies, but against evil rulers and authorities of the unseen world, against mighty powers in this dark world, and against evil spirits in the heavenly places."

How do we defend ourselves against "mighty powers" we cannot see? With spiritual armor the world doesn't recognize.

Ephesians 6:14–17 (NLT) says, "Stand your ground, putting on the belt of truth and the body armor of God's righteousness. For shoes, put on the peace that comes from the Good News so that you will be fully prepared. In addition to all of these, hold up the shield of faith to stop the fiery arrows of the devil. Put on salvation as your helmet, and take the sword of the Spirit, which is the word of God."

Truth and righteousness are not abstract concepts when it comes to our protective belt and body armor. To protect ourselves from the devil's schemes, we must know that Jesus' sacrifice was sufficient for our sins and that God has given us His righteousness as a gift. With this truth comes peace, since nothing can separate us from God's love. Our faith in God and in His love keeps the devil's lies from doing us harm. Our helmet of salvation is designed to keep these truths in our mind. When we do encounter doubts, we have the Word of God to guide us back to the truth.

God's armor is built on truth. Becoming a faithful man means digging into the truth of His Word daily. The more we do, the more we'll recognize Jesus' sacrifice which gave us God's righteousness which leads to peace in His love for us.

How confident are you in your salvation? Why is truth the key
to defending ourselves against the enemy's schemes?

DAY 7

BE THE MAN WHO DOES THE UNEXPECTED

But I say unto you which hear, Love your enemies, do good to them which hate you, Bless them that curse you, and pray for them which despitefully use you.
LUKE 6:27–28 KJV

In his memoir, *Callus on my Soul*, black comedian and civil rights activist Dick Gregory wrote:

> *Last time I was down South, I walked into this restaurant. This white waitress came up to me and said, "We don't serve colored people here." I said, "That's all right, I don't eat colored people. Bring me a whole fried chicken." About that time, these three cousins came in. You know the ones I mean, Ku, Klux, and Klan. They said, "Boy, we're givin' you fair warnin'. Anything you do to that chicken, we're gonna do to you."*
>
> *So I put down my knife and fork, picked up that chicken, and kissed it.*

Dick Gregory's humorous response defused the tense situation. It was a perfect example of doing the unexpected.

Christianity (with its basis of being dependent on and dedicated to God's glory) will always be in tension with the world (with its basis of being independent and dedicated to an individual's glory). As such, Christians will experience rejection, violence, and hate simply for being Christians. The world expects us to answer in kind—rejection for rejection, violence for violence, hate for hate. But Jesus shows us a better way.

In order for the world to see the difference God makes in our lives, we must do the unexpected. We must love our enemies, do good to those who hate us, bless those who curse us, and pray for those who wish us ill. We must pick up the chicken and kiss it, trusting God even when the world doesn't back down.

How have you experienced the tension of living for God in a world where self-gratification is expected? How can you bless those who curse you today?

DAY 8

BE THE MAN WHO DOESN'T FEAR

*Fear thou not; for I am with thee: be not dismayed; for I am
thy God: I will strengthen thee; yea, I will help thee; yea,
I will uphold thee with the right hand of my righteousness.*
ISAIAH 41:10 KJV

Use your phone's calendar function to remind you. Leave a note on the fridge. Tie a string around your finger. Okay, ready? Take a deep breath and write this down:

THERE'S NO NEED TO BE AFRAID—GOD IS WITH YOU RIGHT NOW.

Every day of your life, God is there to help. So at each moment, you have a choice between two pursuits: do you worry yourself into weakness or turn to God for strength?

Some people make a full-time job out of peddling fear, and they are exceptional salesmen. You'll find anxiety for sale in advertising, the news, and even coffee shop conversations. There will always be something to be concerned about. Pretty soon, you'll find it easy to take up the salesman mantle yourself. But every time an unexpecting customer accepts a worry you know that person doesn't need, it'll only amplify your own.

God hates worry, and it's easy to see why. If you worry even after God has promised to be with you, this implies you've either missed His message or you're still struggling to trust Him.

You can be a man who embraces God's strength. . .but this means rejecting worry in favor of believing God is in control. Remember: He gives you strength, He stays with you, and His help is always on call.

When is the right time to worry? How can a choice to be
anxious function as an invitation to personal chaos?

BE THE MAN WHO WIELDS HIS SWORD

For the word of God is alive and active. Sharper than any double-edged sword, it penetrates even to dividing soul and spirit, joints and marrow; it judges the thoughts and attitudes of the heart.

HEBREWS 4:12 NIV

Making a sword isn't terribly complicated. Blacksmiths start with a chunk of raw iron. The iron must be heated so that impurities bond and float to the surface for easy removal. Iron that is free of impurities, called steel, is easier to shape, being both strong and flexible.

The brick of steel is slowly drawn out by repeatedly being heated and beaten into the shape of the sword. The sword is then heated again and rapidly cooled in oil for additional strength. Once strong enough, it is heated again and the point and edges are thinned and sharpened.

The Roman gladius was a double-edged sword used in Jesus' day. Although single-edged swords were better for swinging, double-edged swords were better for stabbing. And, having two edges, the weapon was dangerous for an enemy to grab at.

Hebrews 4:12 compares the Word of God to just such a sword. Scripture is free from impurities and has been shaped into something both strong and flexible. It is double-edged, intended to pierce hearts, not glance off armor. And when our enemies try to take God's Word away from us, they cannot help but be affected by it as well.

Our sword is not only a defensive weapon against the world. It is most useful when used on ourselves. By allowing the Word of God to pierce our own hearts, to judge our thoughts and attitudes, we become like the sword itself: free from impurities and shaped into something useful by the hands of the master blacksmith.

Our shaping (the heating and hammering of life's difficulties) will never be comfortable, and our sharpening (spending time in God's Word and prayer) will always take time. But being a faithful man requires both.

What impurities do you need to allow God to remove from your life?
How are you being shaped to better serve God's purposes?

BE THE MAN WHO LOVES UNCONDITIONALLY

*This is how we know what love is: Jesus Christ
laid down his life for us. And we ought to lay
down our lives for our brothers and sisters.*
1 JOHN 3:16 NIV

Some people are easy to love. People who are nice to you, whom you find attractive, or who have a good sense of humor. Those who share your interests, language, likes, and dislikes. Relatives, childhood friends, or close acquaintances. All these traits contribute, either consciously or subconsciously, to a person's status in your "loveable" category.

Processing these traits in this manner may help us naturally connect to certain people, but it can also place restrictions on our love.

If you are drawn to someone based on how that person looks, what happens to that love if a disfiguring accident occurs? What if the funny guy you get along with so well suddenly plunges into depression? What if your bowling buddy of multiple decades suddenly stops frequenting the lanes?

Christians are called to love like Jesus loves, which means reaching far beyond our comfortable categories of "loveable" people. And the extent to which Jesus calls us to show love goes way beyond our natural inclinations. As faithful men of honor, we are called to lay down our lives for people who would rather spit than look at us. Why? Because when we love as Jesus has loved us, without expecting love in return, we show the world what love truly is. And even when our love is met with indifference, God sees us acting in His nature toward people He loves as much as us—and no sacrifice on His behalf will go unrewarded.

What aspects about your loved ones make them easy to love?
How can you show love to someone who has none of those aspects?

DAY 11

BE THE MAN WHO STEPS OUT

Then flew one of the seraphims unto me, having a live coal in his hand,
which he had taken with the tongs from off the altar: And he laid it upon
my mouth, and said, Lo, this hath touched thy lips; and thine iniquity is
taken away, and thy sin purged. Also I heard the voice of the Lord, saying,
Whom shall I send, and who will go for us? Then said I, Here am I; send me.
ISAIAH 6:6–8 KJV

David Livingstone was a gifted author, explorer, and missionary to Africa. If that sounds like an impressive resume, you should know Livingston was more willing than he was prepared. He failed his missionary exam and would have been rejected had the missionary board not agreed to give him a rare second chance.

Stepping out of your comfort zone requires a powerful resolve and a deep sense of courage—and that's just the kind of courage the prophet Isaiah had. When God asked for volunteers, Isaiah bravely responded, "I'm right here. I'm willing to go. You can send me."

His journey wasn't easy. While God insisted on leading the people, the people insisted on running away. When God asked them to follow, they played a high-stakes game of hide and seek. But through it all, Isaiah remained faithful to his calling.

This same God who discovered willingness in Isaiah and David Livingstone is asking today, "Whom shall I send?" Often, it's easier to look around and wonder who's going to answer. But have you ever considered that God might be asking *you*?

God is waiting for you to listen, raise your hand, and shout, "I'm right here. I'm willing to go. You can send me."

When was the last time God gave you an opportunity to step out? How did you respond? How can you be more courageous in stepping out to follow God's directions?

BE THE MAN WHO RESPECTS WOMEN

*And he began to speak boldly in the synagogue: whom when
Aquila and Priscilla had heard, they took him unto them,
and expounded unto him the way of God more perfectly.*
ACTS 18:26 KJV

Apollos was a smart guy. According to Acts 18:24 (KJV), he was "an eloquent man, and mighty in the scriptures." But he still didn't have the full picture.

Apollos believed in the teachings of Jesus and strongly declared what he knew, but it wasn't until he arrived in Ephesus and encountered a married couple—Aquila and Priscilla—that he finally came to a full knowledge of Christ's sacrifice and resurrection.

In 1 Corinthians 3:5–6 (NIV) Paul recognizes Apollos as a fellow missionary when he says, "What, after all, is Apollos? And what is Paul? Only servants, through whom you came to believe—as the Lord has assigned to each his task. I planted the seed, Apollos watered it, but God has been making it grow."

But what would have happened if Apollos hadn't listened to both Aquilla *and* Priscilla? The Bible mentions them both, which is interesting because it could have easily left Priscilla out. After all, in ancient times, women stood on the lowest rung of the social ladder. Their testimonies were inadmissible in Jewish courts.

If Apollos had similarly ignored Priscilla's contribution, the message of the gospel would have been hindered. Because he listened, however, he convinced many people that Jesus was the Messiah the Jews had been waiting for (see Acts 18:27–28).

Becoming a faithful man, as Apollo was, means rejecting society's views toward women and respecting them as equal bearers of God's image. It means listening to them, as did Apollos, and giving them opportunities to speak, as did Aquila.

How could you better listen to the women in your life? How could
you create more opportunities for women to be heard?

BE THE MAN WHO LIVES AT PEACE

*Blessed are the peacemakers: for they
shall be called the children of God.*
MATTHEW 5:9 KJV

To understand what it means to live at peace—and to be a peacemaker—
we must first dig into the Hebrew word *shalom*.

To say that *shalom* means "peace" is like saying the ocean is wet.
It is, but it's a lot more than that. Shalom is a multifaceted peace that
encompasses a right relationship with God, a sense of well-being with
others, and a personal feeling of wholeness that is unshakeable by any
circumstance. The key to experiencing shalom isn't found in meditation,
stress reduction, or any other activity; it is found exclusively in the person
and sacrifice of Jesus Christ.

The apostle Paul refers to Jesus as the "Lord of peace" in 2 Thessalonians 3:16 (KJV). And Jesus Himself said in John 14:27 (KJV), "Peace I
leave with you, my peace I give unto you: not as the world giveth, give I
unto you. Let not your heart be troubled, neither let it be afraid."

Because Jesus became the required sacrifice for our sins, we are able
to live in a right relationship with God, to experience shalom in its fullest
sense. Once our heavenly relationship is at peace, we can experience the
internal, personal shalom Jesus described in John 16:33 (NIV): "I have
told you these things, so that in me you may have peace. In this world you
will have trouble. But take heart! I have overcome the world."

Having the peace of God doesn't mean trouble will never come. It
simply means we won't have trouble with the one in charge. And when
we have that kind of peace, we can spread it like water on a thirsty land
until the world is swallowed by the ocean of God's peace.

How does your outward life reflect your inner peace?
How can you be a peacemaker in your community?

BE THE MAN WHO LIVES BY FAITH

Now the one who has fashioned us for this very purpose is God, who has given us the Spirit as a deposit, guaranteeing what is to come. Therefore we are always confident and know that as long as we are at home in the body we are away from the Lord. For we live by faith, not by sight.

2 Corinthians 5:5–7 niv

Near Oregon's Multnomah Falls, faith was on display as a woman dangled over a drop of three hundred feet. The only thing standing between her and doom was a well-placed tree root, which she strongly grasped. Her arms were tiring, and she could find no foothold. She *had* to believe the root would hold—the only other option was unacceptable.

This woman had no guarantee that someone would find her or even be able to help. But as she held on, hope kept her vision of rescue alive.

What a profound picture of your faith in God! As you cling to the root of God's Word, God promises that rescue is coming. He will step in and lift you up, allowing you to share your story with others at the end of your struggle.

"But why," you might ask, "doesn't God let me see into the future?" The answer is simple: if you knew every detail of every experience you'll ever face, then the joy of the journey would be diminished. With nothing left to surprise you, why would you need courage?

It takes a man of faith and courage to believe God's promises when there's no strength left to hang on. Faith doesn't need to know what's next—it just knows who's coming to your rescue.

> How does the Spirit's presence in your life transform your decision making and help you write a new chapter in your story today?

DAY 15

BE THE MAN WHO WELCOMES FORGIVENESS

But Zacchaeus stood up and said to the Lord, "Look, Lord! Here and now I give half of my possessions to the poor, and if I have cheated anybody out of anything, I will pay back four times the amount."
LUKE 19:8 NIV

Luke 19 shares the story of a man who was short on strength. He'd taken on a job that found him collecting tax from his friends and neighbors. In his weakness, he decided to start overcalculating their tax. . .and pocketing the difference. This bad idea, of course, didn't go unnoticed. Soon, Zacchaeus also became short on friends.

One day, Jesus came to town. But when the local buzz pinpointed the street where He'd walk, nobody bothered to save Zacchaeus a space. As a result, the tax collector decided to climb a tree. There, he'd have one of the best views in town!

When Jesus was about to pass by, He stopped under the tree, looked up, and invited Himself to dinner. It was at that meal that Jesus confronted Zacchaeus' weak actions. Somehow, instead of fearfully retreating, this man gained strength from Jesus' words. He changed his thinking and then his actions. He stopped collecting extra tax and provided a refund to everyone he'd taken advantage of.

This unique story is a powerful example of what happens when a man comes to grips with a hard truth, abandons fear, and seeks God's strength. Don't fear being called out by God. Instead, accept His assessment of your weakness and embrace the strength He offers. Don't get mad because you were caught in sin—rejoice because Forgiveness came to town and noticed you.

Why does correction often lead to defensiveness? How can God's assessment of your actions lead to greater inner strength?

BE THE MAN WHO KEEPS ON PRAYING

*And pray in the Spirit on all occasions with all kinds
of prayers and requests. With this in mind, be alert and
always keep on praying for all the Lord's people.*
EPHESIANS 6:18 NIV

If the armor of God is our defense in spiritual battles and the Word of God is our weapon, prayer is our plan of attack.

Many men use prayer as little more than a mealtime ritual, as a last resort in times of crisis, or as a spiritual shopping cart, asking God to cover the payment. In reality, prayer is the most active thing you can do to strengthen your relationship with God.

After listing each piece of God's armor, the apostle Paul writes in Ephesians 6:18 (NIV), "And pray in the Spirit on all occasions with all kinds of prayers and requests. With this in mind, be alert and always keep on praying for all the Lord's people."

Paul didn't leave much ambiguity with how we should pray. On which ocasions? On all occasions. How? With all kinds of prayers and requests. For whom? For all the Lord's people. How often? Always.

A faithful man actively prays. We should certainly thank God for our meals, pray for help in times of crisis, and even go to God with the things we want (as long as what we want is what He wants for us). But our prayer life should never stop there.

We should also pray for forgiveness when we sin. We should lift up the requests of other Christians in prayer. We should pray for God to have His way in our hearts, our families, our work, our future, and our nation. We should praise God for who He is and what He has done.

Don't know how to start? Pray about it!

Which aspect of prayer might be missing from your prayer
life? Is there anything you don't feel like praying about?
(Hint: This is probably the most important thing to pray about.)

DAY 17

BE THE MAN WHO KNOWS HIS INFLUENCERS

Do not be misled: "Bad company corrupts good character."
1 CORINTHIANS 15:33 NIV

Once upon a time, your only friends were the people you hung out with in person. You encouraged one another—in good ways or bad—and it was (usually) pretty easy to see how they were influencing your life.

Today, you can be "friends" online with people you've never met, some of whom may actually be computer programs intent on feeding you disinformation. And here's the unnerving part: the difference between real friends, perfect strangers, and slick artificial intelligence programs isn't always that clear. The ways you are influenced by your online activities and relationships can be difficult to perceive—much more so than if a buddy nudges you with an elbow and suggests robbing a bank.

Regardless of whether your influencers are online or in-person, today's scripture remains true: "Bad company corrupts good character." You must be aware of the company you keep. How well do you know the people you listen to? How do you know you can trust something before you share it? Are your friends encouraging you to love more people in self-sacrificial ways and guard against the threats of this world?

Do not be misled. If you are being influenced by people, social media, or slick marketing more than by God's Word, your character is in danger of being corrupted. If you aren't encouraging your friends to live holy lives of love and integrity, you might be the corrupting influence. Today, take some time and pray that God would reveal who has influence over you. . .and how you can influence others for Him.

Who would you say your biggest influencers are? Over whom might you have influence?

BE THE MAN WHO STANDS STRONG

It was by faith that Noah built a large boat to save his family from the flood. He obeyed God, who warned him about things that had never happened before. By his faith Noah condemned the rest of the world, and he received the righteousness that comes by faith.

HEBREWS 11:7 NLT

Imagine the curiosity that Noah's neighbors must have felt as they watched him and his family build a massive boat on dry land. And imagine their even greater bewilderment once animals began to arrive!

This project took more than a hundred years to complete. Day after day, Noah and his sons took hammers in hand, knowing their neighbors didn't understand what they were doing or why. The Bible doesn't say that Noah was mocked, but it's hard to imagine any other response. The people probably couldn't help tossing in some choice bits of mockery and sarcasm.

Noah had never piloted an ocean vessel before, and he probably wasn't even a carpenter. But it was God who drew up the plans. . .all Noah had to do was obey. For more than a century, this man stood strong. He probably had days in which he wanted to quit, but God's command was clear—and He never suggested that Noah could stop.

God took a story whose end was unknown and combined it with an adventure no one had ever experienced. But this seemingly outlandish plan saved the lives of Noah, his wife, his sons, and a floating zoo.

You can experience the same discovery at the place where God's plan and your purpose collide. Even when people don't understand your need to follow God, all you must do is stand strong.

Is anything preventing you from standing unashamed as a Christian?
How does Noah's story inspire you to keep following God?

BE THE MAN WHO TRADES WEAKNESS FOR STRENGTH

Now all glory to God, who is able, through his mighty power at work within us, to accomplish infinitely more than we might ask or think.
EPHESIANS 3:20 NLT

We remember people who go above and beyond. Those who don't have to help but do it anyway. Those who lend their expertise without being asked. Those who jump to carry others' burdens, choosing to walk with them shoulder to shoulder.

But sometimes, going above and beyond is impossible, no matter how hard you try. You can barely take care of yourself, let alone help someone through a tough time. In these times, who's remembering you? God. (No surprise there.)

He knows the struggle you face. But He also knows that when you want to check out, the real answer is to check in with Him. He goes above and beyond for you. He helps, lends expertise, and stands with you.

The strength you need isn't found in a gym, an energy drink, or a list of all-natural vitamins. No, you benefit from a very unfair trade. It can feel like trading in an old, broken-down station wagon for a brand-new luxury SUV. The deal is straight across with no payments and free maintenance for life.

God wants your anxiety and worry—in exchange, He offers strength and peace. Sound too good to be true? Rest assured: it's true. God calls this gift *grace*. It's more than you deserve, but it's just one set of gifts God gives to help you live a thriving life, even in the soil of personal disappointment.

Be a strong man who started out weak. Accept the strength trade today.

Have you accepted God's gift of strength and given up your willingness to stay weak? How does this trade seem better than what you deserve?

BE THE MAN WHO GIVES CHEERFULLY

You must each decide in your heart how much to give.
And don't give reluctantly or in response to pressure.
"For God loves a person who gives cheerfully."
2 Corinthians 9:7 NLT

Seeds are incredible. When planted in good soil and nourished by sunlight and water, seeds become plants—which, in turn, make more seeds, enabling one small seed to grow exponentially in number within a short time.

In his second letter to the church at Corinth, Paul uses this agrarian example to illustrate generosity. Second Corinthians 9:6-8 (NLT) says, "Remember this—a farmer who plants only a few seeds will get a small crop. But the one who plants generously will get a generous crop. You must each decide in your heart how much to give. And don't give reluctantly or in response to pressure. 'For God loves a person who gives cheerfully.' And God will generously provide all you need. Then you will always have everything you need and plenty left over to share with others."

God has blessed us with resources to grow His kingdom. Whenever we plant generously with the resources He's given, our increase will be exponential.

What does this have to do with giving *cheerfully*? Planting seeds isn't a fun process. It's hard work! But a farmer can be cheerful because he knows his seeds will become a harvest. And just like with actual plants, the harvest is God's responsibility, not ours.

While generosity is often associated with finances, God has given us resources which have nothing to do with our bank account. We can be generous with our time, our attention, and our help. We can loan our tools and share our food. We can even be generous with our compliments.

Whenever we give cheerfully to others, God will ensure we have enough to keep giving.

What resources could you give cheerfully to others?
How have others given cheerfully to you?

DAY 21

BE THE MAN WHO PRIORITIZES OTHERS OVER SELF

Don't be concerned for your own good but for the good of others.
1 CORINTHIANS 10:24 NLT

Have you ever heard of a "helper's high"? Scientists have discovered that acts of altruism can release endorphins—brain chemicals that make people happy—in similar ways to exercise. It literally feels good to do good. Unfortunately, these "highs" are short-lived. If we're to live out the command in today's scripture, we're going to need the bigger picture instead of relying on the "helper's high."

When we live for the good of others instead of self-gratification, we learn true gratitude. As we shift our focus off ourselves and onto others—willfully ignoring the ways we are left out, forgotten, or let down—we become intentional about including others, remembering the details of their lives, and being present when we're needed.

It's like when you buy a car and suddenly start seeing that make and model all over the place. Those other cars were always there, but you didn't notice them until you could relate to their drivers. In helping others, you start noticing the ways that others have helped you.

The best part is that God doesn't ask us to help others alone. He fills our needs when we pour out ourselves for others. As we help them, He helps us. Psalm 54:4 (NIV) says, "Surely God is my help; the Lord is the one who sustains me."

God has designed us to feel happy when we do good for others and shift our focus off ourselves, but it takes His help to stay the course. Today, as you seek opportunities for service, pray for His strength to sustain you. Don't worry about your own needs. As you set the example for others, you'll likely find your own needs either taken care of by someone else. . .or forgotten altogether.

When was the last time you experienced a
"helper's high"? How can you help someone today?

DAY 22

BE THE MAN WHO MOVES FORWARD

Thus saith the LORD, which maketh a way in the sea, and a path in the mighty waters; which bringeth forth the chariot and horse, the army and the power; they shall lie down together, they shall not rise: they are extinct, they are quenched as tow. Remember ye not the former things, neither consider the things of old. Behold, I will do a new thing; now it shall spring forth; shall ye not know it?

ISAIAH 43:16–19 KJV

Plenty of movies involve someone whose good, problem-free life is torn apart by a worst-case scenario. The rest of the movie often features the protagonist overcoming roadblocks on his quest to get back to the good old days.

God, however, doesn't think this way. His map for your life doesn't loop back to the place right before your failure; instead, it stretches onward, using that failure as a springboard to reach even greater heights than before.

God's plan for your life requires courage. After all, complacency is much easier than adventure. That's why some people stick with their jobs, even when better opportunities present themselves. There is security in what is familiar.

But God, in a burst of superior wisdom, has forged a way through the ordinary, and the destination is amazing! The road will be rough, and you might sometimes think you've taken a wrong turn. But when you trust God and move forward, you'll look back one day, convinced He led you to a better place.

Your story isn't a movie, so trading your new life for old habits will always be unwise. Getting started may be the hardest—but most important—step you take.

Do you ever struggle with embracing your new life over the old?
If so, what will it take to adjust your vision toward the goal?

BE THE MAN WHO'S AMAZED BY GOD'S STRENGTH

The LORD made the earth by his power, and he preserves it by his wisdom. With his own understanding he stretched out the heavens. When he speaks in the thunder, the heavens roar with rain. He causes the clouds to rise over the earth. He sends the lightning with the rain and releases the wind from his storehouses.

JEREMIAH 10:12–13 NLT

Talk to a meteorologist long enough, and you'll hear things like "a strong midlevel warm air advection will be aided by an upper-level divergence" and "a vigorous upper level trough may erode the mid-level warm pool." These seemingly incomprehensible phrases, however, usually boil down to something like "It's going to be a nice day" or "Watch out for storms this evening."

You don't have to understand the language of a meteorologist to know that weather can be crazy. Whether it's lightning, thunder, rain, hail, wind, or snow, you can't control the weather. No matter how many times you revert to childhood and sing, "Rain, rain, go away. Come again some other day," the weather doesn't care. All that'll do is confuse and annoy the people at the local convenience store who are waiting out the storm.

Weather is a powerful reminder of God's strength. He created weather and now preserves it, even when it gets severe. He tells thunder when it's time to boom. He tells lightning when it's time for a real display. He even has a storehouse for wind.

When you are going through your own seasons of trouble, try focusing on a storm in your past that's been long overshadowed by sunny days. Then remember this one truth: God is bigger than any storm, no matter how ferocious.

Does weather cause you to trust God more?
How can it remind you of God's strength?

BE THE MAN WHO ANTICIPATES JESUS' RETURN

*"It will be good for those servants whose master finds them watching
when he comes. Truly I tell you, he will dress himself to serve, will
have them recline at the table and will come and wait on them."*
LUKE 12:37 NIV

Jesus told us to keep watch for His return. That alone should be enough of a reason to do so, since Jesus was God in the flesh. But Jesus didn't just give us a command. He also told us a story to show what kind of God He is.

Jesus said in Luke 12:35–38 (NIV), "Be dressed ready for service and keep your lamps burning, like servants waiting for their master to return from a wedding banquet, so that when he comes and knocks they can immediately open the door for him. It will be good for those servants whose master finds them watching when he comes. Truly I tell you, he will dress himself to serve, will have them recline at the table and will come and wait on them. It will be good for those servants whose master finds them ready, even if he comes in the middle of the night or toward daybreak."

The servants' job was to be ready whenever their master returned. They didn't need any additional incentive. But the master did reward the prepared servants by trading places with them at his arrival.

Becoming a faithful man means keeping watch for Jesus' return, not just because He told us to but because we also know He rewards obedience. We need to be dressed and ready with our lamps burning bright, no matter how late we think it might be.

How are we to dress? Revelation 19:8 (NIV) describes our garments as "righteous acts of God's holy people." And how can we keep our lamps bright? Matthew 5:16 (NIV) says, "In the same way, let your light shine before others, that they may see your good deeds and glorify your Father in heaven."

What righteous acts can you do to make sure you're dressed?
What good deeds can you do to shine God's light?

BE THE MAN WHO MENTORS THE NEXT GENERATION

Train up a child in the way he should go:
and when he is old, he will not depart from it.
PROVERBS 22:6 KJV

If you've ever heard a sermon about parenting, today's verse may sound familiar. It shows up in Christian wall art, social media memes, and a hundred other places. In fact, it's so pervasive that the words may have lost some of their meaning. Although the command to "train up a child in the way he should go" is definitely a parent's responsibility, it is not exclusively so. Every man should look for opportunities to pass on his spiritual knowledge and training to the next generation, whether bound by ties of blood or not.

Mentorship can take many forms. If you are looking for an easy avenue to speak God's truths to kids, churches are a good place to start. Most children's ministry directors would love to have solid male volunteers looking to serve as teachers and leaders in their ministries.

There are also plenty of mainstream organizations looking for volunteers to spend time with kids. Kids with troubled pasts, special needs, or absent fathers are particularly in need of mentors who will pour love into them.

If you're already a family man, consider how you might mentor your children's friends. Is your house a natural place for your kids to hang out? Are you making time in your schedule to focus on their interests? How are you inviting them into the things that interest you? And most importantly, how are you using those opportunities to teach them about God's goodness and the ways they can grow more like Him?

Today, pray that God would bring to mind someone you can train in godliness—as well as the understanding you'll need in order to train that person well.

What skills might you teach to the next generation?
What benefits do you think you'd experience as a mentor?

BE THE MAN WHO IS KHAZAK VE'EMATZ

"Be strong and very courageous. Be careful to obey all the law my servant Moses gave you; do not turn from it to the right or to the left, that you may be successful wherever you go. Keep this Book of the Law always on your lips; meditate on it day and night, so that you may be careful to do everything written in it. Then you will be prosperous and successful. Have I not commanded you? Be strong and courageous. Do not be afraid; do not be discouraged, for the LORD your God will be with you wherever you go."

JOSHUA 1:7–9 NIV

In the Hebrew language, the English words *strong* and *courageous* are spoken as *khazak ve'ematz.*

Whenever a Hebrew heard these words, that person would likely automatically think of Joshua's story. When Joshua took Moses' place in leading the people into the promised land, he was undoubtedly intimidated. After all, not even Moses—whom God used to set the people free—could get the people to the land God had given them. How could Joshua have expected to succeed where such a noble man had failed?

That's when God commanded Joshua to *khazak ve'ematz*—be strong and courageous. God gave this command more than once, driving home the point that neither fear nor discouragement was welcome. God, who could do the impossible, was with him.

Today, exercise your faith and choose to follow God. It doesn't matter what language you speak or what dialect you understand—the concept behind the words *strong* and *courageous* is universal.

The God with whom you walk is bigger than any obstacle that stands in your way.

> Do fear and discouragement ever hinder your walk with God? If so,
> how can you work on being stronger and more courageous?

BE THE MAN WHO CELEBRATES GOD'S STRENGTH

Then God said, "Let us make mankind in our image, in our likeness."
GENESIS 1:26 NIV

Director Frank Capra delivered a movie in the mid-1940s that did little to capture the attention of movie goers at the time. The movie might've been forgotten entirely if it hadn't been picked up by television and replayed every Christmas.

The story follows Jimmy Stewart's character, George, as he experiences many troubles and setbacks. All his dreams seem to end in disappointment. One day, he decides he's had enough—but just before George can make a terrible decision, a self-described angel arrives to show him what life would be like without him.

As it turns out, George's trouble has brought strength not only to himself but to those around him. Without him, things are much worse. The town's name is changed, and everyone is somehow harder and more calloused.

Unfortunately, this beloved movie has no real-life counterpart. You can't really look at what life would be like without you. And even if you tried to speculate, your faulty conclusions might make you even more depressed!

However, maybe your pity party can transform into a celebration if you pay attention to the things God has said about you. He made you, He loves you, and He sent His Son to die for you. He created you with a purpose, making you a part of His grand plan. He has chosen to be with you, and He'll never leave. He wants to impact the world with your life—a story only you can share.

God wants to make the world a better place because you are here. He has a plan for you—will you cooperate?

How is strength linked to God's purpose for you? Why should pity parties always give way to celebrations of God's goodness?

BE THE MAN WHO SAYS WHAT HE MEANS

"All you need to say is simply 'Yes' or 'No'; anything
beyond this comes from the evil one."
MATTHEW 5:37 NIV

In the United States, incoming presidents often take the oath of office by placing their left hand on a Bible while swearing to uphold the Constitution. George Washington began the practice on April 30, 1789, and presidents have continued it into modern times.

According to *The New Yorker* contributor Hannah Rosefield, the use of oath books in a legal setting dates back to ninth-century England, when certain transactions were conducted at the altar with participants swearing on a gospel book. A few centuries later, English courts adopted the practice. Rosefield writes, "By placing a hand on the book and then kissing it, the oath-taker is acknowledging that, should he lie under oath, neither the words in the Bible nor his good deeds nor his prayers will bring him any earthly or spiritual profit. In time, this became standard legal procedure—all witnesses swearing to tell the truth, the whole truth, and nothing but the truth—and made its way into American courts. British witnesses today still take their oaths 'by Almighty God,' as American oath-takers conclude theirs with 'so help me God.'"

We might be tempted to affirm the practice of swearing our truthfulness by the Bible or by invoking God's name, but doing so isn't biblical.

In Matthew 5:33–37, Jesus prohibits taking oaths. He wants His followers to have such integrity that their truthfulness is never called into question. A truly faithful man says what he means and keeps his word. When his integrity is intact, his words will be believable.

Next time you feel tempted to swear something is true, remember how trustworthy most politicians are and ask yourself if the oath will boost your credibility.

Do you ever say things like, "No really, I'm telling the truth"?
What are some better ways to convince people?

BE THE MAN WHO REJOICES IN SUFFERING

Not only so, but we also glory in our sufferings, because we know that suffering produces perseverance; perseverance, character; and character, hope. And hope does not put us to shame, because God's love has been poured out into our hearts through the Holy Spirit, who has been given to us.
ROMANS 5:3–5 NIV

Disasters come in many shapes: hurricanes, floods, fires, divorce, disease, injustice, and violence. You can probably supplement this list with your own personal experiences. Unfortunately, these disasters rarely come in small, easy-to-process bits. There's often a domino effect.

Getting sick can lead to missing work, which can lead to financial distress, which can complicate relationships, and so on. It's easy to feel hopeless in such circumstances if you don't have a proper view of suffering.

Suffering need not lead to hopelessness when you realize God has designed it with a different kind of domino effect in mind. In His design, suffering provides opportunities for men to push through the pain—with God's help—and persevere. When we refuse to let suffering thwart our good deeds, we show the kind of character God inspires. When the world sees His character in us, they'll see the hope that comes with salvation.

Suffering allows us, as followers of Christ, to experience a crucial aspect of Jesus' life. Therefore, we should consider it a privilege. Philippians 1:29 (NIV) says, "For it has been granted to you on behalf of Christ not only to believe in him, but also to suffer for him."

Is it really possible to have joy in the midst of suffering? Yes, because through suffering, we can show the world that our destiny as God's children lies far beyond the pain we currently endure—that our lasting joy overshadows the temporary griefs this world inflicts.

Which "domino effect" is obvious in your life when you suffer?
How might suffering better connect you to Jesus' experience?

BE THE MAN WHO HUMBLY RESISTS

Do you think the Scriptures have no meaning? They say that God is passionate that the spirit he has placed within us should be faithful to him. And he gives grace generously. As the Scriptures say, "God opposes the proud but gives grace to the humble." So humble yourselves before God. Resist the devil, and he will flee from you.

JAMES 4:5–7 NLT

Motivation plays a huge role in your life story. It's the very thing that gives you the desire to become a faithful man—without it, you'll be stuck cowering in a corner, incapable of following God's positive change.

To be humble before God, you must be motivated to see God as bigger, wiser, and bolder than you are. And to resist the devil, you must be motivated to follow God.

The problem for most men is that when the devil makes his debut, they blindly accept his invitation. The devil doesn't want you to seek God, so he'll make fun of you for thinking you need Him. And once Satan convinces you that you don't need God or that God is withholding good things from you, that's when he has you right where he wants you. To resist his influence, you must believe that the enemy's words, though they sound like silk, are actually filled with venom.

Thankfully, God's resources can motivate you to resist. And whenever that happens, the devil gets really uncomfortable. He can't stay long when God is welcome.

Whatever you believe deep down is what determines the direction you'll go. . .and whom you'll follow to get there.

Do you have a strong motivation to follow God and resist the devil? If so, how is this motivation evidenced in your life?

BE THE MAN WHO ISN'T A LONE WOLF

Two are better than one; because they have a good reward for their labour.
ECCLESIASTES 4:9 KJV

Does the idea of being a lone wolf appeal to you? Going it alone sounds like something men are supposed to do. Pulling yourself up by your bootstraps seems like a worthy story to share with grandchildren. Self-reliance seems like something to be proud of.

Yet God has created you for relationship. Friendships are important. Shared burdens result in efficiency. Working with someone brings encouragement. Receiving help boosts your confidence for the task at hand.

A great illustration can be found in a very unusual object: the disposable diaper. Because these diapers contain a certain polymer, they have uses that most people never consider. Perhaps the strangest: you can use a new diaper as your antiperspirant! Because the diaper is absorbent and has a fresh scent, it's helpful for drying things out and leaving you smelling fresh all day long. Other uses include keeping cut flowers fresh, preventing fires, and improving the hardness of cement.

Peanut butter complements chocolate, marshmallows complement hot cocoa, and tacos complement almost anything. Who's complementing you? Do you have a friend who just seems to make you better?

These questions are not meant to minimize God's strength but to point out one of the ways He can strengthen you. Knowing that someone has your back can change the way you feel about any challenge. Confidence comes when friends stand together.

Why do you think God made friendships so important?
Do you have an "Ecclesiastes 4:9" friend? Can you be one?

BE THE MAN WHO RUNS FOR THE PRIZE

Don't you realize that in a race everyone runs,
but only one person gets the prize? So run to win!
1 CORINTHIANS 9:24 NLT

At the time of Paul's missionary journeys, the city of Corinth hosted the biennial Isthmian Games, second only to the Olympic Games in popularity. The Isthmian Games were an ancient festival of athletic and musical competitions held in honor of the Greek god Poseidon. The victors of each competition were crowned with a pine wreath.

In his letter to the church at Corinth, Paul borrowed the imagery of the Isthmian Games to teach a spiritual truth. First Corinthians 9:24–27 (NLT) says, "Don't you realize that in a race everyone runs, but only one person gets the prize? So run to win! All athletes are disciplined in their training. They do it to win a prize that will fade away, but we do it for an eternal prize. So I run with purpose in every step. I am not just shadowboxing. I discipline my body like an athlete, training it to do what it should. Otherwise, I fear that after preaching to others I myself might be disqualified."

The faithful man runs with "purpose in every step." Intentional in action and consistent in attitude, he keeps his eyes on the eternal prize.

Philippians 3:13–14 (NLT) says, "No, dear brothers and sisters, I have not achieved it, but I focus on this one thing: Forgetting the past and looking forward to what lies ahead, I press on to reach the end of the race and receive the heavenly prize for which God, through Christ Jesus, is calling us."

Successful athletes discipline themselves, giving up junk food and regularly training for their sport. Successful Christians discipline themselves too. Refusing to dwell upon past sins, they run forward in grace, committing their steps to God's glory.

Are you looking backward or forward as you run? What practices
might you need to drop in order to run more freely?

DAY 33

BE THE MAN WHO PATIENTLY WAITS ON GOD

Wait on the LORD: be of good courage, and he shall strengthen thine heart: wait, I say, on the LORD.
PSALM 27:14 KJV

Waiting might sound like a passive activity. In reality, it's anything but.

Consider a military sniper who waits poised and attentive for the target to come into range. The sniper isn't sleeping or playing around. He waits and watches and listens. In fact, he isn't even waiting alone. Snipers work with someone called a "spotter," whose job is to equip the team with necessary gear, communicate with their commanders, and review the mission objectives.

The spotter "has already done the job as a shooter," says Staff Sergeant Christopher Rance, a sniper course team leader for the US Department of Defense. "He already has a mastery of the shot process. He's the one who's identifying the actual target. He's. . .relaying that information to the shooter, giving him those proper firing commands, and basically assessing that the sniper team is firing on target so, if they were to miss, he's making that quick second-shot correction, relaying that info to the shooter, and hopefully eliminating that threat as they see fit."

When we wait on the Lord, we are to wait as the sniper does, listening to the commands of someone who has been there before us, who sees the bigger picture, and who can clean up our mistakes when we fail. Who is our spotter? God Himself.

Jesus has experienced life on earth and is master over sin. God not only sees the bigger picture but directs all things together for His good. The Spirit intercedes with the Father on our behalf and communicates directly to our souls.

We can strengthen our hearts by waiting attentively for God's will to be done. Let's pay attention to what our spotter is telling us instead of passively watching the world move by. Are you waiting, actively and intentionally, on the Lord?

How might you wait more attentively when it comes to doing God's will? What do you think His mission objectives are for your life?

DAY 34

BE THE MAN WHO DOES SOMETHING

Only be thou strong and very courageous, that thou mayest observe to do according to all the law, which Moses my servant commanded thee: turn not from it to the right hand or to the left, that thou mayest prosper withersoever thou goest. This book of the law shall not depart out of thy mouth; but thou shalt meditate therein day and night, that thou mayest observe to do according to all that is written therein: for then thou shalt make thy way prosperous, and then thou shalt have good success.

JOSHUA 1:7–8 KJV

It's been said that meditation is the art of doing nothing. But what if meditation instead means filling your mind and spirit with so much good news that the lingering bits of nothing get washed away?

If time is of the essence, then engaging in worthless pursuits doesn't make sense. The meditation that God describes may be more aptly compared to a jeweler's act of examining a diamond through a magnifying lens. Whenever you search for brilliance and clarity in God's Word, dwelling on it in the process, you will replenish your appreciation for God. That way, you'll have something to believe in rather than nothing worth talking about.

When you know what God says and understand what He wants, you won't miss what He wishes for you to learn and do. Also, by closely reading a scripture passage—as well as the verses around it for context—you'll leave with a gem that can impact your understanding of God's truth.

Meditate when you wake up, when you make your morning commute, and when you struggle to sleep at night. Your spiritual success may well depend on it.

> Do you ever think meditation is a waste of time? If so,
> how can you turn it into the art of doing something?

BE THE MAN WHO KNOWS WHEN TO HUSH

*Then they sat on the ground with him for seven days
and nights. No one said a word to Job, for they saw
that his suffering was too great for words.*
JOB 2:13 NLT

Sometimes, the worst thing you can do for someone is talk. You see someone struggling and you want to help, so you fill the silence with words that end up only causing pain.

Guys are wired to be fixers. If you can provide a solution for what's bothering a friend, then you can put it behind you and move on. But often, this "solution" is just a best guess. . .and that's not what friends need. Sometimes, they just need to hear these four words: "I'm here for you."

Job's friends started that way. They recognized his suffering was too big for words to heal. But the longer they endured silence, the more awkward they likely felt. You might know what that's like. You meet a friend who's quiet, and perhaps it isn't long before the silence grows too loud. Your jaw suddenly unhinges, spilling out obviously unhelpful words, but you can't make it stop. The words flow as freely as opinions at Thanksgiving dinner, and the awkwardness explodes.

Just like adult children who don't want their parent's advice unless they ask for it, so too are your hurting friends. They might need a friend who's content to just be there for them. You can add or diminish strength based on what you choose—or refuse—to say.

Why is it so hard to wait in silence?
How can ongoing conversations diminish strength?

DAY 36

BE THE MAN WHO DENIES HIMSELF

Then said Jesus unto his disciples, If any man will come after me,
let him deny himself, and take up his cross, and follow me.
MATTHEW 16:24 KJV

Death by crucifixion wasn't fun. In fact, the word *excruciating* was invented just to describe how painful it was. If it had been pleasant, Jesus wouldn't have asked for another way.

Mark 14:36 (NIV) records His prayer in the Garden of Gethsemane on the night of Judas' betrayal: "'*Abba*, Father,' he said, 'everything is possible for you. Take this cup from me. Yet not what I will, but what you will.'"

Jesus submitted His future to God, understanding the grave necessity of the cross yet still refusing to run. He lived out the command He gave to His disciples in Matthew 16:24 by denying Himself and taking up His cross to pay for the world's sin.

Life isn't always fun. There will always be jobs we'd rather not do. If washing dishes or folding clothes isn't your cup of tea, it's still better than the cup Jesus drank when He died for our sins. When we deny our wants to serve others, we take up our cross. When we give up our rights for someone's convenience, we take up our cross. When we lift others up instead of stealing the spotlight, we take up our cross.

Faithful men find ways to serve others sacrificially, stepping outside their comfort zones to pass on God's undeserved love. Is it fun? No. Is it excruciating? Sometimes. The greater the pain, however, the better we will understand what Jesus endured for us.

What potentially helpful job do you dislike the most? How can
you deny yourself to better understand Jesus today?

BE THE MAN WHO USES WORDS WISELY

*Watch your tongue and keep your mouth shut,
and you will stay out of trouble.*
PROVERBS 21:23 NLT

"Big talk" among guys is common to the point of expectation. It starts small—"My dad is stronger than your dad!"—and grows from there. The problem comes when these big words are put to the test. Often, the speaker's arrogance is stripped away by reality; however, even when his boasting is warranted, the pride itself leaves a sour taste in people's mouths.

The wise man keeps his mouth shut and lets his actions speak for themselves. As Proverbs 27:2 (NLT) says, "Let someone else praise you, not your own mouth—a stranger, not your own lips."

It's time for men to stop talking big. As Jesus said in Matthew 12:36 (NLT), "You must give an account on judgment day for every idle word you speak." Our words may well come back to haunt us.

Given how potent our words are, here's a rough guide for how to use them well.

When to speak up: when sharing the gospel, praising God, speaking truth, defending the innocent, communicating in love, and building others up.

When to stay silent: every other moment.

Before your day begins, before you've had your morning coffee to kickstart your brain, pray this prayer from Psalm 141:3 (NLT): "Take control of what I say, O LORD, and guard my lips."

When was the last time your words got you into trouble?
Can you think of ways you can use your words more wisely?

BE THE MAN WHO CAPTURES THOUGHTS

I beg you that when I come I may not have to be as bold as I expect to be toward some people who think that we live by the standards of this world. For though we live in the world, we do not wage war as the world does. The weapons we fight with are not the weapons of the world. On the contrary, they have divine power to demolish strongholds. We demolish arguments and every pretension that sets itself up against the knowledge of God, and we take captive every thought to make it obedient to Christ.

2 CORINTHIANS 10:2–5 NIV

There is something appealing to men about the life of a warrior. Warriors are brave men of valor, and their lives represent purpose and adventure. They are aligned with a cause, and they have a leader to follow.

You are called to be a "word warrior." This war isn't physical, nor does it involve vanquishing those who hold different opinions. Rather, it involves compassionately challenging bad ideas with God's truth.

This battle starts by challenging your own thinking. It will be hard to convince anyone of God's truth if you don't believe (or know) it yourself. Therefore, take your own thoughts captive, interrogate each one, and contrast them with what God actually said. Don't settle for secondhand accounts. Your belief should come from a personal knowledge of God's Word.

God's enemy will try to challenge your convictions, setting up shop in your mind and disputing each truth you interrogate. He will be an advocate for the status quo. He is pleased whenever there's a mismatch between what you think and what God says.

Don't let the enemy stop you from entering truth's doors—be the warrior that God calls you to be today.

Do you have any thoughts that contradict God's Word?
If so, how can you challenge them?

BE THE MAN WHO RECOGNIZES STRENGTH'S VALUE

"The LORD will guide you always; he will satisfy your needs in a sun-scorched land and will strengthen your frame. You will be like a well-watered garden, like a spring whose waters never fail."
ISAIAH 58:11 NIV

Excessive worry prevents you from enjoying life. "But," you may say, "being pessimistic means I'm never disappointed." Fair enough. But even if you're wrong and good things do come, you immediately assume this good fortune won't last.

Instead of enhancing life, worry makes it much smaller. It taps into today's strength and bleeds it dry. And when you throw what little strength you have left to the wind, worry will return tomorrow.

Who wants a small life? Who wants their joy to shrink like cooked bacon? Who looks at their deficiencies and thinks, *I want even less*? If you're one of the millions who would shout, "No one!" then there is good news: you don't have to settle for such a scaled-down, unsatisfying life.

"Runt-of-the-litter living" is not the life for you! If God supplies abundantly, stop behaving like you're living in spiritual poverty. If He loves, stop acting like you're rejected. If He lives, stop assuming there's no hope.

It's easy to tell the difference between a well-nurtured garden and an abandoned one. If your life is a garden, don't set up an umbrella when God sends the rain.

Strength is easy to lose, but it can also be replenished. You might make strength-depleting choices, but don't forget the choices that bring restoration. God can provide more than you started with.

What threatens to loosen your grip on strength? Why is this course of action so alluring sometimes? Why is it a lie?

DAY 40

BE THE MAN WHO ENCOURAGES OTHERS

So encourage each other and build each other up,
just as you are already doing.
1 THESSALONIANS 5:11 NLT

When tragedy strikes—whether natural disaster, death, or destruction of property—grief is a natural response. However, while grief has its place, not everyone knows how to move past it.

A faithful, purpose-driven man always shares hope in tragedy. He encourages the grief-stricken by empathizing with their pain, meeting their needs, and showing them—by example—his eternal perspective.

When tragedy struck the church of Thessalonica, they didn't know how to grieve, so Paul wrote, "And now, dear brothers and sisters, we want you to know what will happen to the believers who have died so you will not grieve like people who have no hope" (1 Thessalonians 4:13 NLT).

Our hope is in Jesus and the enduring salvation He gives.

God can—and does—cause good to spring from bad situations. But before we quote Romans 8:28 to the grieving ("And we know that God causes everything to work together for the good of those who love God and are called according to his purpose for them"), we must quote Romans 12:15–16 to ourselves ("Be happy with those who are happy, and *weep with those who weep*. Live in harmony with each other. Don't be too proud to enjoy the company of ordinary people. And don't think you know it all!") (All verses NLT, emphasis added).

We won't always know what to say or how to build others up, but our quiet presence should communicate God's love. The greatest needs of our community are met whenever we show people our hope of a glorious future beyond all grief. Encouragement starts with listening and ends with sharing our hope.

How has someone shared hope with you before? What are some
practical ways to meet someone's need in times of loss?

BE THE MAN WHO BOASTS IN THE LORD

Therefore, as it is written: "Let the one who boasts boast in the Lord."
1 CORINTHIANS 1:31 NIV

There's always that guy who knows a guy. Need a new transmission? He knows a guy. Need a deal on lumber? He knows a guy. Need a cake decorated with a superhero driving a monster truck through a herd of angry dinosaurs? He knows a guy. He might not be the richest, smartest, or most talented guy out there, but he is well-connected.

According to the Bible, our connections matter more than our innate abilities. Actually, there's only one connection that truly matters to the faithful man: "This is what the LORD says: 'Let not the wise boast of their wisdom or the strong boast of their strength or the rich boast of their riches, but let the one who boasts boast about this: that they have the understanding to know me, that I am the LORD, who exercises kindness, justice and righteousness on earth, for in these I delight,' declares the LORD" (Jeremiah 9:23–24 NIV).

When you compare yourself to the Creator of all things, every trace of pride dissolves. You will never be richer, smarter, or more talented than God, but He has still known, chosen, and loved you for who you are. Therefore, God's love for you is the only thing you can brag about, and even then, it should come with the realization that God's love extends not just to you but to everyone.

So feel free to tell the world about your connection to God so that they can be connected too. Need a Savior who loves people even while they reject Him, who forgives every wrong thing they've done, who freely gives wisdom to those who ask, and who works all things together for the good of those who love Him? You know a guy, and He wants you to share that connection with everyone else you know.

Do you tend to boast sometimes? If so, how might you repurpose these boasts to tell someone about your connection to God?

BE THE MAN WHO SEES HIMSELF CLEARLY

*"Why worry about a speck in your friend's eye when you have a log in
your own? How can you think of saying to your friend, 'Let me help
you get rid of that speck in your eye,' when you can't see past the log in
your own eye? Hypocrite! First get rid of the log in your own eye; then
you will see well enough to deal with the speck in your friend's eye."*

MATTHEW 7:3–5 NLT

At some point, someone will say something that you know is not true.
Many trustworthy people might believe the lie and pass it on as solid
intel. Consequently, misinformation will be accepted without challenge.

When you recognize a falsehood, you might be tempted to jump up,
shout the person down, and tell everyone the truth. If you do, however,
most people will be more inclined to remember your awkward outburst
than they will the lie. Your own fault will have overshadowed the fault
you sought to correct.

Jesus' metaphor of the log and speck has everything to do with perspective. If you have a large object in your eye, your window of vision
shrinks dramatically, altering your perception of the world around you.
Similarly, when you have a big sin in your life, you should be able to
notice it. But instead, it creates a blind spot around your own sin while
amplifying whatever tiny sins you spot in anyone else.

Confronting your own sin takes humility and courage. But not only
will it improve your own spiritual eyesight, it will make you compassionate when dealing with the sin you see in others.

Do you spend time working on your own spiritual vision?
How compassionate are you when it comes to the sins of others?

BE THE MAN WHO AVOIDS WRONG PLACES

*Blessed is the man that walketh not in the counsel of the ungodly,
nor standeth in the way of sinners, nor sitteth in the seat of the
scornful. But his delight is in the law of the LORD; and in his law
doth he meditate day and night. And he shall be like a tree planted
by the rivers of water, that bringeth forth his fruit in his season; his
leaf also shall not wither; and whatsoever he doeth shall prosper.*

PSALM 1:1–3 KJV

Weakness comes when you walk, stand, or sit in the wrong place. It's not really a matter of location—it's a matter of company. It can be exhausting to spend your time with "spiritual leeches" who seem bent on ridding you of spiritual strength.

God says you're a blessed man if you let Him steer you away from these ungodly scorners and toward His Word instead. It's like when a tree is transplanted from the arid desert to the edge of a rushing river. Where it once fought for every available ounce of strength, it now grows mighty through abundance.

Choosing generosity in place of selfishness has the same effect. Have you ever seen the satisfaction on someone's face when that person gives a gift that's well received? When a guy goes out of his way to help someone who needs it? This type of action transforms people from weak and malnourished to strong and thriving.

A man's strength depends on where he walks, stands, and sits. Weakness always follows the wrong choice. But even then, there's no mistake too big for God to fix.

Have you ever witnessed the weakness that comes from having the wrong companions? How can God's Word lead you toward improved strength?

BE THE MAN WHO SEES THE BIG PICTURE

"Don't store up treasures here on earth, where moths eat them and rust destroys them, and where thieves break in and steal. Store your treasures in heaven, where moths and rust cannot destroy, and thieves do not break in and steal. Wherever your treasure is, there the desires of your heart will also be."
MATTHEW 6:19–21 NLT

In the 1960s, Dr. Walter Mischel conducted a psychological experiment known as the "marshmallow test." The experiment was designed to test how a child's self-control might affect later life outcomes. Children were placed in a room with a marshmallow (or a cookie, pretzel, or other candy in later experiments) and told if they could resist the temptation for a certain amount of time, they'd get a second treat. Mischel's team then followed a few of these children through the years and found that those who waited were more likely to have successful futures.

In a 2018 study based on Mischel's research, Dr. Tyler W. Watts varied the sample of children to include less-privileged households, better matching the racial and economic makeup of the United States' population. While this updated study revealed a plethora of other factors that can impact a child's future success, delayed gratification still retained its importance.

Delayed gratification isn't a shortcut to success, but it is the first step. Matthew 6:20 encourages us to store up eternal treasures in heaven instead of fleeting treasures on earth. Mark 8:36 (NLT) sums it up this way: "And what do you benefit if you gain the whole world but lose your own soul?"

If we're part of God's family, our soul is secure. But without an eternal perspective, we'll accumulate our treasures in the wrong place. Our lives on earth are just a blip on eternity's radar, so we should have no problem using our current resources to bring others to God. We're not striving for another marshmallow. We're striving for real, eternal rewards!

How does an eternal perspective help you make better daily decisions? How good are you at delayed gratification?

BE THE MAN WHO LEADS HIS FAMILY WELL

An elder must be blameless, faithful to his wife, a man whose children believe and are not open to the charge of being wild and disobedient.
TITUS 1:6 NIV

In his letter to Titus, the apostle Paul outlined some attributes the young pastor should look for when placing men in leadership over the fledgling church of Crete. Today's verse identifies some of these attributes: leaders must be above reproach in their behavior, faithful as husbands, and godly examples for their kids. In short, they must lead their families well.

This kind of leadership cannot be achieved by demanding obedience. If an imposing command to obey God's laws were enough, the Israelites would've never suffered through the wilderness after God gave them the Ten Commandments. They saw the power of God in action, but they still struggled to align their hearts with His.

No, to lead his family well, the faithful man must live humbly before God, following Him as he wants his family to follow himself. He cannot expect godly children if he is not showing them how and why to live a godly life in a wicked world.

This is no easy task today, but neither was it simple in Paul and Titus's time. The city of Crete was every bit as fallen and depraved as today's society. Titus 1:12 (NIV) says, "One of Crete's own prophets has said it: 'Cretans are always liars, evil brutes, lazy gluttons.'"

If the standard to find men of value who are above reproach was given to Titus in such a society, we have no excuses not to be such men today. And before anyone thinks this call to lead his family well doesn't apply to him because he is unmarried or childless, think again. All of God's children are called to follow His example and, in so doing, set an example for others to follow.

Is your character and reputation above reproach?
Are you living as an example you'd like others to follow?

DAY 46

BE THE MAN WHO HAS A LONG VIEW

For which cause we faint not; but though our outward man perish, yet the inward man is renewed day by day. For our light affliction, which is but for a moment, worketh for us a far more exceeding and eternal weight of glory; while we look not at the things which are seen, but at the things which are not seen: for the things which are seen are temporal; but the things which are not seen are eternal.

2 CORINTHIANS 4:16–18 KJV

If you tell a struggling friend, "Don't worry. You'll get over it," you may technically be right, but you might have to look for a new friend. Most people don't take kindly to such platitudes.

Yet when God expresses this sentiment, it's not a platitude. He doesn't criticize the hurt He sees in others but instead compassionately reminds them that their struggles won't last forever. Bad times will come to an end. In the eye of the storm, it's hard to see what God is doing, but this temporary pain will provide an unimaginable payoff.

God is the absolute best at transforming worst-case scenarios into exceptional outcomes. He can make scars beautiful. Restoration is possible to those who are broken, battered, and forgotten.

Courageous men understand that eternity is forever, so the relatively short life span we live here means very little compared to all the good that is yet to come for us who love God and live for His kingdom.

So take a long view. Remember that whatever you face will not be faced forever and that your reward can never be invaded by trouble. You live a short time here. . .but forever with God.

Do you sometimes find it hard to remember that trouble is a short-term issue? How can you remind yourself that bad days will never last?

BE THE MAN WHO OPENS HIS TOOLBOX

Tell them to use their money to do good. They should be rich in good works and generous to those in need, always being ready to share with others. By doing this they will be storing up their treasure as a good foundation for the future so that they may experience true life.
1 Timothy 6:18–19 NLT

Spiritual math is strange. Somehow, you can take God's strength, give His strength to those who need it, and walk away with more than you started with!

God doesn't forbid spending time with nonbelievers. He actually wants you to help them. But there's a big difference between using His strength to introduce people to Him and merely joining the crowd described in Psalm 1—the ungodly, sinners, and scornful. Even among non-Christians, you stick with God's agenda. You don't relax your standards or let down your guard. Your strength diminishes when you decide to use God's Great Commission as an invitation to jump back into the life you wisely left. If you aren't with the unbelieving to extend the offer of God's rescue, then it may be time to get out. The longer you stay, the weaker you'll become.

But when you take the right approach, everything from your finances to your presence can be a tool that God uses. Your generosity and readiness to help will get people asking why. When you do this, 1 Timothy 6 says that you are storing up treasure, building a good foundation and experiencing true life.

Faithful men understand they're on a mission. They know their choices have consequences, their actions matter, and their strength can always improve.

Why does God care if you store, build, and experience the right things? How can you prioritize God's commission and then seek the strength to do what He asks?

BE THE MAN WHO MEMORIZES SCRIPTURE

Thy word have I hid in mine heart, that I might not sin against thee.
PSALM 119:11 KJV

In the Internet Age, the need to memorize has decreased significantly. Why commit things to memory when you can find them on your smartphone? While memorizing trivial facts may be a waste of time, hiding God's Word in our hearts is not. By memorizing scripture, we become more like the author Himself.

But how do we do it? What's the best method for memorization?

According to Michael Nielson—an Australian quantum physicist, science writer, and computer programming researcher—the answer is simple: flashcards.

The concept of spaced repetition—taking a break between learning sessions to better recall the information later—may not be new, but it's still effective. On Twitter, Nielsen said, "The use of spaced repetition memory systems has changed my life over the past couple of years. Here's a few things I've found helpful: I've memorized about nine thousand cards, over two years. The single biggest change is that memory is no longer a haphazard event, to be left to chance. Rather, I can guarantee I will remember something, with minimal effort: it makes memory a choice.

"Rule of thumb: if memorizing something will likely save me five minutes in the future, into the spaced repetition system it goes."

The next time you're sipping coffee, eating lunch, or waiting for a meeting to start, use the time to memorize scripture. The more you get into God's Word, the more God's Word gets into you. And the more that happens, the less you'll be tempted to sin, because you'll be looking at the world through God's truth.

What verses have you already memorized? How can
remembering God's Word help you avoid sin?

BE THE MAN WHO SHOWS SELF-DISCIPLINE

For God has not given us a spirit of fear and timidity,
but of power, love, and self-discipline.
2 Timothy 1:7 nlt

There's a reason you can almost always find Wrigley gum in the grocery store checkout aisle.

Back in the 1950s, the Wm. Wrigley Jr. Company commissioned the Stanford Research Institute to study impulse buying. In 1962, Stanford researcher Hawkins Stern published "The Significance of Impulse Buying Today" in the *Journal of Marketing*, forever changing the layout of grocery stores. Due to Stern's research, Wrigley gum moved from the main aisles to the checkout, where people are more likely to buy it because the stress of grocery shopping has weakened their willpower.

The ability to control our impulses, whether they include buying checkout aisle candy or engaging in less innocent activities, is known by many names: self-discipline, self-control, willpower, resolve, and so on. According to today's scripture, this quality is a gift God has provided us. This doesn't mean you won't struggle against temptation—it means God has granted you His strength to overcome your weakness in that moment.

However, self-discipline doesn't usually develop overnight. Rather, it's like a muscle that gets stronger with use. Denying temptation once will make it easier to deny that temptation in the future. And remember, you aren't doing this alone. Willpower and prayer work hand in hand in fighting temptation. Inviting God into your struggle honors Him with your desire for holiness and pleases Him because you are wise enough to humbly ask.

Next time you are in the grocery store checkout line and feel tempted to indulge in your desires, pray for discipline to avoid temptation—and set your mind on higher things.

What temptation are you dealing with today? How can you couple prayer with willpower in order to maintain your self-discipline?

DAY 50

BE THE MAN WHO DISCOVERS STRENGTH

I can do all this through him who gives me strength.
PHILIPPIANS 4:13 NIV

Many verses need a little context to understand them. Philippians 4:13 is no exception.

Often, people gain comfort through a surface level reading of this verse. They believe that God will give them the strength to do *anything*— that there's nothing they can't accomplish. But what happens if you factor in the previous verse? Philippians 4:12 says, "I know what it is to be in need, and I know what it is to have plenty. I have learned the secret of being content in any and every situation, whether well fed or hungry, whether living in plenty or in want" (NIV).

Clearly, Paul didn't mean you can dream up anything you want and God has to give it to you. God does want you to dream big, but He never offers a blank check. Rather, Paul's words came from a specific place of courageous wonder.

Sometimes, the apostle ate well; other times, he went hungry. There were good days and days that seemed doomed from the start. However, instead of complaining to customer support whenever he encountered some supply chain issues, Paul simply said, "I can do all this through him who gives me strength."

He recognized that no one is wired to get through hard days alone— God's help is required. So during these bad times, God's comfort was imperative. His compassion was Paul's rock of refuge, which reminded him that God's dream was worth following and that His ultimate plan dwarfs even the most wonderful of days.

Do you sometimes complain when you don't get exactly what you want?
If so, how can you learn to lean more fully on God's comfort and help?

BE THE MAN WHO FINDS SECURITY

You created my inmost being; you knit me together in my mother's
womb. . . . Your eyes saw my unformed body; all the days ordained
for me were written in your book before one of them came to be.
PSALM 139:13, 16 NIV

Every man who's ever existed has one thing in common—*insecurity.*
Some are better at masking it than others, but all men ask themselves at
some point, "Do I measure up?" You want to know if you fit into a plan—
any plan. You want to know if your life is going to impact someone—
anyone. You want to know if God ever thinks about you—any thoughts.

Psalm 139 is your answer. Before your body even had form, God
stitched you together. He knew how long you'd live before you took a
breath. He knows the path you should take before you think to ask. He's
got a book with your story written inside. None of your choices take Him
by surprise.

If you're too insecure to even admit your insecurity, take heart: your
perspective can change. God's got a lock on security, and He says you
obtain that security when you obtain Him. You don't have to wonder if
you are important to God. You can be secure knowing that you are. . .and
always will be.

You were not an accident—you were created. You were not unknown—God saw you. You are not unrecognized—God has a book with
your story.

A man of faith and strength first understands his weakness, and then
he understands that insecurity is nothing more than a terminated position—a career God has replaced with trust.

How does insecurity play a role in your view of life? Do you find it easy to deny
your insecurity? Why is it important to admit that you are sometimes insecure?

BE THE MAN WHO CONTENDS FOR THE FAITH

Dear friends, although I was very eager to write to you about the salvation we share, I felt compelled to write and urge you to contend for the faith that was once for all entrusted to God's holy people.

JUDE 3 NIV

Contend isn't a word you hear every day. It means "to fight, compete, or engage in rivalry." It comes from the Latin word *contendere*, a word which combines "with" and "to stretch." If you've ever seen a wrestling match, you've seen what it means to contend.

Jude, the half-brother of Jesus, urged all believers to contend for the faith, to fight for Christianity. Fighting isn't usually considered a Christian ideal. After all, Jesus says in Matthew 5:38–39 (NIV): "You have heard that it was said, 'Eye for eye, and tooth for tooth.' But I tell you, do not resist an evil person. If anyone slaps you on the right cheek, turn to them the other cheek also."

However, when it came to defending the faith, Jesus was no pacifist. John 2:13–16 (NIV) says, "When it was almost time for the Jewish Passover, Jesus went up to Jerusalem. In the temple courts he found people selling cattle, sheep and doves, and others sitting at tables exchanging money. So he made a whip out of cords, and drove all from the temple courts, both sheep and cattle; he scattered the coins of the money changers and overturned their tables. To those who sold doves he said, 'Get these out of here! Stop turning my Father's house into a market!'"

When evil people persecute us, we should always turn the other cheek. But when false teachers or corrupt spiritual leaders attack our belief in Christ, it is our duty as faithful men to fight back with truth, actively contending for our faith.

What do you do when you hear someone who claims to be a Christian speaking lies about the faith? How can you know when someone is teaching falsely?

DAY 53

BE THE MAN WHO KNOWS HIS BODY IS GOD'S

*For ye are bought with a price: therefore glorify God in
your body, and in your spirit, which are God's.*
1 Corinthians 6:20 KJV

The core message of salvation is extremely simple: the Son of God lived a perfect life, sacrificed Himself to pay the penalty we deserved, and then rose again, telling us that we can be children of God if we simply believe. This invitation has been offered to all people. It's mind-blowing!

However, here's the complex part: God's free gift of salvation cost Jesus everything, and when we accept that gift, we become the thing that Jesus bought. God welcomes us into His family and gives His Spirit to live inside us, but in the process, we must bargain away certain freedoms.

Nothing belongs to us anymore. Not our souls. Not our bodies. Not our minds. Nothing.

Let that sink in.

Now, before you start thinking you somehow got the short end of the stick or that you were tricked into accepting a gift that came with such costly conditions, consider this: what were you doing with all that freedom *before* accepting God's gift of salvation?

You were most likely living for yourself, giving into every temptation and digging yourself deeper into the hole of sin. The whole reason we needed salvation is because we were doing such a lousy job with our freedom. The adversary loves trying to convince us that we had more fun before we were God's, but the truth is that sin always makes us miserable. Freedom to sin is nothing more than the freedom to crawl back into the devil's chains, from which Christ freed us at the cross.

You are not your own. You have been bought with Christ's blood and invited into God's family. As such, it is your duty to respect Jesus' sacrifice with your body, soul, and mind, using them all for His glory instead of your own pleasure.

How does the knowledge that salvation cost Jesus His life affect your view of salvation? What can you do when the adversary tempts you toward his "freedom"?

BE THE MAN WHO IS AN ESSENTIAL ANALYST

If there be therefore any consolation in Christ, if any comfort of love,
if any fellowship of the Spirit, if any bowels and mercies, Fulfil ye my joy,
that ye be likeminded, having the same love, being of one accord, of one
mind. Let nothing be done through strife or vainglory; but in lowliness
of mind let each esteem other better than themselves. Look not every
man on his own things, but every man also on the things of others.

PHILIPPIANS 2:1–4 KJV

Computers can seem a lot like human intellect—that's because human intellect developed them. They analyze data and compute a response. The better the data, the better the analysis. These devices aren't prone to snap judgments, prejudice, or personal preference. They only respond to data and not what motivated the data.

God wants you to be one of His analysts. Whenever you see that someone has a need, pray to God, and He will help you calculate how to respond.

It's often easy to let your personal desires control your response as you ignore any certain data associated with the needs of others. God, however, has an essential analyst update—His Spirit—that allows you to take this extra data into account and respond with empathy and compassion. Some people can't seem to be courageous in helping because they haven't accessed this essential upgrade.

You are more than a computer—you are flesh and bone analyzing flesh and bone, so what you discover will be more than hard facts and bottom lines. Being an essential analyst brings you to a place of connection with those you are learning to care about.

How good are you at analyzing the needs of others?
What can you do to extend kindness to those who need help?

BE THE MAN WHO DOESN'T BETRAY THE BETRAYER

It is not an enemy who taunts me—I could bear that. It is not my foes who so arrogantly insult me—I could have hidden from them. Instead, it is you—my equal, my companion and close friend. What good fellowship we once enjoyed as we walked together to the house of God.

PSALM 55:12–14 NLT

Betrayal can't come from an enemy—you have to be friends first. Betrayal does the unthinkable because it's an act you don't expect.

Nestled a third of the way through the book of Psalms is a chapter (Psalm 55) that deals with a betrayal David once had. David lamented that it was more bearable to have an enemy taunt him (remember Goliath?) than a friend. A foe could insult him, but it was more damaging from someone he thought he could trust.

When the one who knows your secrets shares them, trust dissolves. When that person lies about you, a friendship is broken. When a friend insults you, a storehouse of good memories is shaken out into a violent wind. It's hard to recover from a betrayal. It hurts. It leaves you weak. It makes you ponder all the things you would've done differently if you'd known then what you know now. You can no longer recommend that person for a job in good conscience, and you might secretly hope God will return the favor to this former friend. Even worse, you might try to take matters into your own hands, and the accumulated anger will leave you spiritually bankrupt.

When God says to pray for your enemies—to refuse to repay evil for evil—it's not because He wants to let them off the hook. Rather, He doesn't want you to place yourself on a brand-new hook. Their betrayal doesn't modify God's orders.

Why is it easy to seek an evil end for a betrayer? How can you process the pain of betrayal to discover a better answer?

BE THE MAN WHO TRUSTS THE ONE HE FOLLOWS

The LORD is my light and my salvation—whom shall I fear?
The LORD is the stronghold of my life—of whom shall I be afraid?
When the wicked advance against me to devour me, it is my
enemies and my foes who will stumble and fall. Though
an army besiege me, my heart will not fear; though war
break out against me, even then I will be confident.
PSALM 27:1–3 NIV

Pick a cause—any cause. It could be one that you or a friend identifies with or cares deeply about. Now that you have that cause in mind, how do its supporters show that it's important to them? Some might send a check, others might volunteer to help bring awareness to the cause, and still others might boycott anything that's opposed to the cause, writing letters to the newspaper or posting online about their disapproval. Rarely, however, will someone die for a cause.

King David had a cause, and that cause was God. Because the king stood for God, God helped him. Eventually, the king concluded that his confidence could find secure lodging in God's goodness. Armed with God's love and protection, he could face a whole army of foes.

And he did. Often.

When you allow your life to represent the cause of Christ, any adversity along the way just draws you closer to the one you follow.

The willingness to stand for this cause is the wisdom to be confident.

How much do you believe in the cause of Christ? What can you
do today to demonstrate your full devotion to this cause?

BE THE MAN WHO ASKS OTHERS TO PRAY FOR HIM

Pray for us. We are sure that we have a clear conscience and desire to live honorably in every way.
HEBREWS 13:18 NIV

A man with a clear conscience and a desire to live honorably can accomplish great things for God. However, evil loves a good challenge—and there's no challenge greater than a man ready to accomplish great things for God. So each Christian man must be wary of the devil's traps and willing to ask for help.

The first and oldest trap for a righteous man is pride, the sin that led to Lucifer's downfall. If you think you've got it all together or that you can maintain a holy lifestyle under your own power, you're stepping right into the trap. You can't live for God without God's active assistance.

The second trap is self-pity. You are trying so hard to live for God, but you don't see things changing for the better. Lazy people get promoted around you. Rich people get richer through dishonesty. And no one thanks you for any of your hard work. Aren't you justified in feeling a little sorry for yourself? Nope! Remember Romans 5:3 (NIV): "Not only so, but we also glory in our sufferings, because we know that suffering produces perseverance."

The best way to avoid these traps is to immerse yourself in God's Word and ask for help. Prayer connects your needs to the one who perfectly provides. When you ask others to pray for you, you are connecting with folks who will encourage you, keep you accountable, and bring your needs before God. Requesting help isn't a sign of weakness; it's a mark of wisdom.

Has asking for help ever felt like weakness to you? When your conscience is clean and your desires are for God, have you noticed any traps?

BE THE MAN WHO SHARES THE LOAD

Share each other's burdens, and in this way obey the law of Christ.
GALATIANS 6:2 NLT

Golfers hire a caddy when they want someone else to carry their clubs. People hire moving companies when they need their belongings moved from one location to the next. A family might hire someone to do some light housekeeping or care for an aging family member or young child whenever the need arises. All these are examples of people who share another's burdens—yet only when they're asked.

What about when nobody asks. . .but you know it's the right thing to do?

Take eleven-year-old Davyon, for instance. He has always wanted to become an emergency medical technician when he grows up. Apparently, he just couldn't wait. One day at lunch, he came to the rescue of a choking student and helped dislodge the food. Later the same day, he helped rescue a neighbor from a burning house. Davyon is an example of someone who kept his eyes peeled for ways to help share another person's burden. In his case, he also saved two lives.

Have you made a habit of stepping up to share someone's load? Being a Christian doesn't mean you'll never have time for yourself—it simply means widening the scope of your interests to include others.

Selfishness refuses to include others and laments every occasion when one's personal time and space is breached. But God asks for a different response. His love is for all people everywhere, and He's in the business of saving lives and transforming hearts. Because He shares your burdens, He asks you to do the same.

Relationships are just that important to Him.

How has someone else shared a burden you faced? How has God?
What might motivate you to share someone else's burden?

DAY 59

BE THE MAN WHO LETS GOD JUDGE

When they hurled their insults at him, he did not retaliate;
when he suffered, he made no threats. Instead,
he entrusted himself to him who judges justly.
1 PETER 2:23 NIV

It's the theme of countless movies and television shows: revenge. To borrow a phrase from 1970s singer B. J. Thomas, "somebody done somebody wrong"—and the second somebody's going to make the first one pay.

As Christian men, we know that Jesus taught His followers, "Love your enemies and pray for those who persecute you" (Matthew 5:44 NIV). Why? "That you may be children of your Father in heaven" (verse 45 NIV).

But even as Christian men, we're very much a part of this broken world. We don't even need the influence of thousands of hours of movies and television shows to make us want revenge. . .though all those "I'll get you back" storylines certainly haven't helped.

A truly faithful man, however, does not pursue vengeance. He knows that the Lord has said, "It is mine to avenge; I will repay" (Romans 12:19 NIV). He knows that even Jesus, the perfect, all-knowing, all-powerful God, chose not to lash out at the people who were killing Him. He never threatened or retaliated, though He could have wiped out His enemies with a sniff, a blink, or the flick of the hand. Instead, Jesus "entrusted himself to him who judges justly"—God the Father.

Vengeance makes for an exciting climax to a movie. But in real life, it generates even more pain and trouble. The strong man is the one who—like his Lord—leaves the paybacks in God's hands.

How does knowing Jesus was betrayed help you rethink your reactions to a betrayer? Why is God's judgment worth more than any other opinion?

DAY 60

BE THE MAN WHO LEARNS FROM MISTAKES

As a dog returns to its vomit, so fools repeat their folly.
PROVERBS 26:11 NIV

According to the American Kennel Club, a dog's sense of smell is far keener than a human's, but their sense of taste is roughly one-sixth as powerful as ours. So when a dog finds something that smells like food, they eat it—even if it's vomit. They still taste it, but they don't seem to mind. In fact, it may remind them of their puppyhood.

As puppies are weaned off their mother's milk, they learn to eat regurgitated food. Since it's partially digested already, it's easier for their bodies to handle. Eating vomit may be disgusting for us, but for dogs, it's natural.

In Proverbs 26:11, the Bible compares a dog eating vomit to fools coming back to their folly. It's a good comparison. Folly comes naturally to fools.

King David wrote in Psalm 51:5 (NIV): "Surely I was sinful at birth, sinful from the time my mother conceived me." However, though we naturally sin in our youth, we were never meant to stay there. Ephesians 2:3–5 (NIV) says, "All of us also lived among them at one time, gratifying the cravings of our flesh and following its desires and thoughts. Like the rest, we were by nature deserving of wrath. But because of his great love for us, God, who is rich in mercy, made us alive with Christ even when we were dead in transgressions—it is by grace you have been saved."

Sadly, many of us digest sin all too easily. Deadening our spiritual taste buds, we crave the things of the flesh. A faithful man allows God to sharpen his palate so that he doesn't confuse vomit for nourishing food. Folly may be natural for fools, but it's disgusting among God's children.

Is there a specific sin you are still tempted by? How can
you sharpen your palate for God's nourishment?

BE THE MAN WHO WALKS THE EXTRA MILE

*"If anyone wants to sue you and take your shirt, hand over
your coat as well. If anyone forces you to go one mile, go with
them two miles. Give to the one who asks you, and do not turn
away from the one who wants to borrow from you."*

MATTHEW 5:40–42 NIV

In a more distant past, it was normal to conscript someone into forced
labor. *Conscription* means the compulsory enlistment for a service to be
performed. More recently, this word was used to describe the draft that
brought young soldiers into the armed forces. Both meanings suggest
involuntary service.

Jesus knew this kind of service was a normal part of life in His
culture. Therefore, He told His disciples that if they found themselves
forced to help someone, they shouldn't stop at the bare minimum. Rather,
they should set the bar much higher and do even more than they were
asked. This response didn't stem from a desire for recognition—it proved
they were Christians who represented God. After all, if they were to treat
others as if they were accommodating God Himself, then why would it
matter if anyone was paying attention?

Think about what your life would be like if God behaved like we do
sometimes. Would He say, "Sorry, I can't help you right now. I'm on the
clock"?

Never! That's just not who He is.

Other people's needs will never be met if you lack empathy. God
tells us that we should go above and beyond to help others. After all, isn't
that what He did for us?

> When you answer someone's call for help, do you go beyond
> what's needed or stop once the minimum is reached? How
> does God's example help you see the right response?

DAY 62

BE THE MAN WHO GAINS STRENGTH IN THE TELLING

"Give his people the knowledge of salvation
through the forgiveness of their sins."
LUKE 1:77 NIV

Before Jesus gave the Great Commission, John the Baptist told people to turn away from sin and toward a friendship with God. And before John the Baptist was born, his father Zechariah, who was a priest, spoke the words written in Luke 1:77.

God was Jesus' father, but Zechariah would've been known as Jesus' uncle. The Bible doesn't say how close John and Jesus were, but they shared the same message—God's salvation must come through forgiveness. This forgiveness inspires strength because it releases guilt, restores hope, and mends your broken relationship with God.

If forgiveness does all that, why would you keep it to yourself? You might feel comfortable and safe in the silence. You might assume telling others about Jesus is a job for someone else. But after Jesus rose from the dead, every disciple kept telling this amazing truth. If those who heard and believed had stopped adding links to the information chain, it would have been broken centuries ago. But that didn't happen. The strength of the message continues to be shared by people like you.

This strength comes in two forms: (1) the strength God gives you to share His amazing gift and (2) the strength you receive from speaking about it.

A faithful man of strength accepts God's boldness and then embraces the strength that comes when he shares "the knowledge of salvation through the forgiveness of. . .sins."

Today, gain strength in the telling.

Have you ever experienced this two-tier gift of strength by telling people about Jesus? If so, what did you learn?

BE THE MAN WHO DOESN'T LET POLITICS GET IN THE WAY

Show proper respect to everyone, love the family of believers, fear God, honor the emperor.
1 PETER 2:17 NIV

Nero ruled over Rome for fourteen years—AD 54 to 68—during the rise of the early church. He was the emperor Peter and Paul referenced in many of their letters. For the first few years of Nero's reign, he seemed like a pretty benign leader. He surrounded himself with good advisors and showed respect for the Senate. But when his main advisors died or retired, Nero fell into immoral and criminal behavior, going down in history as the emperor who burned down part of the city to make room for his palace. Nero then blamed the fire on the Christians, and he reportedly had them burned alive as human torches to light his gladiatorial games.

This was the emperor that Peter—who himself would be martyred by Roman hands—told his readers to honor in today's scripture. Honor *that* emperor? Really?

Yes. Political viewpoints are no reason to dishonor someone.

Peter opens the verse with encouragement to honor *everyone*. He closes it by including Nero specifically. Whatever crimes Nero committed, he was a man made in the image of God. It was God alone who was to be feared, not the emperor.

Nero's reign of terror caused many Christians to flee their homes, and Christianity spread around the world. Would Christians have chosen a different path to disseminating the gospel? Probably, but God chose to place Nero in the emperor's seat, and it resulted in many new nations coming to God.

Do you disagree with someone? Are you experiencing suffering at someone else's hand? Honor the person and fear God—He will work out the rest.

Do you regularly pray for people with opposing viewpoints? How else might you honor them?

BE THE MAN WHO PERFORMS ACTS OF KINDNESS

We know what real love is because Jesus gave up his life for us. So we also ought to give up our lives for our brothers and sisters. If someone has enough money to live well and sees a brother or sister in need but shows no compassion—how can God's love be in that person? Dear children, let's not merely say that we love each other; let us show the truth by our actions.

1 JOHN 3:16–18 NLT

A man's courage is never stronger than when he's doing something that defies expectation. If greed is the common response, then a courageous man shows generosity. He may experience ridicule, but he also understands that God has a different set of rules for His family. If following those rules makes him seem peculiar, then so be it.

Kindness rarely makes the headlines, but it's constantly impacting families around the world. Some churches have even tried increasing acts of kindness by giving their members money and asking them to use it exclusively for others. These churches hope that this investment will help their congregation experience first-hand the joy that intentional acts of kindness bring. Many members will return with stories about what God did when they used their gift.

Kindness can be a good way for you to show God's selfless, heart-changing love to people who doubt it exists. Actions like walking someone's dog, generously tipping a waiter, or paying for a stranger's meal may be small, but they make a very visible point. When others see it, maybe they will also see the God who inspired it.

When was the last time you saw kindness make a positive impact? Why did that happen? Do others see God's love in your own kindness?

DAY 65

BE THE MAN WHO BUILDS WITH SUCCESS

They go from strength to strength.
PSALM 84:7 KJV

God's strength may seem like an impossible acquisition.

Matthew 25 contains the story of three men who were managers of their employer's business holdings. The boss gave all three a certain amount of money to invest while he was away. Two of these men managed to double their investment. (The Bible doesn't say how.) One success led to more success as they wisely used what they were given. The third, however, essentially put the cash in his mattress. He chose to live in fear of his employer, making inaction his permanent address.

Psalm 84 echoes this story's theme when it describes success as a grand procession toward God, with one strength leading to another strength. It's fitting, therefore, that this chapter is found in the middle of the Psalms near the center of the Bible.

This procession is all about victory and overcoming—about honoring a good God who offers free samples of strength for those who start their spiritual journey and keeps growing it from there. So bring on the celebration!

Building blocks of God's strength are assembled through acts of trust. Without trust, we're left with nothing but weakness. Our "God blocks" fall apart, replaced by the fear we thought we'd left behind so long ago.

So today, be a man who accepts God's strength. Don't even think of going without it.

Does it help you to think of accepting God's strength one challenge at a time?
How might one moment of God's strength lead to a stronger life of faith?

BE THE MAN WHO BELONGS TO THE KINGDOM OF HEAVEN

Jesus answered, "My Kingdom is not an earthly kingdom. If it were, my followers would fight to keep me from being handed over to the Jewish leaders. But my Kingdom is not of this world."
JOHN 18:36 NLT

In His earthly life, Jesus could have been King of this world. He had the power to make it happen. This was what the nation of Israel had wanted ever since God promised them a Messiah. Jesus could have pivoted His teaching and miracles toward political ends. He could have marched to Jerusalem, claimed David's throne, and overthrown the Roman empire.

It wasn't just the people of Israel who thought Jesus should do this. When the devil tempted Jesus in the wilderness, it was with the promise of ruling the world.

Jesus could have done this, but He chose not to. Why? Because Jesus had a bigger kingdom in mind. He wanted to usher in the kingdom of heaven. He didn't want to overthrow Rome, a temporary power on eternity's spectrum; Jesus wanted to overthrow sin and death itself!

And He did. The coronation ceremony occurred when Jesus was given a crown of thorns. His sacrificial death brought everlasting life to those who trust in Him. His kingdom is here and now, and we are His subjects.

But sometimes, we forget our allegiance. Like the Israelites who wanted Jesus to overthrow Rome, we get caught up in temporal things. We need to stop treating Jesus like an earthly king and instead recognize His spiritual reign.

If you have accepted Jesus as your Lord, stop ignoring His kingdom. Everyone, from pauper to president, will someday bow at His throne— but we are called to bow to Him *now*.

Where does your allegiance lie? What does it look like to be a resident in God's kingdom?

DAY 67

BE THE MAN WHO IMITATES GOD

Imitate God, therefore, in everything you do,
because you are his dear children.
EPHESIANS 5:1 NLT

Has anyone ever mistaken your voice for your dad's over the phone? If you're biologically related, some similarity probably exists. Even if you aren't, you may have learned the same verbal habits—pronunciations, pauses, and so on—your dad uses.

Now, have you ever tried to imitate someone else's voice? Maybe you've done an impression of Arnold Schwarzenegger from the Terminator movies ("I'll be back"). Or maybe it was some politician with a memorable catchphrase ("I am not a crook," "No new taxes," "Yes we can!").

Knowing a few lines isn't enough for a successful imitation, though. To get it right, you must pitch your voice properly, drop the same syllables, speak with the same accents, pause in the same places, place emphasis on the right words, and practice, practice, practice. It all starts with listening, and it ends with others recognizing the voice.

The same can be said of imitating God. It isn't enough to know a few of His lines from the Bible. It starts with listening to Him carefully, knowing Him fully, then trying to do what He does. It means loving unconditionally, forgiving completely, and providing for others' needs, even when it costs you everything. And it means doing it all the time.

Fortunately, you have the same family advantage that makes it possible to sound like your earthly father. With the Spirit of God dwelling inside you, it will be easier to act like the Almighty because you won't need to act at all. Listen to the Spirit, read God's Word, and pray for God's guidance as you go through your day. When you do, others will see the imitation for what it really is: family resemblance.

In which ways is it natural for you to imitate God? Are there any areas in which you might need to practice for others to see the resemblance?

BE THE MAN WHO IS LION-BOLD

The wicked flee when no man pursueth:
but the righteous are bold as a lion.
PROVERBS 28:1 KJV

Darkness falls and evil creeps into the heart of our world. That's not the tagline for a new movie—it's a simple truth that the Bible addresses repeatedly. Jesus said, "Light is come into the world, and men loved darkness rather than light, because their deeds were evil" (John 3:19 KJV). The apostle Paul urged Christians in Rome, "Let us therefore cast off the works of darkness, and let us put on the armour of light" (Romans 13:12 KJV).

When people do the wrong thing, they often try to hide it. Whenever they choose to sin, they want to conceal any evidence in the darkest part of their hearts.

People who sin don't want to get caught. They seal their lips, close their heart, and distance themselves from people who care about them. They run when no one chases and live in constant fear of being exposed. They believe their life will be destroyed if they're caught, so they cower in terror.

On the opposite end of the spectrum is the courageous man. His inscription reads, BOLD AS A LION. This description refers not to pride but to truth. He knows that the path to forgiveness lies in God's embrace, so he freely runs toward it.

The brave, strong, and courageous are bold like lions simply because God has rescued them from the darkness and brightened them with His love.

How "lionlike" are you today?

Have you abandoned darkness in favor of light?
How can you learn to be more lion-bold?

DAY 69

BE THE MAN WHO ABANDONS HIS OLD ADDRESS

My old self has been crucified with Christ. It is no longer I who live,
but Christ lives in me. So I live in this earthly body by trusting
in the Son of God, who loved me and gave himself for me.
GALATIANS 2:20 NLT

When you sell your house or move out of a rental property, it's natural to take all your belongings. You don't leave some things just in case you want to go back someday, and you don't leave one room untouched so that you'll have a place to visit. No, you take everything. Why? Because your address has changed. The old house is no longer home. You don't live there anymore.

This is how we should treat the separation between our old life and the new. Yet too often, we find ourselves knocking on the door to a house that's no longer ours, wanting to spend time in rooms we left behind. We won't find strength in this dilapidated place—only fear at every turn. The doors creak and so do the floors. This shack doesn't even feel like home, so why do we spend so much time here?

Strength is found when we move forward in our friendship with God. When we leave the past in the past and know our future lies elsewhere. When we resist the urge to turn from God's provision, back to the weakness that no longer defines us.

You may know you have a different future, but emotions can make you think there's something special you've left behind. Any return you make, however, will be a less-than-satisfying reunion. So do everything you can to remember why you left it in the past—your feet weren't made to walk that path again.

> When do you feel the pull to revisit your past life
> the most? Why is it important to resist a return?

BE THE MAN WHO KILLS RUMORS

Fire goes out without wood, and quarrels disappear when gossip stops.
PROVERBS 26:20 NLT

The ability to build a roaring fire isn't a prerequisite for manliness, but there is something inherently testosterone-enhancing about setting a carefully stacked pile of wood ablaze.

However, whether your ideal campfire starts as a "teepee" (dry tinder in the center, pencil-thin kindling arranged in a cone around the tinder with forearm-sized pieces of fuel wood on the outermost layer) or a "log cabin" (dry tinder and kindling arranged teepee-style with fuel wood stacked in a square around it), there won't be much of a fire without wood.

The same is true for rumors. Remove the fuel and the rumor dies. Stop repeating what you've heard from others, and gossip will cease.

James 1:26 (NLT) says, "If you claim to be religious but don't control your tongue, you are fooling yourself, and your religion is worthless."

It isn't enough to idly listen while someone spouts rumors to us—a faithful man douses the flames of gossip with the water of truth. Proverbs 20:19 (NIV) says, "A gossip betrays a confidence; so avoid anyone who talks too much." When others tell you a story about someone else, tell them you'd rather hear it from the source. Tell them it isn't right to talk about people behind their backs. Tell them if they can't control their tongues, you'll have to avoid them altogether.

Listening to gossip only adds fuel. And besides, if someone gossips to you about others, that person probably gossips to others about you.

There's nothing manly about stoking the fires of gossip. Instead, speak the truth in love. Build an actual bonfire, inviting your friends over to discuss things openly. Lead by example. Kindle camaraderie, not rumors.

How can social media be used to quench gossip, not fuel it?
Have you ever betrayed someone's confidence by spreading gossip?

BE THE MAN WHOSE LOVE IS GENUINE

Don't just pretend to love others. Really love them.
Hate what is wrong. Hold tightly to what is good.
ROMANS 12:9 NLT

Barbara Erni, born into poverty in 1743, was determined not to die poor. Instead, she died by beheading, the last person to be executed in Liechtenstein before the tiny country outlawed the death penalty in 1987.

You see, Erni had developed quite a scam in order to escape poverty. She would travel from inn to inn across the Liechtensteinian country-side, lugging a large treasure chest or satchel behind her. At each inn, she would beg the innkeeper to keep her treasure chest in the most secure room in the inn, preferably where the innkeeper's own valuables were stored.

At night, the innkeeper would lock her chest in the room—but in the morning, the chest, the innkeeper's valuables, and Erni would all be missing. Her secret? She didn't work alone. Inside the chest was a man with dwarfism who would pop out at night and load the chest with whatever valuables struck his fancy before the duo took off for the next inn, where they would repeat the trick.

Barbara Erni's con worked for fifteen years before she was caught and condemned. Her chest hid secrets, and her innocent requests concealed her true motives.

Now let's consider your life story. Are you hiding secrets in your chest? Are you forthcoming about your motives? When you profess to love someone, is your love genuine or does it mask a desire to get something in return? Christian love is, at its core, selfless. There must be no hidden agendas or ulterior motives. You cannot show love to someone else when evil intentions lie within.

Take a moment right now to examine your heart. Ask the Lord to reveal any greed, lust, or selfishness that might lie buried within. It is time for love to be genuine.

> Are there any hidden motives in your heart? How does
> genuine love differ from a love that's in word only?

DAY 72

BE THE MAN WHO LIVES WITHOUT FEAR

Remember those in prison, as if you were there yourself. Remember
also those being mistreated, as if you felt their pain in your own
bodies. . . . God has said, "I will never fail you. I will never
abandon you." So we can say with confidence, "The LORD is my
helper, so I will have no fear. What can mere people do to me?"
HEBREWS 13:3, 5–6 NLT

Imagine yourself as a six-year-old boy with a loving teenage brother. You think of him as your protector and defender. There's no reason to be afraid when someone bigger and stronger, with much more authority, is watching out for you. "Big brother" can keep the bullies away, make decisions you don't know how to make, and offer companionship when you really need a friend. Hopefully, he's always available when you need him.

It's nice to have help when bad things happen, but there is no better help than that which comes from the God who made you. When life's bullies show up, you can say, "When you mess with me, you mess with *Him*." That might cause bullies to reconsider their plans.

Faithful, courageous men are convinced that no one will ever exceed God's strength, cause Him to back down, or have a more authoritative name. They know that God's presence ensures a positive outcome.

You can be courageous under pressure when you remind yourself, "God helps me and I'm not afraid. People can never hurt me more than God loves me!"

What frightens you more than anything else? How can you remind
yourself that God is bigger than even your worst scenario?

BE THE MAN WHO ESCAPES HIS IMAGINATION

*"Do not worry about your life, what you will eat or drink;
or about your body, what you will wear. Is not life more
than food, and the body more than clothes?"*
MATTHEW 6:25 NIV

Walter Mitty is the fictional protagonist of two movies bearing his name. In both stories, he has a mediocre job and is rather clumsy and confused. All his strength comes through his fantastical daydreams. But when Walter finally engages with reality, the shackles of his imagination grow less powerful. The worry he once embraced is transformed into strength.

When you stop looking at all the "what ifs" in life and pay attention to the "what *is*," there'll be a big shift in how you perceive things. This is no substitute for God's strength; instead, it's a great way to stop working against God and continually insisting that life is against you.

Worry is worthless—God's Word says so. If you're thirsty, there's water. If you need clothes, there are plenty of shops to choose from. Life is more than a designer label or a packaged bottle of water. When you get mired in the specifics, you miss out on the adventure happening all around you. You start looking like a detective who's hauling the world's largest magnifying glass.

As a man of faith and strength, you can cooperate with God. So take your thoughts captive and interrogate them in the light of God's Word—not the faulty glow of your imagination.

How often have you allowed your imagination to convince you things are worse than they actually are? When was the last time you measured your thoughts using the Bible's teachings? How might you use this strategy more?

BE THE MAN WHO SHINES FROM THE HILLTOP

*Let your light so shine before men, that they may see your
good works, and glorify your Father which is in heaven.*
MATTHEW 5:16 KJV

When Jesus gave the Sermon on the Mount, He used the geographical features of the land to impart God's truth.

In Matthew 5:14–16 (KJV) Jesus said, "Ye are the light of the world. A city that is set on an hill cannot be hid. Neither do men light a candle, and put it under a bushel, but on a candlestick; and it giveth light unto all that are in the house. Let your light so shine before men, that they may see your good works, and glorify your Father which is in heaven."

The ancient city of Hippos sat on a hill toward the southeastern end of the Sea of Galilee. As one of the cities of the Decapolis, Hippos was a Greco-Roman cultural center. Also, due to its naturally advantageous position, the city was fortified as a military outpost and would have been difficult to conquer. In fact, it took an earthquake, centuries after Christ walked the earth, to finally destroy it.

When Jesus compared His followers to a city on a hill, His original audience would have immediately thought of Hippos. Its position was obvious, and that was part of its strength.

When we engage in ungodly deeds, we cover God's light and rob Him of glory. A faithful child of God, however, draws strength from his identity in Christ, and his faith is illuminated by his actions—like a city on a hill.

As Hippos was a cultural center for Greeks and Romans, Christians should live as cultural centers for God's values, representing Him in regions that need His light.

Are you shining God's light or covering it up? How can
you let your light shine more brightly before others?

BE THE MAN WHO RESPECTS
THE LIMITS OF OTHERS

*I know and am convinced on the authority of the Lord Jesus
that no food, in and of itself, is wrong to eat. But if someone
believes it is wrong, then for that person it is wrong.*
ROMANS 14:14 NLT

Many people assume that the Amish believe using electricity is a sin,
but the truth is more complicated than that. It may surprise you to learn
the Amish use power drills, air nailers, gas-powered refrigerators, and
solar-powered electric fences. The problem isn't the electricity itself; it's
being connected to—and reliant on—the electrical grid.

Since we're just traveling through this life, they might say, it is best
not to get caught up in the things of this world, many of which are currently made possible by electricity (and in more recent years, the Internet). Some Amish communities have developed workarounds allowing
for the use of electricity while staying off the grid. In each instance, they
think long and hard about how each new technology will affect their
community before adopting it.

Now let's compare the Amish to a techno-savvy megachurch with
all the newest technologies. The megachurch is firmly connected to the
grid in the hope of reaching the lost through the use of new equipment.

Which group is right? Any good answer can come only through
respect and love. If you respect a person's limits, you'll neither force anything on someone nor treat that person with disrespect. If you love someone, you can show your love by refraining from whatever activities that
person might view as wrong.

Whether you agree with them or not, take time today to pray for
your fellow Christians.

What other situations can you think of where love and respect
should outweigh your opinions? In what ways can you show
forgiveness when someone inadvertently offends you?

BE THE MAN WHO HAS ASTONISHING UNDERSTANDING

*When they saw the courage of Peter and John and realized
that they were unschooled, ordinary men, they were astonished
and they took note that these men had been with Jesus.*
ACTS 4:13 NIV

Dan had a background in broadcasting and a lifelong friendship with Jesus. So when a congregation needed a sermon for the weekend, they asked him to preach. Without a formal education, Dan stepped behind the pulpit, drew a deep breath, and began speaking about things he felt certain God had been teaching him. He enjoyed the experience. When he was asked again, it was easier to say yes. Eventually, Dan became the pastor of a small church. It wasn't a full-time job, and he had no formal degree, but he served with an equal blend of passion and perseverance. He embraced this role until he died.

Dan followed in the footsteps of Peter and John. It's easy to forget that these disciples weren't traditional religious leaders—even the people who heard them speak struggled to believe it. After all, the duo spoke as men who knew what they were talking about!

Yet these men were just ordinary fishermen until Jesus asked them to do something new. Courage allowed them to follow the call.

You can be courageous in sharing what you know with your family, friends, and coworkers. God didn't lock His saving grace behind a wall of education. You don't need a few letters after your name to share His story. Like Dan, Peter, and John, you have opportunities every day to share good news, no matter what you do for a living.

Have you ever backed down from telling people about God
because you thought you lacked the right education? Have you
devoted yourself to lifelong learning at Jesus' feet?

BE THE MAN WHO REDEFINES *NEED*

God will generously provide all you need. Then you will always have everything you need and plenty left over to share with others.
2 Corinthians 9:8 nlt

What if you never had to worry about whether your life could be successful? What if strength was assured? What if you knew all your needs would be supplied? How would the answers to these three questions change the way you live?

Good news: with God, those questions are already answered! But it's human nature to still view them as "what ifs." And this uncertainty keeps messing with our ability to feel secure. We want assurances (and God gives them), but we can't seem to believe this kind of security exists. We've experienced the feeling of seemingly not having what we need, and we hate this feeling so much that it's hard for us to leave our life in someone else's hands.

So when we read 2 Corinthians 9:8, we might ask—with just a touch of sarcasm—"So what's the catch?" Phrases like "everything you need" and "plenty left over" make us wonder if God's looked at our bank account lately.

But *need* doesn't have a fixed definition in the human mind. Today, you might believe you need a car. But there was a time when cars didn't exist, so no one ever felt they needed them. Universal needs include things like air, water, food, love, hope, and forgiveness. But were those the things you thought of when you read the word *need*?

God knew you would need Him, and He meets that need every day. If you adjust your list of true needs, you'll see God has never failed to meet them.

Do you let God decide what you really need? How might readjusting the way you think of need change the way you think of God?

BE THE MAN WHO PULLS HIS WEIGHT

For even when we were with you, we gave you this rule:
"The one who is unwilling to work shall not eat."
2 THESSALONIANS 3:10 NIV

Work is not a consequence of sin. Genesis 2:15 (NIV) says, "The LORD God took the man and put him in the Garden of Eden to work it and take care of it."

Thorns are a result of sin (see Genesis 3:17–19), but work itself is good. However, since work is often difficult, some people refuse to do it. While many people are truly unable to work, inability and unwillingness are two vastly different things.

In his letters to the church at Thessalonica, Paul taught the value of hard work in this fallen world, and he led by example. He says in 1 Thessalonians 2:9 (NIV), "Surely you remember, brothers and sisters, our toil and hardship; we worked night and day in order not to be a burden to anyone while we preached the gospel of God to you."

Paul also called out those unwilling to follow his example. In 2 Thessalonians 3:6 (NIV) he writes, "In the name of the Lord Jesus Christ, we command you, brothers and sisters, to keep away from every believer who is idle and disruptive and does not live according to the teaching you received from us."

If we allow others to provide for us while refusing to pull our own weight, we abuse their kindness, portraying Christianity as a haven for laziness. Our hard work has no effect on our salvation, but our salvation should inspire us to work hard.

Hard work is an honorable thing. In the garden of your life, work the soil by the sweat of your brow. . .and God's seeds of love and faithfulness will grow in you.

What do you like most about your work? How can you
pray for a better mindset about the work you dislike?

BE THE MAN WHO KEEPS
NO RECORDS OF WRONGS

Above all, love each other deeply, because love covers over a multitude of sins.
1 PETER 4:8 NIV

Let's talk about grudges. After reading too many sugar-coated, spiritual self-help books where the author advises readers to forgive and forget, Sophie Hannah decided to write a book set in the real world, *How to Hold a Grudge*. For Hannah, holding grudges is just part of life, and to deny this impulse is to deny part of a person's humanity.

She's got a point. People are natural grudge holders. It *is* part of humanity, and anyone who thinks forgiving and forgetting are simple is sugar-coating the situation with unrealistic expectations. Such forgiveness is likely nothing more than a facade, behind which a grudge is smoldering in unhealthy and unresolvable ways.

So should people just hold grudges? Nope.

Whatever inspired the grudge needs to be resolved. If you don't drag the problem into the light, it will fester in the darkness. Merely saying you've forgiven someone but not addressing the matter at hand is like slapping a Band-Aid on a gaping wound and hoping for the best.

Too often, today's scripture is quoted by well-intentioned people who want to skip over the hard work of cleansing the wound. They don't realize that to "love each other deeply" is more than a solo, mental experience. Covering a multitude of sins through love is grueling work that involves multiple people who address and resolve past wrongs.

You aren't allowed to ignore offenses and call it love. To put past mistakes in the past, you must let them heal; otherwise, they will become future problems. Seek out wise counsel in how to proceed. Bring a mediator to work through the issues. Once it is resolved, move on.

The end goal is to turn former grudges into future wisdom, ensuring that a record of wrongs never prevents the good that can be done.

How can you address the wrongs committed against you so that you can move on? If you've committed wrongs against others, how can you address them?

BE THE MAN WHO SEEKS AUDIENCE WITH GOD

For we have not an high priest which cannot be touched with the feeling of our infirmities; but was in all points tempted like as we are, yet without sin. Let us therefore come boldly unto the throne of grace, that we may obtain mercy, and find grace to help in time of need.
HEBREWS 4:15–16 KJV

The boss sits in his office, reviewing paperwork and rubbing his temples. A sigh occasionally escapes his lips, and displeasure is etched across his face.

Would this be a good time to step into his office to ask for a raise?

Maybe not. Instead, you read the room, choosing to keep your head down and avoid disrupting your boss at all costs. Maybe you'll ask some other time.

Many people refuse to pray because this is how they view God. *It's a bad time to talk*, they think. *He's got too much on His plate right now. He'll get upset if I bug Him.*

But God isn't like that. He doesn't worry, and nothing surprises Him. He doesn't have to contemplate business strategies or the latest news. He can pay full attention to whomever is courageous enough to get in touch. There is no bad time to pray, no hurt that can't be discussed, and no concern that will bother God. He's given you the right to consult with Him at any time about anything. He brings a listening ear to the table and then adds His mercy and grace. They are all yours.

So today, step up, speak out, and stand strong, seeking God's help when you need it most. There is no reason to delay. You have His permission.

Pray.

How similar to your boss is your idea of God?
Do you feel courageous when seeking His help?

BE THE MAN WHO WISELY ENLISTS

Fight the good fight of the faith. Take hold of the eternal life to which you were called when you made your good confession in the presence of many witnesses.
1 TIMOTHY 6:12 NIV

Is surrender a sign of weakness or strength. . .or both?

Think of a soldier. For him, surrendering to the enemy would be a sign of weakness. But each day, the same soldier must surrender his own plans and desires to the orders of his commander. That's a sign of strength.

So for a soldier, the second kind of surrender happens first. After that, *surrender* becomes a foreign word. Similarly, you were called to fight a good and faithful fight for God. And when you love God, there's no need to back down. When you serve Him, there's no need to call in sick. When He tells you to stand, you stand. You follow a new plan, so the thought of abandoning your post should never cross your mind.

People pay attention to your new life because they want to see how it works for you. If you walk away, the observer might conclude that God can't really change anything. In other words, God would get blamed for your choice. How fair is that?

A faithful man—a strong Christian soldier—understands that what he abandoned will never be worth more than the companionship of other soldiers. He also knows that being a soldier isn't about physical strength—it's about agreeing to follow and obey the God he enlisted to serve.

His reward? An existence that never ends, even after he breathes his last.

> Why must you surrender to God before you can refuse to surrender to anything else? Why is the battle cry of "No surrender" an appropriate response for God's soldiers?

BE THE MAN WHO HOLDS BACK ANGER

Fools vent their anger, but the wise quietly hold it back.
PROVERBS 29:11 NLT

Getting cut off in traffic. . .being held up in the grocery aisle. . .sitting next to a talker in the theater. We all have things that make us angry.

Being angry, in itself, isn't sin. How we deal with anger could be, though.

Proverbs 29:11 (NLT) says, "Fools vent their anger, but the wise quietly hold it back." This doesn't mean we should always swallow our anger—that just causes an ulcer. It means we shouldn't let rage rule our actions.

"Think before you speak," is more than good parental advice. It's the top anger management tip in an article by the Mayo Clinic. Second on the list: "Once you're calm, express your anger."

These tips fit well with what the Bible teaches. Ecclesiastes 7:9 (NLT) says, "Control your temper, for anger labels you a fool." And Ephesians 4:26–27 (NLT) says, "'Don't sin by letting anger control you.' Don't let the sun go down while you are still angry, for anger gives a foothold to the devil."

It's healthy to take a moment to calm down when we're riled. But when we try to ignore what's bothering us, we do more harm than good. It's always best to address our anger while we still remember what we're angry about.

Faithful men deal with their frustration in healthy ways, knowing that God will bring justice in the end. You can either trust Him and let go of your anger, or your anger will lead you to sin. The choice is yours.

What makes you angry? How can you address your anger and give it to God?

BE THE MAN WHO KNOWS WHERE HIS WEALTH IS

*Honor the LORD with your wealth and with
the best part of everything you produce.*
PROVERBS 3:9 NLT

While the children of Israel were still wandering around the wilderness, God commanded the practice of giving their firstfruits—the first and best of their crops—back to Him as an offering. (For further understanding, check out the firstfruits ceremony outlined in Deuteronomy 26:1–11.) They didn't yet have farmland or crops to give. They had only the promise of the promised land, but that was all they needed because they knew who the giver really was.

All things belong to God.

First, *He* created them. Hebrews 11:3 (NLT) says, "By faith we understand that the entire universe was formed at God's command, that what we now see did not come from anything that can be seen."

Second, it was created *for* Him. Colossians 1:16 (NLT) says, "For through [Jesus] God created everything in the heavenly realms and on earth. He made the things we can see and the things we can't see—such as thrones, kingdoms, rulers, and authorities in the unseen world. Everything was created through him and for him."

Since God made everything for Himself, it is foolish to think anything belongs to us. God may allow us to borrow things—such as wealth—from His creation, but it always remains His.

All earthly success comes from God. It is meant to be seen as evidence that He keeps His promises, and it is to be used for furthering His kingdom. Deuteronomy 8:18 (NLT) says, "Remember the LORD your God. He is the one who gives you power to be successful, in order to fulfill the covenant he confirmed to your ancestors with an oath."

Just remember, earthly success is not designed to last. It's easy to hold lightly to the wealth of this world when your true wealth is in God Himself, the Creator of all things.

To what are you holding tighter—the giver or His gifts? How are
you honoring the Lord with the wealth He's entrusted to you?

BE THE MAN WHO ACCEPTS STRENGTH

I give you thanks, O LORD, with all my heart; I will sing your praises before the gods. I bow before your holy Temple as I worship. I praise your name for your unfailing love and faithfulness; for your promises are backed by all the honor of your name. As soon as I pray, you answer me; you encourage me by giving me strength.
PSALM 138:1–3 NLT

Courage is not generally required when you do only the things you want to do. If you want to say something rude to someone, there's probably no need to access courage. When choosing to buy something you want, you simply pull it off the shelf and pay for it.

If these personal choices come naturally, then why do we need courage? You need courage whenever you're embracing the change that God brings to your heart. God has a new direction for you, and it takes courage to "walk in newness of life" (Romans 6:4 KJV).

A courageous man knows he is on a mission. His quest began the day he was brave enough to believe that God was more than a child's bedtime story. This adventure requires courage, and the strength found in that courage is his for the asking.

Discouragement, however, is far easier to accept, especially when you're challenged to rise above the average and do something special for God. That's why God's encouragement is so important—it helps you fulfill your purpose with passion and endurance.

God offers strength, so it just makes sense to accept it. He answers prayer, so you should pray. God can and will finish what He started, so be courageous and let Him complete the work He wants to do in your life.

Have you accepted God's strength to complete your quest?
How can His courage inspire you to rise above what's "normal"?

BE THE MAN WHO SEPARATES KNOWLEDGE FROM WISDOM

"God also gave Joseph unusual wisdom, so that Pharaoh appointed him governor over all of Egypt and put him in charge of the palace."
ACTS 7:10 NLT

Wisdom is an important aspect of strength; acting foolish, on the other hand, is usually seen as weakness. You can know lots of stuff and still be considered foolish. Why? Because whereas knowledge is useful for winning trivia games, wisdom is knowing what to do with what you know. It's essential for making quality decisions.

One of those wise men of the Bible is Joseph. This man was the second youngest of his brothers, who all hated him and sold him into slavery. To make matters worse, he was then accused of a crime he didn't commit, placed in jail, and forgotten by the only man who could've helped secure his release. Not exactly the best soil for wisdom to grow! But the Bible says God was with Joseph through it all.

In fact, God's strength, found in the "unusual wisdom" of Joseph, was instrumental in turning his bad circumstances into incredible outcomes. By the time the story reaches its pinnacle, the worst famine in recent memory was raging. . .and Joseph was the second in command of an entire country. The wisdom God gave him allowed him to implement a national rationing plan that saved people from many countries. And when Joseph had the chance to pay his brothers back, his God-given wisdom led him to do something unexpected instead—he gave them a new home in Egypt, where they'd have enough food to withstand the bad years.

How might you explain the difference between wisdom and knowledge? Why should you gain strength from God's wisdom?

BE THE MAN WHO TRUSTS GOD

*Trust in the LORD with all thine heart; and lean
not unto thine own understanding. In all thy ways
acknowledge him, and he shall direct thy paths.*
PROVERBS 3:5–6 KJV

Have you ever bought a new bottle of ketchup to replace the one you couldn't find, only to find the old one immediately afterward? The inability to see things right in front of us is, sadly, one of the things men are known for. But science may have finally explained why.

"What we pay attention to is largely determined by our expectations of what should be present," says Christopher Chabris, a cognitive psychologist who co-authored *The Invisible Gorilla*.

The title of Chabris's book is inspired by a YouTube video that instructs its viewers to count the number of times a basketball is passed between people wearing white shirts. While the viewers are focusing on the basketball, most completely miss the man in a gorilla suit who walks across the screen.

As Chabris notes in his book, our minds don't work the way we think they do. Without expecting something, we're unlikely to pay attention to it, he says, and "when we are not paying attention to something, we are surprisingly likely to not see it."

It is no wonder, then, that the Bible tells us not to lean on our own understanding. If we can miss ketchup bottles and gorillas that are right in front of us, we can also overlook God's guidance in our life. But as Chabris noted, when we learn to pay better attention and discount our assumptions, we'll be better prepared to see things as they truly are.

Purpose-driven, faithful men trust God more than their own viewpoint. We must acknowledge Him in order to see His true and perfect plan for us.

Have your expectations ever altered your perspective?
How can you better trust God's viewpoint over your own?

BE THE MAN WHO KEEPS HIS WORD

Whatever your lips utter you must be sure to do, because you made your vow freely to the LORD your God with your own mouth.
DEUTERONOMY 23:23 NIV

Stuff happens.

Let's say a buddy of yours is moving this weekend and you volunteer to help. The weekend hits, but before you can help your buddy, your lawn needs to be mowed. It's been raining for the last few days, but today is beautiful. While mowing, you notice a patch that hasn't grown well, even with all the recent rain, so you get out the grass seed and some soil and the sprinkler. But as you retrieve the sprinkler, you see how dirty your car is and think, *I should probably wash that today since the weather is so nice.* So you find the other hose, but it has a leak that needs to be fixed. . .and on and on.

At the end of the day, you remember your buddy. You feel a bit bad that you didn't show up, but you justify it. After all, it's not like you were goofing around.

Stuff happens. So is it really a big deal when we break our word?

Practically speaking, it is. When you forget or ignore the promises you've made, people are less likely to believe you next time. Broken trust can take a long time to heal.

Spiritually speaking, it's *definitely* a big deal when we break our word. When God's children vow to do something, the vow is witnessed by God. Breaking a person's trust reflects on God. What would someone think if you broke a promise then invited that person to church? That person might conclude that church people don't really care about their responsibilities to others, as long as the church's offering plates stay full.

So when you say you are going to do something, do it—even if stuff happens. You don't want your broken promises to prevent someone from coming to God.

How likely are you to rely on people who have broken their word before?
Do you have any neglected promises that you can start fulfilling today?

BE THE MAN WHO DOESN'T JUST WATCH

Be on your guard; stand firm in the faith; be courageous; be strong.
1 CORINTHIANS 16:13 NIV

When you watch a sporting event on television, what do you see in the stands? You undoubtedly spot numbered jerseys, foam fingers, and special headgear—whether corn cobs or cheese wedges or dawg masks. If you could visit those fans' homes, you'd probably find logo cups, pennants, or even a game-worn jersey or pair of socks in a frame. Real fans take pride in living vicariously through the actions of players they've likely never met.

But there's a much more important game—the game of life—that beckons you. God is inviting you to step away from the sidelines and engage in the rough and tumble of the actual contest. You'll need more courage and strength than you can summon on your own, so expect your great coach's assistance. You won't just be a fan—you'll be out on the field, embracing the quest with these instructions in mind:

1. Be on your guard: opposition is coming, so keep your eyes peeled and have your response ready.
2. Stand firm in the faith: believe that God has already won the victory.
3. Be courageous: fear has no place on this field.
4. Be strong: your coach will transform your weakness into the strength you need.

You can't be a Christian and just watch from the sidelines. There's a playbook to study. There's work to be done. There are teammates to support and encourage. Go get into the game!

Which of the four game instructions is the hardest for you?
What is your motivation to follow God's playbook?

BE THE MAN WHO SEES BEYOND "AVERAGE"

Then the LORD said to Moses, "See, I have chosen Bezalel son of Uri, the son of Hur, of the tribe of Judah, and I have filled him with the Spirit of God, with wisdom, with understanding, with knowledge and with all kinds of skills—to make artistic designs for work in gold, silver and bronze, to cut and set stones, to work in wood, and to engage in all kinds of crafts."
EXODUS 31:1–5 NIV

People can, intentionally or unintentionally, place workers in categories. If a man works in an office, people may see him as more important than one who wears a hard hat and gets his hands dirty. They might even assume there's an intelligence gap between the two. This distinction usually isn't said aloud, and some might not even be aware they're making it.

Exodus 31 doesn't say a lot about Bezalel, but we do know he was someone who worked with his hands. He probably had callused hands and dirt beneath his broken fingernails. Yet God did something remarkable. He didn't dismiss this hardworking man or indicate he had no value. No, He specifically told Moses that this man was important. God said, "I have filled him with the Spirit of God, with wisdom, with understanding, with knowledge and with all kinds of skills."

This man's skill was inspired by the God who created everything. God Himself gave this artisan the ability to create with wisdom.

Today, gain strength and perspective from this lesser-known Bible hero, knowing that God has a plan for you as well.

Why is it easy to categorize people based on their occupation?
What is the best remedy for such an attitude?

BE THE MAN WHO HATES EVIL

Hate evil and love what is good; turn your courts into true halls of justice. Perhaps even yet the LORD God of Heaven's Armies will have mercy on the remnant of his people.

AMOS 5:15 NLT

Murder is evil—there's not much debate about that. But is it evil to simply wish someone were dead? Adultery is wrong. But how wrong is it to fantasize about someone other than your wife? When it comes to right and wrong, we tend to visualize things on a spectrum. We think of murder as worse than hatred and adultery as worse than viewing pornography.

The truth is less nuanced than we'd like to think. Sin is sin, even when it pretends to be harmless.

In Matthew 5:21–22 (NLT), Jesus says, "You have heard that our ancestors were told, 'You must not murder. If you commit murder, you are subject to judgment.' But I say, if you are even angry with someone, you are subject to judgment! If you call someone an idiot, you are in danger of being brought before the court. And if you curse someone, you are in danger of the fires of hell."

And in Matthew 5:27–28 (NLT), He adds, "You have heard the commandment that says, 'You must not commit adultery.' But I say, anyone who even looks at a woman with lust has already committed adultery with her in his heart."

Until we start viewing sin as evil—not on a spectrum but as its own category—we will not hate it as we should. Faithful men understand that to downplay sin is evil in itself. The effects of sin are devastating, and nothing about it is redeemable. That is why we needed to be rescued from sin instead of merely redirected toward good.

Do you hate evil? How can your actions and attitude show your views on good vs. evil?

BE THE MAN WHO DOES RIGHT BEFORE GOD AND MAN

*For we are taking pains to do what is right, not only
in the eyes of the Lord but also in the eyes of man.*
2 CORINTHIANS 8:21 NIV

Remember the last fundraiser you took part in? Maybe you were a student selling candy bars for a school trip. Maybe you washed cars to raise funds for disaster relief. Or maybe you did jumping jacks or ran in a race or competitively ate hot dogs—all with the goal of raising money for some charity.

If, after you've done all that work to raise funds, some unscrupulous person were to steal the money, wouldn't you be a little bothered? No, you'd probably be furious! How dare someone steal money from school children, disaster victims, and charities!

In his second letter to the Corinthians, the apostle Paul goes into fundraising mode. In chapters 8–9, Paul describes other churches' generosity toward those in need. He expresses his appreciation for the Corinthians' giving nature, tells how he and Titus are trustworthy men, and explains how the Corinthians' gift will bless both the recipients and the givers. The one strategy he doesn't try is coercion. "Each of you should give what you have decided in your heart to give," he writes, "not reluctantly or under compulsion, for God loves a cheerful giver" (2 Corinthians 9:7 NIV).

Honorable men are above reproach when it comes to how they use money, especially when that money belongs to other people. They do what they say they'll do, making sure each gift is given to its intended recipient. Not only does this honesty please God, it makes it easier for people to trust those who work in God's name.

What kinds of people do you trust the most? How might
you build up this degree of trust with others?

BE THE MAN WHO HELPS RESTORE COURAGE

Paul said unto Barnabas, Let us go again and visit our brethren in every city where we have preached the word of the LORD, and see how they do. And Barnabas determined to take with them John, whose surname was Mark. But Paul thought not good to take him with them, who departed from them from Pamphylia, and went not with them to the work.
ACTS 15:36–38 KJV

A recurring storyline in police procedurals finds a well-respected officer nursing bitterness toward a partner due to a betrayal. The veteran officer never wants to work with that partner again, but they are predictably forced back together through a very specific set of circumstances. The betraying officer, we learn, was either misunderstood or has grown up since they last worked together, and the rest of the movie (and usually the sequel) functions as a buddy cop drama.

A similar plot ran deep in the missionary world of the apostle Paul and his friend Barnabas. They were the veterans of the early missionary program, and several rookies were advancing through the ranks. Then came John Mark, who betrayed the veterans by leaving before the work was done. No note. No apology. No postcard from home.

You can probably understand why Paul was not especially thrilled when Barnabas proposed bringing John Mark back!

But Barnabas showed courage in brokering the return, Paul showed courage in eventually accepting him again, and John Mark showed courage in coming back—despite the intense awkwardness he knew would follow. In the end, Paul instructed Timothy, "Take Mark, and bring him with thee: for he is profitable to me for the ministry" (2 Timothy 4:11 KJV). God's restoration doesn't leave the willing behind.

> Are you still reeling from a shocking and hurtful betrayal?
> If so, how might you offer forgiveness to that person today?

BE THE MAN WHO RECOGNIZES GOD'S STRENGTH

*There is a man in thy kingdom, in whom is the spirit of the holy gods;
and in the days of thy father light and understanding and wisdom, like
the wisdom of the gods, was found in him. . . . Forasmuch as an excellent
spirit, and knowledge, and understanding, interpreting of dreams, and
shewing of hard sentences, and dissolving of doubts, were found in the same
Daniel, whom the king named Belteshazzar: now let Daniel be called.*

DANIEL 5:11–12 KJV

Daniel was a man who, at any point, could probably be voted as the smartest in the room. Of course, God was wiser than Daniel, but Daniel was sold out to following God—so God gave him a wisdom that was unmatched in the world at the time.

When Daniel spoke, he calmed fear and inspired trust with his convincing arguments. He understood the world around him and the God who made that world. God even helped him interpret dreams. Daniel's lifelong pursuit of God put him in the ranks of the wisest men who've ever lived. As those around him immersed themselves in a smelly marinade of jealousy, spite, and vindictiveness—trying their best to ruin the reputation of a good man—Daniel stood out as a faithful man of strength. Feel free to read the book of Daniel to see who succeeded.

A faithful man knows that his "God wisdom" doesn't depend on the opinions of the jealous, spiteful, and vindictive. These people don't like anything that reminds them of their imperfection. God's wisdom can do that—but it can also point them toward a strength that only He can supply.

How can becoming wise make you more aware of God's strength?
Do you employ this wisdom in your everyday life?

BE THE MAN WHO LOVES HIS NEIGHBOR

*"The most important one," answered Jesus, "is this: 'Hear, O Israel:
The Lord our God, the Lord is one. Love the Lord your God with
all your heart and with all your soul and with all your mind and
with all your strength.' The second is this: 'Love your neighbor
as yourself.' There is no commandment greater than these."*
MARK 12:29–31 NIV

A neighbor is someone who lives next door. . .or a million miles away. A neighbor is someone who mows your grass when you're away. . .or someone whose dog poops on your lawn. Everyone is your neighbor, whether you like them or not. You are called to love them all.

But since loving everyone all the time is a difficult concept to grasp, let's focus on our literal neighbors for now. If no one lives directly next to you, think of acquaintances with whom you regularly interact. How can you love these people?

The first step is knowing their names. If you've lived next to them for so long that asking their name is embarrassing, get over it. A faithful man swallows his pride to love his neighbor. If you need an excuse to ask your neighbor's name, bring a gift, explaining how you would like to be a better neighbor.

The second step is to see your neighbors as people, ignoring the annoying things they might do. They might be the type who revs their truck engine after bedtime; if so, find common ground by asking them about their truck's make and model.

The third step is finding ways to serve them. Think of Jesus' parable about the Good Samaritan (see Luke 10:25–37 if you need a refresher). In this story, the good neighbor is the one who serves the needs of the injured traveler. We are to serve in the same way.

Once you master loving your actual neighbor, see how you can grow your neighborhood.

How can you get to know your neighbors better? How can you serve them?

BE THE MAN WHO BELIEVES THE IMPOSSIBLE

For with God nothing shall be impossible.
LUKE 1:37 KJV

Today's verse comes from the passage in Luke where the angel Gabriel foretells Jesus' birth to Mary. The young virgin understandably struggled with the idea of having a baby. That's not how biology works. Impossible!

Mary's life was about to change drastically. Her engagement to Joseph was endangered by this unexpected, impossible pregnancy. Jesus' arrival had the potential to utterly destroy her future. In fact, it seemed impossible that she'd come through the experience intact. But look at how she reacted.

Mary responded, "Oh, how my soul praises the Lord. How my spirit rejoices in God my Savior! For he took notice of his lowly servant girl, and from now on all generations will call me blessed. For the Mighty One is holy, and he has done great things for me" (Luke 1:46–49 NLT).

How could a holy God send His Son as a sacrifice to save this wicked world? It was impossible! What about Jesus' miracles, which testified to humanity that He was genuine? Also impossible. And the way God sends His Spirit to dwell inside those who accept His gift of salvation? Even more impossible. Yet God has done all these impossible deeds—and He never quits. A thousand impossibilities are realized each morning before your feet hit the floor!

It's time to believe and rejoice in the impossible God we serve. If you ever worry that your relationship with Jesus could destroy your life, look at Mary's example and rejoice. God has chosen you to be blessed. The Mighty One is ready to do great things for you! And if it all seems impossible, that's because it is. But even the impossible is possible for God.

Are you afraid of the impossible ways in which Jesus might change your life? If so, how can you entrust Him with that fear?

BE THE MAN WHO KNOWS THE OVERCOMER

Jesus asked, "Do you finally believe? But the time is coming—indeed it's here now—when you will be scattered, each one going his own way, leaving me alone. Yet I am not alone because the Father is with me. I have told you all this so that you may have peace in me. Here on earth you will have many trials and sorrows. But take heart, because I have overcome the world."

JOHN 16:31–33 NLT

Life is filled with good news and bad news—and sometimes, they can both rush in all at once. You welcome the good and wish the bad would take a vacation. So far, however, it hasn't booked a trip.

Jesus spoke the truth in love, and He sugarcoated nothing. He gave some bad news first: the disciples would never escape trouble and sadness. But then the good news: this trouble didn't need to affect them. He never said He would overcome trouble in the future—no, Jesus said it was *already* overcome.

It's pretty clear that if trouble can't get the best of Jesus, then He's worth knowing, following, and obeying. You can allow this knowledge to change the way you think and strengthen you on your weak days. There's very little to be gained from wallowing in self-pity.

Yes, trouble is a common adversary to every man, but Jesus is an uncommon victor who can't be intimidated. Because you know the Overcomer, you too can overcome. He did what no one else could so that you can be free from worry and fear. Someday, when you meet God in heaven, your trials and sorrow will become eternally past tense.

So today, feel free to choose the best response: courage.

Do you ever see your troubles as good news in disguise? Why is it important to acknowledge that trouble has been overcome?

BE THE MAN WHO SPEAKS ONLY TRUTH

Stephen, a man full of God's grace and power, performed amazing miracles and signs among the people. But one day some men from the Synagogue of Freed Slaves, as it was called, started to debate with him. They were Jews from Cyrene, Alexandria, Cilicia, and the province of Asia. None of them could stand against the wisdom and the Spirit with which Stephen spoke.

ACTS 6:8–10 NLT

How do you react when you are confronted with a truth that opposes your actions and plans? When pitted against conventional wisdom, truth wins. . .but this victory is hardly ever easy to accept.

Today's passage describes a group of men who arrived from various parts of the world. They thought they were pretty smart, so when they heard about Stephen, they organized a public debate. These well-traveled men would show the world how smart they were and why it was foolish to listen to Stephen's words. Each of their arguments was perfectly designed to crush Stephen and debunk what he had to say about Jesus. It would be a courtroom smackdown for the ages.

Stephen, however, had some impressive credentials too. He possessed grace and power. He performed miracles. So when this tag team of at least four men showed up to put Stephen in his place, they were rudely surprised. Because they didn't possess God's wisdom, they in turn missed out on God's strength: "None of them could stand against the wisdom and the Spirit with which Stephen spoke."

God's strength was manifested through Stephen's firm conviction. It showed up because he refused to accept any pet theory that contradicted God's wisdom by even the smallest degree.

How can accepting God's truth to the exclusion of all other wisdom improve your spiritual strength? Have you accepted this truth?

BE THE MAN WHO PRAISES OTHERS

Do not withhold good from those to whom
it is due, when it is in your power to act.
PROVERBS 3:27 NIV

Doing a job well feels better when someone praises you for it. Whether you've nailed a presentation at work, baked the perfect loaf of bread, or caught a fish the size of a Buick, it means more when someone notices. And yet, we sometimes choose to withhold praise from those who have earned it.

Why? Maybe we're too wrapped up in ourselves to see the achievements of others. Or maybe we don't want to draw attention to their accomplishments for fear that our own won't measure up.

As faithful men, we are called to praise what is praiseworthy, being kind whenever possible. Proverbs 3:27 (NIV) says, "Do not withhold good from those to whom it is due, when it is in your power to act."

Praising the accomplishments of others reveals things about you too: You value expertise. You're detail oriented. You're a positive person. You share your opinions, making it easier for others to share their opinions with you.

Of course, you should never give someone false praise or withhold constructive criticism. Proverbs 27:6 (NIV) says, "Wounds from a friend can be trusted, but an enemy multiplies kisses."

When we compliment someone, it should be true, helpful, and genuine. The same three characteristics apply to criticisms as well. The difference is that praise should be given freely in public, but criticism should be reserved solely for the person with whom we find fault.

If you're pleased when people notice the good things you do, be the man who notices the accomplishments of others. Always be ready to say, "Good job."

When was the last time you gave someone a compliment?
What are some qualities you appreciate about someone else?

DAY 99

BE THE MAN WHOSE REPUTATION PRECEDES HIM

Paul went first to Derbe and then to Lystra, where there was a young
disciple named Timothy. His mother was a Jewish believer, but his father
was a Greek. Timothy was well thought of by the believers in Lystra
and Iconium, so Paul wanted him to join them on their journey.
ACTS 16:1–3 NLT

As Paul went from town to town proclaiming the gospel of Christ, he stayed on the lookout for leaders who might further the ministries he started. Timothy was one of these. He came to Paul's attention because of his solid reputation, even though he had some obstacles to overcome.

Timothy was Jewish according to Hebrew law, but his father was Greek. This fact raised questions about the authenticity of Timothy's faith, yet Paul probably saw this as an advantage. Timothy embodied the kind of ministry Paul was aiming for: reaching out to the Jews first by preaching in the synagogues, yet welcoming all—regardless of their national or religious origins—into the arms of the church.

But it wasn't Timothy's parentage that primarily drew Paul's attention; it was his reputation. What began as a good report from a group of believers grew into a parental relationship between Paul and Timothy, as evidenced by his letter to the young church leader.

Second Timothy 1:3–4 (NIV) says, "I thank God, whom I serve, as my ancestors did, with a clear conscience, as night and day I constantly remember you in my prayers. Recalling your tears, I long to see you, so that I may be filled with joy."

Paul trusted Timothy because his reputation preceded him. Does your reputation as a believer precede you? If Paul were to come on a missionary journey through your town, would he identify you as a leader? Have you overcome any obstacles to your trustworthiness so that others can see you as a genuine believer?

If not, it's never too late to start repairing your reputation.

Is there anything about your reputation that might dampen your
Christian witness? If so, how might you faithfully work to overcome it?

BE THE MAN WHO IGNORES FOOLISH ADVICE

The serpent was more crafty than any of the wild animals the LORD God had made. He said to the woman, "Did God really say, 'You must not eat from any tree in the garden'?" The woman said to the serpent, "We may eat fruit from the trees in the garden, but God did say, 'You must not eat fruit from the tree that is in the middle of the garden, and you must not touch it, or you will die.'"" "You will not certainly die," the serpent said to the woman.

GENESIS 3:1–4 NIV

You probably know a guy who has opinions on every subject you bring up. He's the armchair quarterback of wisdom. He has no real experience in the field or evidence to back up his claims, but that doesn't stop him from endlessly offering advice. You might even hesitate to bring up anything at all when he's around.

The serpent of Genesis is the first recorded example of a know-it-all. When the first woman told him what God had said, the serpent replied with an "Oh, really?" He presented himself as an expert on the subject, and the woman believed his explanation over God's command.

Courage works to discard bad intel and accept direct orders. It chooses to believe truth and not some new, creative interpretation of the truth. It trusts God and rejects whatever contradicts Him. You are in connection with the God who really does know it all, so you don't have to be held hostage by the best guesses of other people.

Crafty speech will always twist the truth and lend credibility to unfounded theories. The serpent started the trend in a garden, and it's been growing ever since.

Will you be a disciple of deception, or will you know a lie when you see one?

> Why is it sometimes easy to be deceived? How can you
> show faithfulness by seeking—and believing—the truth?

BE THE MAN WHO BEARS FRUIT

*But the Holy Spirit produces this kind of fruit in our lives: love,
joy, peace, patience, kindness, goodness, faithfulness, gentleness,
and self-control. There is no law against these things!*
GALATIANS 5:22–23 NLT

Apple trees and pear trees are both members of the Rosaceae family of plants. Know how to tell them apart? Look at the fruit. Apple trees produce apples. Pear trees produce pears.

Want to know how to tell Christians from non-Christians? The same way: look at their fruit.

Galatians 5:19–23 (NLT) explains the difference this way: "When you follow the desires of your sinful nature, the results are very clear: sexual immorality, impurity, lustful pleasures, idolatry, sorcery, hostility, quarreling, jealousy, outbursts of anger, selfish ambition, dissension, division, envy, drunkenness, wild parties, and other sins like these. Let me tell you again, as I have before, that anyone living that sort of life will not inherit the Kingdom of God. But the Holy Spirit produces this kind of fruit in our lives: love, joy, peace, patience, kindness, goodness, faithfulness, gentleness, and self-control. There is no law against these things!"

In Matthew 12:33 (NLT), Jesus says, "A tree is identified by its fruit. If a tree is good, its fruit will be good. If a tree is bad, its fruit will be bad."

Before you start examining other people's fruit though, remember God is the fruit inspector, not us. He is the farmer who cultivates the soil, and we must be willing to allow Him to work in us. When we submit to God, we'll start bearing the right kind of fruit.

Jesus, in John 15:5 (NLT) says, "Yes, I am the vine; you are the branches. Those who remain in me, and I in them, will produce much fruit. For apart from me you can do nothing."

Do you exhibit sinful fruit or the fruit of the Spirit? How might
you allow God to cultivate spiritual fruit in your life?

BE THE MAN WHO IS CLEAN, INSIDE AND OUT

*"It's not what goes into your body that defiles you;
you are defiled by what comes from your heart."*
MARK 7:15 NLT

Have you ever used an automated car wash? It's like going on a low-thrill amusement park ride. You drive into a darkened tunnel with flashing lights, surrounded by water jets and spinning brushes and long, noodly cloth strips that slap the dirt from your car. Then comes the giant blow dryer that makes water droplets climb your windshield and fly off the back of your trunk. Finally, you emerge, fresh and clean, sunlight glinting off your shiny exterior.

But is your car truly clean?

The outside—the part that other people see—may be spotless, but if the inside is filled with desiccated french fries, sticky spots of spilled soda, and moldy fast-food packaging, it isn't anywhere near clean. Buying an air freshener won't help. What your car needs is a good detailing service—one that removes the seats, wet vacuums everything, and uses toothpicks and cotton swabs to get the dirt out of tight places.

What does that mean spiritually? Just this: it doesn't matter how clean you keep your exterior—the parts of your life others can see—if your interior is a mess.

Jesus says in Mark 7:21–22 (NLT), "For from within, out of a person's heart, come evil thoughts, sexual immorality, theft, murder, adultery, greed, wickedness, deceit, lustful desires, envy, slander, pride, and foolishness."

Any efforts to clean your interior by yourself will amount to hanging up an air freshener and hoping no one notices the filth. You must allow God to come in, clean every part, and throw out the garbage. Only then will you be ready to welcome others into your car and help them on their own journey toward Jesus.

Do you have any "spilled soda" areas in your life? If so,
what's stopping you from letting God detail your life today?

BE THE MAN WHO KNOWS HIS FATHER

Ye have not received the spirit of bondage again to fear; but ye have received the Spirit of adoption, whereby we cry, Abba, Father. The Spirit itself beareth witness with our spirit, that we are the children of God: And if children, then heirs; heirs of God, and joint-heirs with Christ; if so be that we suffer with him, that we may be also glorified together. For I reckon that the sufferings of this present time are not worthy to be compared with the glory which shall be revealed in us.
ROMANS 8:15–18 KJV

Have you ever noticed how fear is self-perpetuating? One fear, when indulged, seems to circle back around with three or four more in tow. Before long, fear can become overwhelming and debilitating.

But if fear enslaves then courage brings freedom. God's Spirit will always work with your spirit to eliminate worry even during alarming situations. Since you've accepted God's payment for the sin debt you owe, what could you possibly fear? Your past is forgiven. Your present is a work in progress. Your future is assured.

Because God is your Father, you have a change in status. You are an heir to the heaven He has created for His family. You are not a black sheep, a charity case, or a lost cause. God has released you from the bondage of fear, sin, and death. You have hope for a future without fear.

Courage understands that you exist in a temporary assignment and that there's more to this life than a dash on a tombstone. Each day, you have the chance to reject fear, follow courage, and embrace faithfulness.

This is no fool's errand—it brings strength now and hope for eternity.

Do you sometimes give up God's blessings by holding on to fear?
If so, how can you drop this fear and trust God as a good Father?

BE THE MAN WHO'S CONTINUALLY BEING REMADE

I am certain that God, who began the good work within you,
will continue his work until it is finally finished
on the day when Christ Jesus returns.
PHILIPPIANS 1:6 NLT

Lots of men excel at good intentions. They start projects and *almost* complete them. . .but then set them aside to do something else. Eventually, they have a dozen or more mostly finished jobs on the back burner. "I'll get around to it someday," they tell themselves.

There are remodeled rooms all over the world in which the work is 95 percent complete, but the lack of trim or new door hardware keeps it from perfection. In such cases, those few small steps to the finish line may never occur.

God is better than good intentions. When He starts the project of remaking men like us, no delays, backordered supplies, or diminished interest will force Him to stop—His work is over only when we're finished. And that won't happen until Jesus comes back, so God stays pretty busy.

Gain strength from knowing you're more than an abandoned, half-finished project. You are a work in progress! And this progress isn't a weekend warrior event. Every day, God leads you in new directions, inspiring better choices with greater compassion. He can do for you what you can't do for yourself.

Now is not the time to give up. Now is the time to celebrate the "future you" with the God who finishes what He starts.

Do you live knowing that God isn't finished
with your life? Why is that important?

BE THE MAN WHO EXHIBITS EMOTIONAL INTELLIGENCE

Rejoice with them that do rejoice, and weep with them that weep.
ROMANS 12:15 KJV

Feelings aren't your enemy. Some men just don't know what to do with them. Psychologist Marc Brackett—founder of the Yale Center for Emotional Intelligence and author of *Permission to Feel*—says avoiding emotions can be disastrous.

To begin properly facing our feelings, we can employ the system Brackett developed to teach emotional intelligence skills in schools: R.U.L.E.R.

- *Recognize*: The first step toward dealing with emotions is to recognize we have them. When a situation raises your hackles, don't shrug it off.

- *Understand*: Once you recognize an emotion, look for clues as to why you are feeling it. What just happened? Are your feelings connected to a similar past experience?

- *Label*: Discard the words *good* and *bad* as descriptions of how you're feeling. Expand your vocabulary. Get specific. In *Permission to Feel*, Brackett writes, "We know from neuroscience and brain imaging research that there is real, tangible truth to the proposition that 'if you can name it, you can tame it.'"

- *Express*: This is where many men fail, either by hiding their feelings or by expressing them in the wrong way at the wrong time.

- *Regulate*: Emotional regulation is a way to control your feelings so they don't control you.

As faithful men of purpose, we must embrace emotions and deal with them intelligently. Then we can better reflect God's patience and understanding to the world around us.

How emotionally intelligent are you? On which area of the R.U.L.E.R. system can you improve?

BE THE MAN WHO'S A MODEL FOR HIS KIDS

He giveth power to the faint; and to them
that have no might he increaseth strength.
ISAIAH 40:29 KJV

If you have children (or might someday), know that they want to look up to you. They want to see you as a role model they can trust. But what happens if you portray yourself as *too* strong. . .as a man who never gets things wrong? What if they see your weakness but know you'll never admit it?

For most men, it sounds wrong to admit their weakness to their kids. They'd rather portray themselves as brave, courageous, and strong. But insecurity has a way of exposing the very lie it tries to hide. You can't *wish* strength into existence. You can't consume a dose of "instant strength" like some muscled sailor man who loves his spinach. Your kids know it, even when you won't admit it.

How do they know? Because they know themselves. They struggle. They fight burning tears of anger. They sense that life is out of control.

So admit that you struggle too. Get real about the impact life has on you. You don't have to go into every little detail, but your children need to know that it's normal to feel hurt, scared, and confused when life is at its toughest.

What if your children never know your strength comes from God? What if all they see is you trying to pull yourself up by the proverbial bootstraps? What if your anger suggests you won't accept their compassion?

Let your kids know that it's okay to feel out of control—that this situation is exactly why they should ask God for help. That can be their response. Is it yours?

Do you try to let your children see your need for God's help? Why might it be a good idea to allow your children to hear you asking God for assistance?

BE THE MAN WHO CHOOSES TO BLESS

David gave his son Solomon the plans for the portico of the temple, its buildings, its storerooms, its upper parts, its inner rooms and the place of atonement. He gave him the plans of all that the Spirit had put in his mind for the courts of the temple of the LORD and all the surrounding rooms, for the treasuries of the temple of God and for the treasuries for the dedicated things. . . . David also said to Solomon his son, "Be strong and courageous, and do the work. Do not be afraid or discouraged, for the LORD God, my God, is with you. He will not fail you or forsake you until all the work for the service of the temple of the LORD is finished."

1 CHRONICLES 28:11–12, 20 NIV

In Jewish culture, it's normal for a father or grandfather to pass a blessing to his son or grandson. This act spoke life into the youth and gave them more defined possibilities for their lives. David, King of Israel, chose this method of blessing his son Solomon in this often-overlooked passage.

Having been through challenge after challenge, David bore both heart wounds and battle scars. Yet whenever he'd let his life wander, he had made a habit of returning to God.

Solomon would be next in line. Therefore, David chose to equip his son with a blessing that carried three lessons:

1. Be strong and courageous: God had given him purpose and strength for his future.

2. Do not be afraid or discouraged: fear had no place in his actions.

3. God will not fail or forsake: even after David died, Solomon would receive instruction and advice from a King greater than his father.

David offered the blessing, Solomon was blessed, and God perfectly lived up to all that the new king could expect—and more!

What impact would a blessing like this have on your life?
How can you use God's blessing to impact a new generation?

BE THE MAN WHO GAINS STRENGTH BY SERVING

*If anyone speaks, they should do so as one who speaks the very words
of God. If anyone serves, they should do so with the strength God
provides, so that in all things God may be praised through Jesus Christ.
To him be the glory and the power for ever and ever. Amen.*

1 PETER 4:11 NIV

Your mouth says words you don't mean, utters promises you won't keep,
and speaks phrases that offend. Speak "God words" instead. Your body
language expresses discomfort, sends bad signals, and shows your disdain
for serving others. Get "God strength" and serve. Don't speak words that
only share your opinion—speak words that glorify God. You don't serve
people; you work for the God who wants people to know He lives. That's
why He asks you to serve Him by serving others.

Men who keep to themselves and refuse to serve grow weaker for
their lack of involvement. Strength evaporates in the world of "I don't
wanna." Unlike schoolhouse games, where everyone hopes to be picked
first, some men see things they could do in God's name but hope for
someone *else* to do it. They hope the assignments run out before their
name is called. They might even devise a plausible excuse for turning a
task down.

God will ask others to do what you will not, but it will always be
your missed opportunity. Why champion a cause but choose something
else instead? Why stress the importance of spreading the gospel when
you sit blissfully ignorant of the person sitting next to you? Face it: the
adventure of the Christian life is reduced when you place your willingness on "standby" mode.

A faithful man steps up, speaks, and serves.

> Why do you think the act of speaking and serving is so important
> to God? What can you do today to make the concept personal?

BE THE MAN WHO FINDS PURPOSE IN STRUGGLE

But he said to me, "My grace is sufficient for you, for my power is made perfect in weakness." Therefore I will boast all the more gladly about my weaknesses, so that Christ's power may rest on me. That is why, for Christ's sake, I delight in weaknesses, in insults, in hardships, in persecutions, in difficulties. For when I am weak, then I am strong.

2 CORINTHIANS 12:9–10 NIV

Say your name out loud, and then follow it with the words "is weak." Feels good, doesn't it? No? Well, that's understandable—nobody wants to feel that way.

The apostle Paul, however, was secure enough in his spiritual walk to admit that he was weak, that insults didn't faze him, that hardships were to be expected, and that persecutions no longer caused him to run.

How is that possible? you might think. *Did Paul have a martyr complex?*

No. He just had a good grasp on what's important.

Paul didn't prefer these abysmal conditions. As a child, he didn't dream of one day wading through an endless slog of trials. But he endured these conditions for one reason—the gospel of Christ.

Without a purpose, Paul would've had zero courage for these trials. He would've found it easy to run away. But in running away, he would've missed some profound encounters with God—and an opportunity to impact billions in the future with his life's story.

All of your suffering has a purpose, even when you don't know what the purpose may be. Christ is the master planner, and He doesn't always share His secrets. You may discover some of them in time, or you may not.

All you need is courage. . .and the simple faith to believe that God is using your trouble for good.

Do you find yourself running whenever trouble comes your way? If so, how can you gain a sense of purpose to provide the courage you need?

BE THE MAN WHO TRUSTS GOD'S STRENGTH

The LORD is my light and my salvation; whom shall I fear? the LORD is the strength of my life; of whom shall I be afraid? When the wicked, even mine enemies and my foes, came upon me to eat up my flesh, they stumbled and fell. Though an host should encamp against me, my heart shall not fear: though war should rise against me, in this will I be confident. One thing have I desired of the LORD, that will I seek after; that I may dwell in the house of the LORD all the days of my life, to behold the beauty of the LORD, and to enquire in his temple.

PSALM 27:1–4 KJV

A lot of things are out of your control—store prices, unsafe drivers, unexpected home repairs, a medical diagnosis. The one thing you *can* control is how you respond. Your response should be informed by the great Gift Giver, whose commands encourage you to think differently about your struggle.

Every day, the headlines tell stories of intimidation and fear. There is always someone who wants you to believe that you don't belong, you don't count, you can't win. God, however, doesn't want you to be afraid of bullies. He wants you to be courageous because His biggest strength is love. This love dispels fear wherever it's found.

God's light illuminates your path, so why would you be afraid? God's strength is greater than any mischief a person can devise—so why see anyone as an enemy? Men of faith and courage are impressed by the God who dispels fear. Such men can make new choices and leave fear without a place at the table.

Have you ever feared someone who threatened or intimidated you? How can following God's directions lead you to send back any fear you may receive?

BE THE MAN WHO EXECUTES GOD'S PLAN

I can of mine own self do nothing: as I hear, I judge:
and my judgment is just; because I seek not mine own will,
but the will of the Father which hath sent me.
JOHN 5:30 KJV

Jesus never strayed from the heart of God. He was no loose cannon. He did not go rogue. Jesus was revolutionary, but only compared to the sinfulness of man. Every single person violated at least one of His laws. No one was perfect; everyone was flawed. But here's the truly revolutionary part—Jesus' sacrifice satisfied the justice we deserved. . .and gave us forgiveness instead!

God had a plan, and Jesus executed the plan. God had a will, and Jesus had a willingness. If Jesus hadn't sacrificed His human body to pay the sin debt of every human in history, His forgiveness would be out of reach. But He pulled off this impossible rescue mission to perfection.

The strength He showed, even in the mundane moments of His life, proved that the same potential exists in you. He chose to be committed to God's plan—so can you. He obeyed God's direction—so can you. He did the hard things with God's help—so can you.

You haven't been left without an example—without a reassurance that following God is truly possible. You've not even been left with a reasonable doubt about God's love for you. God said you needed forgiveness, and Jesus agreed. . .then He made forgiveness possible.

Gain strength in God's rescue plan.

How does knowing you have an example improve your strength while following God? How can your response to God's plan alter your willingness to act?

BE THE MAN WHO SEEKS THE ESCAPE ROUTE

*There hath no temptation taken you but such as is common to man:
but God is faithful, who will not suffer you to be tempted
above that ye are able; but will with the temptation also
make a way to escape, that ye may be able to bear it.*

1 CORINTHIANS 10:13 KJV

Sometimes, the game is rigged.

One example of this theme that shows up often in books and films is known as "Morton's Choice." The phrase refers to John Morton, the fifteenth-century Archbishop of Canterbury and Lord Chancellor under Henry VII. To justify tax increases, Morton claimed that those living extravagantly could obviously afford them while those who lived within their means were good at saving money and could obviously afford them too. Choice, as a result, became an illusion—both decisions ended up with the same result.

Fortunately, there's usually a way to outsmart Morton's Choice. Consider this riddle: A master sits across from his pupil. The master has a cup of tea in one hand and a cane in the other. He says, "If you manage to take my tea, I will beat you with the cane. If you fail to take my tea, I will beat you with the cane." So what should the pupil do? He should take the cane.

Silly riddles aside, we are often faced with seemingly unwinnable moral scenarios. In these scenarios, is it really best to take the lesser of the two evils?

The game is never rigged against God. God always wins. In fact, He already won the battle on Calvary's cross. As such, He's provided us access to Him, leading us through whatever moral dilemmas we face.

When the way forward seems like a trap, step back and pray for wisdom. There may be a third option that God is just waiting to show you until you prove faithful to His guidance.

Can you think of any times when the game has been rigged against you? How could stepping back from the situation have helped?

BE THE MAN WHO CONFRONTS DOUBT WITH MERCY

*Immediately the boy's father exclaimed,
"I do believe; help me overcome my unbelief!"*
MARK 9:24 NIV

Have you ever been in school with someone who just didn't understand what the teacher was saying? The whole class is ready to move on to the next assignment when one guy raises his hand and says, "I don't get it."

It's tempting to be frustrated with slow learners, but making them feel bad about asking questions only ensures they'll never understand the concept. They may hear the class groaning and resolve never to ask questions again.

Coming to Christ is a lot like that.

For some, becoming a Christian is as easy as addition. For others, it's like doing long division with irrational numbers and x's and y's thrown in. In those cases, the best thing a believer can do is be patient with the one struggling with doubts as that person comes to Christ. Jude 22 (NLT) says, "And you must show mercy to those whose faith is wavering."

Being judgmental toward someone who wants to understand Christianity is only going to turn that person off to who Christ is. It's not only counterproductive, it's the opposite of how Christ acted in the same situation.

In Mark 9:14–29, the disciples were unable to help a boy possessed by an evil spirit. So the boy's father timidly asked Jesus if *He* could drive it out. Jesus didn't turn the man away without helping. He gave the father a reason to believe.

Are you ever frustrated when people struggle to believe what you take for granted? How can you go beyond simply quoting the Bible to them?

BE THE MAN WHO KNOWS WHAT HE IS

See what great love the Father has lavished on us, that we should be called
children of God! And that is what we are! The reason the world does not
know us is that it did not know him. Dear friends, now we are children of
God, and what we will be has not yet been made known. But we know that
when Christ appears, we shall be like him, for we shall see him as he is.

1 JOHN 3:1–2 NIV

Many television movies are based on a tried-and-true formula: A boy
meets a girl, and both try to convince themselves they are just friends.
Suddenly, one of them realizes he or she has fallen in love—but then
sees the other person talking to an old flame. In frustration, the disappointed lover leaves the scene, determined to forget the other person.
But then events bring them back together again, and the movie ends in
a sweet kiss.

God's love for you is different. No made-for-television plot could
ever hope to capture it. He offers to make everyone His child, but each
story will follow a different path.

God's love breaks down barriers of resistance and invites long conversations. This love paid for a priceless but necessary gift. God's love sent
you an invitation and waited for you to accept.

When you do accept His love, Luke 15:10 says that "there is rejoic-
ing in the presence of the angels of God" (NIV).

Knowing your identity will powerfully encourage your heart. Stand
up, embrace confidence, and discover joy. You are God's redeemed and
forgiven child, and He never misunderstands you. He won't rush out,
even if it seems you are rejecting Him. You needed to be found, so He
didn't stop until you were.

Now that's a great plot!

> What part of God's redemptive story in your life makes you feel most
> grateful? How can God use your story to introduce Himself to others?

BE THE MAN WHO REMEMBERS GOD'S FAITHFULNESS

*The LORD will work out his plans for my life—for your faithful love,
O LORD, endures forever. Don't abandon me, for you made me.*
PSALM 138:8 NLT

Psalm 138:8 could be considered a nonessential prayer. God had already promised to never leave His people. The psalmist surely knew this, but it didn't change the fact that he sometimes felt he was on the verge of abandonment.

It's possible to doubt God's promises, even if you know all His other words have come true. You might pray the beginning part of today's verse—"The LORD will work out his plans for my life"—with the courage of a lion. . .and then follow up that bold statement by begging, "Oh, by the way, please don't leave me."

You might believe God was faithful in the past but wonder if it was a limited time offer. You know God has answered your prayers, but maybe He's too busy this time. You ask for help, but you also wonder if you're pressing your luck.

Gain strength by knowing you can ask God. Even if He says no, your honest question will not bother Him or cause Him to turn away. His faithfulness lasts forever. It's doesn't waver with inflation, political upheaval, or personal opinion.

You should never treat God with disrespect, but even if you do, this won't change His faithfulness to you. Remember: mankind's rebellion was why Jesus came to make things right between us and God. He didn't wait for humanity to achieve perfection—He knew that's not possible. Instead, Jesus' perfection makes up for it.

Today, follow the psalmist's example and remember that God is *always* present and faithful. He's here right now. And in that knowledge, gain new strength.

Where is God when you beg Him to never leave?
Why is this important to remember?

BE THE MAN WHO WORKS OUT HIS SALVATION

Therefore, my dear friends, as you have always obeyed—not only in my presence, but now much more in my absence—continue to work out your salvation with fear and trembling, for it is God who works in you to will and to act in order to fulfill his good purpose.

PHILIPPIANS 2:12–13 NIV

In his letter to the Philippians, Paul encouraged Christians to work out their salvation with fear and trembling.

But wait! Doesn't 1 John 4:18 (NIV) say, "There is no fear in love. But perfect love drives out fear, because fear has to do with punishment. The one who fears is not made perfect in love"? Is Paul suggesting we should be afraid because our salvation isn't sure? Doesn't salvation involve recognizing God's perfect love for us?

Let's view it from another angle.

Athletes work out. They don't work for a new body; they work the bodies they have. They train their bodies through exercise, shedding fat and building muscle while being careful of what they consume. They are motivated by an internal desire that overpowers their desire to eat junk food and be lazy.

Similarly, Christians don't work for salvation. There's nothing we can do to earn God's love (see Ephesians 2:8–9). We train our minds and hearts through spiritual exercise, shedding sinful choices and building love for others while being careful of what we consume. We're motivated by something stronger than a desire to be healthy. Philippians 2:13 says it is God who works in us, motivating us to fulfill His good purpose.

The fear and trembling we experience while we "work out" our salvation is simply our recognition of God living within us. We don't fear God's wrath—Jesus has already taken our punishment—but we do treat God's presence with the respect and gravity He deserves.

In exercising our spiritual muscles for others, we strengthen our relationship with God, fulfilling His will in our lives.

How are you working out your salvation? What is a spiritual exercise you could improve on?

BE THE MAN WHO PAYS HIS DEBTS

The wicked borrow and never repay, but the godly are generous givers.
PSALM 37:21 NLT

Debt is a simple concept to get, but it's much harder to get out of. As soon as you borrow more than you can repay, you enter a dangerous cycle. Having money problems impacts your mental health, which makes it harder to make wise financial decisions, which leads to bigger money problems, which worsens your mental health. . .and on and on.

According to a 2015 study by the Pew Charitable Trusts, "Although younger generations of Americans are the most likely to have debt (89 percent of Gen Xers and 86 percent of millennials do), older generations are increasingly carrying debt into retirement. Eighty percent of baby boomers and more than half (56 percent) of retired members of the silent generation hold some form of debt."

Debt itself isn't evil, but it can do bad things to people who unwisely enter into it: it can lead to acts of desperation, prevent future generations from accessing good educational opportunities, and fuel discord in relationships.

The Bible calls those who borrow and never repay "wicked." They take money they haven't earned and live as though the bills will never come due. The generous, on the other hand, are considered "godly." They give away money they've earned, expecting nothing in return.

Being a faithful man of honor means figuring out how to avoid the cycle of debt in order to be generous with your God-given resources. It's difficult to freely give your earned income when debt-collectors are banging on your door. And with the vast majority of the nation in some kind of debt, it would be easy to justify a bit of stinginess since so many other people are in the same situation as you.

However, this is simply unacceptable. Treat debt like the four-letter word it is and commit yourself to being as generous with others as God has been with you.

Do you have debts that are affecting your generosity? If so, what expenses might you cut back on in order to pay these debts and give charitably to those in need?

BE THE MAN WHO FINDS COURAGE IN WAITING

Teach me how to live, O LORD. Lead me along the right path,
for my enemies are waiting for me. Do not let me fall into their hands.
For they accuse me of things I've never done; with every breath they
threaten me with violence. Yet I am confident I will see the LORD's
goodness while I am here in the land of the living. Wait patiently for
the LORD. Be brave and courageous. Yes, wait patiently for the LORD.
PSALM 27:11–14 NLT

You've received good news: you're entitled to a tax refund! This news gives you a shot of boldness and confidence, and you immediately start formulating plans for what you will buy. But as the days go by and the refund doesn't appear, your confidence begins taking a back seat to fear. You find yourself refreshing your online bank page or taking one more look in your mail slot. Still nothing. How long must you wait?

It should come as no surprise that God often feels the need to remind you to wait for Him. His timing is very different from yours. He's not on the clock—He knows exactly when to show up with what you need.

Bold confidence comes with a unique blend of trust, patience, and a good memory. God has been good before, He is now, and He will be again. Don't spend any time trying to outthink Him—you'll never anticipate His next move. You may not see it when you take the first step or the hundredth, but just know that His move will be amazing.

Pay attention and keep waiting.

Have you ever felt like you've waited too long for God?
Why is patience linked to courage?

BE THE MAN WHO STANDS AND RESISTS

*For we are not fighting against flesh-and-blood enemies, but against
evil rulers and authorities of the unseen world, against mighty powers
in this dark world, and against evil spirits in the heavenly places.*

EPHESIANS 6:12 NLT

What do you think of when you picture yourself as a soldier in God's
army? Lots of gear and body armor? Boot camp and early morning drills?
A physical enemy? A lifetime of veteran discounts?

None of these are entirely accurate. God's soldiers come in all shapes,
sizes, ages, and cultures. They may be transferred and recommissioned,
but they don't retire. Our enemy isn't another person—it's an army of
spiritual powers.

This type of warfare can sound ominous, but that's just what the en-
emy wants you to think. God's command to His soldiers remains simple:
Stand and resist. If you do this, the enemy will step away from the fight.
When you refuse to run, he eventually will.

You'll never gain strength by sitting and welcoming the enemy to a
conversation. This is one of the easiest ways for the devil to disarm you
and reduce your interest in following God's orders. He'll make it seem
like he's a friend, but the moment you set your shield aside and take
a moment to rest, he will accuse, condemn, and mock you for being a
failure. Your strength as a soldier diminishes with each passing remark
of the enemy.

So today, stand—and resist.

Why does God say that our enemy is not human? How might
that change your opinion of what to stand for—or against?

DAY 120

BE THE MAN WHO VALUES MENTORSHIP

In the same way, encourage the young men to live wisely. And you yourself must be an example to them by doing good works of every kind. Let everything you do reflect the integrity and seriousness of your teaching. Teach the truth so that your teaching can't be criticized. Then those who oppose us will be ashamed and have nothing bad to say about us.

Titus 2:6–8 nlt

One of the best ways to learn is to watch someone who knows what he's doing. Not only does learning from someone else's experience apply to fixing cars and grilling hamburgers, it applies to the Christian life. A faithful man intentionally seeks out experienced Christians to share their wisdom.

Older guys, it is your duty to seek out younger guys who might benefit from your wisdom. If you think you don't know how or what to teach, just stick to sharing what you've learned from the Bible. If you stick to the truth, no one can second guess you.

Younger guys, seek out those who have been where you want to be. Ask them to share their experiences with you. Ask them how they reached that point and what truths they live by daily.

Mentorships can be as lax or as formal as you'd like, but a few ground rules will help them go better. First, discuss your hopes for what the mentorship will look like. How often will you meet? Will you meet by phone, video call, or in person? What kind of information are you hoping to learn from each other? Yes, this is a two-way deal.

Second, be honest with one another. There's nothing to be gained from sharing false information.

Third, be gracious with each other. As with any relationship, there will be miscommunications and mistakes. Fortunately, as Christian men, we can rally around the fact that God has forgiven us, enabling us to fulfill His command to forgive each other.

Do you know someone who could benefit from your experience, or vice versa? How can you touch base with that person this week?

BE THE MAN WHO DOESN'T YELL IN ANGER

A gentle answer turns away wrath, but a harsh word stirs up anger.
PROVERBS 15:1 NIV

What do you do when someone can't hear you? You speak louder. But what about when someone stops listening? For some people, the answer is the same: keep yelling!

Unfortunately, yelling angrily is a surefire way to activate most people's "fight, flight, freeze or fawn" response, making it difficult for their brains to even process the words being yelled. And if people no longer react to your yelling, you've probably lost credibility with them as someone they want to listen to.

The solution? Gentle answers.

If increasing your volume only makes things worse, then using gentle words will make things better. Of course, this won't be an easy change to make. If your go-to solution for however-many years has been yelling, it'll be difficult to retrain yourself.

Your goal is to make communication possible by remembering it's a two-way street. If you want to be listened to, you need to actively listen to the other person. If someone yells at you, resist the urge to yell in return. Show that person the better way by speaking calmly and easing the tension. Once volumes have returned to normal, it'll be easier for both of you to listen to each other's viewpoint.

Speaking louder doesn't make you righter. It might make you easier to hear, but it will definitely make you harder to listen to. Answer thoughtfully with well-chosen words spoken in a respectful tone. Show the kind of love and respect that befits a faithful man.

What do you do when confronted with yelling? Can you think of ways to improve?

BE THE MAN WHO KNOWS
WHEN NOT TO HESITATE

Because all those men which have seen my glory, and my miracles, which I did in Egypt and in the wilderness, and have tempted me now these ten times, and have not hearkened to my voice; surely they shall not see the land which I sware unto their fathers, neither shall any of them that provoked me see it: But my servant Caleb, because he had another spirit with him, and hath followed me fully, him will I bring into the land whereinto he went; and his seed shall possess it.

NUMBERS 14:22–24 KJV

As a younger man, Caleb was part of a spying party Moses sent into the promised land. Ten of these twelve men returned with a report that the land's men were too big. The spies felt like grasshoppers in comparison. Consequently, most decided they should give up on the conquest and settle for wilderness living. Caleb and his friend Joshua, however, thought it was time to take the land that God had said was theirs.

The crowd sided with the doom-and-gloom brigade, so God told the people they could hang out in the wilderness a few more years. Eventually, He would welcome Caleb and Joshua into the promised land, but the other ten wouldn't live to see that day.

Caleb was a faithful man of courage—he believed that if God said the land was theirs, then not even giants could prevail against them.

He was right, of course. He had no good reason to doubt and every reason to trust, so he believed. Caleb would re-enter that land as an old man, settling it with a strength that remained just as potent as it was when he first laid eyes on the land.

Do you sometimes hesitate to take possession of what God says is yours? Does the knowledge that you have an adversary ever cause you to doubt if God can come through?

BE THE MAN WHO KEEPS FRIENDS CLOSE

The LORD is my strength and song, and he is become my salvation: he is my God, and I will prepare him an habitation; my father's God, and I will exalt him.
EXODUS 15:2 KJV

Once upon a time in the fictional world of Hollywood, there was a family that could understand what their dog meant just by listening to him bark. They listened to his vocal emissions and said something like, "What is it, fella? You say Timmy's stuck in a well?" Maybe you have a dog like that—maybe you're certain its insistent barking means something more than a need to go outdoors.

A man in the western United States is thankful his dog showed that level of persistence. The human (unclear if his name was Timmy) tumbled down a steep mountain slope and injured himself. His canine best friend, seeing the problem right away, went looking for help. This dog wasn't much of a barker; he just did some impressive acrobatics that involved a fine display of jumping and spinning. But that urgent display was enough—help was on the way.

Sometimes, God sends you strength through a friend's persistent encouragement. This friend doesn't run away when you fall but gets help when you need it. This is the type of friend described in Exodus 15. But you don't have to meet the perfect person to find the perfect friend— God helps you. He knows the hurt you feel the deepest, and He stays with you and sends His Spirit to assist.

The worst predicament you'll ever face is no trouble for your divine best friend.

Who comes to mind when you think of your best friend?
Why do you need God as a friend more than any other?

BE THE MAN WHO EARNS HIS KEEP

A hard worker has plenty of food, but a
person who chases fantasies has no sense.
PROVERBS 12:11 NLT

Name the movie from this plot: The protagonist has dreams of success, but his family/friends think his dreams are a silly waste of time. Our hero initially abandons his goal in order to get a "real" job, but he's then inspired to chase his dreams anyway. Finally, he succeeds. His dreams are realized. His family/friends admit that they were wrong to doubt.

This is the basic plot for dozens, if not hundreds, of films. Why? Because we can relate to it! What man doesn't want to have his goals of success realized and celebrated, no matter how far-fetched his dreams might seem?

At face value, today's scripture might seem to throw a wet blanket on the "chase your dreams" mindset. The world of the Old Testament was an agrarian society. If farmers didn't work hard to plant crops and care for their animals, society itself would collapse. If a man wanted to have plenty of food, he needed to work for it. Does that mean God wants everyone today to be farmers and cattle ranchers?

No. We don't live in that world anymore. Besides, the Bible doesn't condemn chasing dreams. Joseph chased dreams from the pit of slavery to become the second most powerful man in Egypt. Today's verse is about the wisdom of working hard.

Whether you get a job as a farmer or factory worker, as a librarian or a boxer or a ballerino (that's a male ballet dancer), working hard is a must. God may have planted a special purpose in your heart, but without working hard to achieve that purpose, your dream will remain a fantasy.

Doors will open whenever you work hard. Walk through them, and you'll surely be taken care of.

What dream has God placed in your heart? How might you work hard to achieve it?

BE THE MAN WHO PRAISES GOD

Praise the LORD, all you nations; extol him, all you peoples.
For great is his love toward us, and the faithfulness of
the LORD endures forever. Praise the LORD.
PSALM 117:1–2 NIV

Psalm 117 is the shortest chapter in the Bible, but its message is all-encompassing. The substance is simple, beginning and ending with, "Praise the LORD!"

Why is God praiseworthy? Because of His great love for us. While many psalms sing of either personal matters or Israel's specific needs, Psalm 117 is a chorus for the whole world to sing. The "us" in the psalm refers to everyone. God loves us all, and His faithfulness to us endures forever.

God proved His love by sending His Son to die for the whole world (see John 3:16). First Corinthians 1:9 (NIV) says, "God is faithful, who has called you into fellowship with his Son, Jesus Christ our Lord."

When we have mountaintop experiences and are keenly aware of God's presence, praising Him is easy. When we travel through the valley and feel far from God, we are still called to praise Him. Our feelings and moods do not change God's love or faithfulness. He is always worthy of praise.

In fact, it's more important to praise God when we feel distant because our focus will shift from ourselves to our Creator. Praising God opens a window from our present circumstance to the one who holds our future.

Need some tips for getting started? Psalm 103 offers a whole list: "Praise the LORD, my soul, and forget not all his benefits—who forgives all your sins and heals all your diseases, who redeems your life from the pit and crowns you with love and compassion, who satisfies your desires with good things so that your youth is renewed like the eagle's. The LORD works righteousness and justice for all the oppressed" (verses 2–6 NIV).

What can you praise God for today? How has praising
Him in the valley helped change your perspective?

BE THE MAN WHO KNOWS WHERE HIS BLESSINGS COME FROM

Every good gift and every perfect gift is from above,
and cometh down from the Father of lights, with whom
is no variableness, neither shadow of turning.
JAMES 1:17 KJV

In 1959, songwriter Hy Zaret, best known for writing the lyrics to "Unchained Melody," wrote the words to a little song called "Why Does the Sun Shine?" A few decades later, the band They Might Be Giants re-recorded the song, making it shine anew.

The tune's simple (yet iconic) lyrics playfully and creatively teach the listener some facts about solar science. One segment of the song describes the sun as a huge ball of nuclear gas, much too hot for anything to ever live on its surface. However, the song explains, nothing on Earth could survive without its light.

Aside from the fact that the sun is actually a ball of plasma, not gas, the song is scientifically accurate. We wouldn't be alive without the sun's energy. As Psalm 74:16 (NLT) says, "Both day and night belong to you; you made the starlight and the sun." It is a great example of one of God's gifts.

And just like the sun always shines, whether we see it or not, God is always good. In fact, He is the source of *all* good things. The sun, the moon, the seasons, the food we eat, the family we have, the water we drink—everything comes from God's love for us. It is our job to notice these things and give proper thanks in response.

What are some good gifts God has given you?
How might you praise Him in return?

BE THE MAN WHO UNDERSTANDS ASSURANCE

For those who are led by the Spirit of God are the children of God. The Spirit you received does not make you slaves, so that you live in fear again; rather, the Spirit you received brought about your adoption to sonship. And by him we cry, "Abba, Father." The Spirit himself testifies with our spirit that we are God's children. Now if we are children, then we are heirs—heirs of God and co-heirs with Christ, if indeed we share in his sufferings in order that we may also share in his glory.

ROMANS 8:14–17 NIV

You are not God's foster child. God doesn't just let you spend the day with Him and then make you go back to your old life. No, you are God's *child*.

Do you find this hard to believe? After all, this is God we're talking about. He's surely got more important things to do than spend time with you, right?

Wrong! The Bible says that even His Spirit tells you that you are His beloved child and that He'll never be too busy to listen to you.

God doesn't use your spiritual adoption papers to manipulate you either. So don't live with feelings of spiritual abandonment. These emotions are a lie from Satan. God does not leave or abandon, and He's promised great things to those who love Him.

This is assurance for the insecure, certainty for the doubter, and courage for the cowardly. God knew you before you were born (see Psalm 139:13)—you will never be an imposition to Him.

> Does being assured of God's love enhance your courage? Has the adversary ever tried convincing you that God has abandoned you?

BE THE MAN WHO LOOKS BEYOND GUILT

Look to the LORD and his strength; seek his face always.
1 CHRONICLES 16:11 NIV

When you're off track and held together by the most fragile threads of guilt, you might avoid seeking God. And when people are vocal about rejecting God, ignoring Him may seem like a great way to avoid ridicule. It's easier to stay quiet, place some distance between yourself and God's help. . .and then conclude you've made a *very* big mistake.

When you follow this track, you're both denying yourself new strength and tossing existing strength to the wind. Your threads of guilt intertwine to form a tapestry of weakness. Its ugly style is noticed by all.

People often spend more time running away from God than toward His strength. Jonah was such a person. He wore his guilt and weakness better than most. He spent too much time showing God he had no intention of obeying. Instead of seeking God's face, he chased whatever wind would take him as far away from God's assignment as possible. But since Jonah would not chase God, God chased him. God knew Jonah needed time to think, so He sent a very large fish to find him. After three days inside the fish, Jonah finally agreed to replace his weakness with God's strength and trade his guilt for God's forgiveness.

When you have a chance, read the book of Jonah. It's not a long book, but it proves how worthless it is to reject God's free offer.

Today, God is willing to share His strength with you. Will you accept?

> Why is it so easy to embrace personal guilt? How willing are
> you to accept a strength you'll never obtain on your own?

DAY 129

BE THE MAN WHO DOESN'T COMPLAIN

Do everything without complaining and arguing, so that no one can criticize you. Live clean, innocent lives as children of God, shining like bright lights in a world full of crooked and perverse people.
PHILIPPIANS 2:14–15 NLT

Not only is complaining useless in solving problems, it can often cause more. In a scientific study by Robert Sapolsky—professor of neurology and neuroendocrinology at Stanford University's School of Medicine—it was found that the negativity associated with complaining can actually damage a person's brain.

But if complaining is harmful, why do we keep doing it? Some people complain to relieve stress (ironic, given how much it stresses others out). Some people do it because it offers the illusion of action in a hopeless situation. Others complain because they learned the behavior in childhood.

Even when the reasons seem valid, complaining will not fix our problems or draw people to our cause. The solution to complaining is surrender—not surrendering to the problem but surrendering the problem to God.

When we give our worries to God, we forfeit the right to complain about them. We can claim the peace offered by Jesus in John 16:33 (NLT): "I have told you all this so that you may have peace in me. Here on earth you will have many trials and sorrows. But take heart, because I have overcome the world."

By surrendering our complaints, we recognize God's overwhelming ability to fix what we cannot. When we live without complaint, trusting God with our lives, we will shine as a positive example in a world of negativity.

Are you guilty of complaining instead of trusting God? After surrendering your complaints to God, how can you prevent yourself from taking them back?

BE THE MAN WHO SEEKS UNDERSTANDING

Fools have no interest in understanding;
they only want to air their own opinions.
PROVERBS 18:2 NLT

Some guys treat communication like a one-way street. They see your contribution to the conversation as merely another opportunity for them to think of a reply. You can tell they're doing this whenever their response has nothing to do with what you just said.

These people are terrible conversationalists, and the Bible calls them fools.

"Fools have no interest in understanding; they only want to air their own opinions" (Proverbs 18:2 NLT).

"Fools think their own way is right, but the wise listen to others" (12:15 NLT).

Proverbs 2:2 (NLT), however, gives the remedy to foolishness: "Tune your ears to wisdom, and concentrate on understanding." A good way of showing others you are listening is to concentrate on what they are saying and ignore your inner monologue. If this comes difficult for you, maybe your ears need a tune-up.

Good listeners ask questions based on what the speaker says—which is difficult when the listener isn't listening. Requests for clarification or even repetition are acceptable. And if you got lost in your thoughts, missing part of what the other person has said, be honest and ask for forgiveness. The reason someone is talking to you is because that person values you.

Don't be a fool when it comes to communication, especially when it's with God.

If our prayers are one-sided—if we ignore what God is trying to tell us—we are far from the wisdom and understanding He wants us to have. It's okay to apologize and ask God to repeat Himself. He wants you to understand His love and His will for your life.

Do you consider yourself a good listener? How might you improve your understanding?

BE THE MAN WHO ACCEPTS A STRONG SONG OF SALVATION

I will trust, and not be afraid: for the LORD JEHOVAH is my strength and my song; he also is become my salvation. Therefore with joy shall ye draw water out of the wells of salvation. And in that day shall ye say, Praise the LORD, call upon his name, declare his doings among the people, make mention that his name is exalted. Sing unto the LORD; for he hath done excellent things: this is known in all the earth.

ISAIAH 12:2–5 KJV

Songs. They can be fun, serious, mournful, or wisely filled with worship. You may not pay attention to the words of worship music, choosing instead to focus on the soothing melody; however, the lyrics often beautifully proclaim God's perfection, taking our focus off our petty fears and putting it on divine, majestic truths.

Fear can keep you from honoring or even following God. Fear drains your spirit of strength. You can't hear God's song of salvation when anxiety is screaming in your soul. That's a horrible song to listen to, and it has no natural harmony.

But when you spend time with God, here's what He brings:

- Strength: You don't have it, but He does—and He'll give you all you need.
- Song: God inspires the words and melody that invite you to worship. His songs change you in ways that honor Him.
- Salvation: Without this, you would have neither strength nor a song. Salvation is God's plan to bring you away from the brink of spiritual death.

God's salvation, song, and strength are His gifts, and the faithful man accepts what He offers. So today, join His quest with enthusiasm. This is a life that begins and ends in the presence of God.

How can you draw closer to God through music? Do you frequently remind yourself that salvation is a gift only God can give?

DAY 132

BE THE MAN WHO RESPECTFULLY DEFENDS HIS FAITH

*But in your hearts revere Christ as Lord. Always be prepared to
give an answer to everyone who asks you to give the reason for the
hope that you have. But do this with gentleness and respect.*

1 Peter 3:15 NIV

There's a big difference between defending something and being defensive about it. This difference lies in the stance of the one being attacked. If you are unwisely placing yourself in danger, you are apt to be defensive. But to defend something, you simply have to stand your ground—the high ground—as the attacks fail to meet their mark.

When your faith comes under attack, it should be easy to defend your beliefs with gentleness and respect because you are standing on the truth. Your footing is secure because God is holding you firm, even as your enemies brandish their weapons.

But when you drift away from the truth, when your faith in God slips toward faith in your own abilities, you slide into indefensible territory. You may still claim to believe in Christ's power, but your defenses are hollow. You are falling into the enemy's trap.

Consider the man who acts defensively when questioned about his faith. Instead of answering such questions with humility and truth, he lashes out with pride and suspicion. "How dare you question me about that?" he might say. His defensive tone is exactly what the enemy is counting on. Indignation never brings anyone to faith.

The man who can calmly and truthfully answer questions—or even accusations—is more likely to be heard. Showing respect to others will make it easier for others to show respect to you. And when you are explaining that Jesus Christ is the reason for your hope, it is vital that people can listen to you and recognize the truth on which you stand.

How would you answer someone who asked you why you believe in
Jesus? How might you respond respectfully if someone accused
you of hypocrisy or failure to show Christ's love?

BE THE MAN WHO CALLS ON
THE LORD WITH A PURE HEART

Flee also youthful lusts: but follow righteousness, faith, charity,
peace, with them that call on the Lord out of a pure heart.
2 TIMOTHY 2:22 KJV

The word *pure* comes from the Latin *purus,* which means "clean, clear, or unmixed." In the context of a Christian life, calling on the Lord with a pure heart means coming to God with the whole of our being, not mixing our attention or affections with other things.

In the Old Testament, Moses warned the Israelites against mixing their worship of God with the worship of idols from surrounding nations. If they broke their vows of loyalty to Him in the promised land (as He knew they would), God gave them this warning: "There you will worship man-made gods of wood and stone, which cannot see or hear or eat or smell. But if from there you seek the LORD your God, you will find him if you seek him with all your heart and with all your soul" (Deuteronomy 4:28–29 NIV).

When the Israelites chased the wrong things, they found themselves in captivity. When they chased after God with pure hearts, they found Him.

Paul used the same formula when describing the Christian life to Timothy, his protege. "Flee also youthful lusts: but follow righteousness, faith, charity, peace, with them that call on the Lord out of a pure heart" (2 Timothy 2:22 KJV).

It isn't enough to flee from sin. A faithful man must actively pursue the things of God. We can't run after two different goals, mixing our worship of the Creator with the work of our own hands. We are to pursue righteousness, faith, charity, and peace. Fortunately, we aren't running alone; we are joined by every believer who calls on God with a pure heart.

Are you chasing after God with a pure heart? How can you
encourage fellow believers who run alongside you?

BE THE MAN WHO STANDS FOR RIGHT

However, he did not kill the children of the assassins, for he obeyed the command of the LORD as written by Moses in the Book of the Law: "Parents must not be put to death for the sins of their children, nor children for the sins of their parents. Those deserving to die must be put to death for their own crimes."

2 KINGS 14:6 NLT

Every now and again, the drive-thru employee at a fast-food joint or a coffee shop will say, "Just so you know, the person in front of you paid for your order." It's called "paying it forward," and it can sometimes set off a chain reaction of generosity.

According to a 2020 report, one such chain at the Dairy Queen in Brainerd, Minnesota, lasted for two and half days with over nine hundred cars participating.

It isn't just ice cream that gets paid forward. After King Joash had been murdered by a group of kingdom officials, his son Amaziah was placed on the throne in Judah. Amaziah could have paid forward his vengeance by having the assassins *and* their children killed. Instead, he exacted justice on the group of murderers and let the children live.

Wait a second, you may be thinking. *I can relate to paying it forward at the drive-thru, but I don't often have the opportunity to sentence the children of my father's assassins to death.*

Good point. But here are some more relevant examples: Do you ever wake up cranky and treat others poorly when they don't deserve it? Are you ever tempted to kick the dog when you've had a bad day at work? If so, you aren't acting justly. You aren't standing for what's right.

Do justice. Set wrong things right. Even better, be gracious. Pass good things forward, even when the world has handed you a raw deal. It's better to start a nine-hundred-car generosity chain than a nine-hundred-person grumble fest any day.

How could you pay forward something good? How could you stop yourself before paying forward something bad?

BE THE MAN WHO IS CRUSH RESISTANT

*We have this treasure in jars of clay to show that this all-surpassing power
is from God and not from us. We are hard pressed on every side, but not
crushed; perplexed, but not in despair; persecuted, but not abandoned;
struck down, but not destroyed. We always carry around in our body the
death of Jesus, so that the life of Jesus may also be revealed in our body.*

2 CORINTHIANS 4:7–10 NIV

Divers once called it "the bends." Today, the malady is more often re-
ferred to as "decompression sickness." It's a pressure issue that affects
divers when they go underwater. When the human body takes in nitrogen gas from compressed air, this gas goes into the body tissue with
potentially dangerous effects. If the diver ascends slowly, the nitrogen
migrates to the lungs and gets expelled through normal breathing, but
if the ascension is too rapid, bubbles of nitrogen form, remaining in the
body and damaging nerves and tissue.

There are parallels here to the Christian life. Following Jesus should
make us dramatically different from the people we were before. There are
new pressures that seem bent on crushing us and thoughts that still float
in our minds long after we've set them aside.

Escaping these pressures may seem like a perfect course of action,
but they are really preparing you for your work in God's kingdom. If you
try to rush away instead of allowing God to prepare you for your next
assignment, you'll find yourself with a case of the spiritual "bends."

Just as coal under pressure becomes a diamond, so too can your life
be transformed by life's pressure. God promises that no struggle needs to
be final—and that no pressure needs to destroy you.

Can you recognize God's work through the pressures you've faced?
How can these pressures lead you toward God's purpose?

DAY 136

BE THE MAN WHO CAN STAND

The LORD gives his people strength.
PSALM 29:11 NLT

"When I run, I feel God's pleasure." Many people believe that the famous track star Eric Liddell said these words, but that isn't true: they came from a movie that portrays his life. Even so, Liddell likely would've agreed with them.

Eric was a world class athlete when he ran in the Paris Olympics in 1924. He chose not to run on the Lord's Day—and was disqualified for it. He'd already won in one category and placed third in another, but Liddell gave up the chance to snag a third trophy. Eventually, he left running altogether to become a missionary. Was his decision driven by strength or cowardice? Fear or freedom? A good moral compass or an error in judgment?

It was almost as if God were asking Eric, *Which do you trust more: Me or another shiny neck accessory?* Would this athlete be strong enough to say no to the call of the starting line, or would peer pressure set his feet to running once more? For Eric Liddell, it wasn't the strength to run that he needed—it was the strength to obey. God gave him that strength.

There will be times when you'll need the strength to stand, to fight off the overwhelming urge to collapse in defeat. You'll recognize this strength when you resist what you know is wrong in favor of a strength you're waiting to receive. The decisions you make in difficult situations will demonstrate where your strength comes from. It'll prove what you believe to be true about the God of strength.

Why is there no such thing as a break from obedience?
How can obedience improve your strength?

BE THE MAN WHO CHOOSES FRIENDS CAREFULLY

Walk with the wise and become wise,
for a companion of fools suffers harm.
PROVERBS 13:20 NIV

In a 2014 study about friendship, researchers Michael L. Lowe of Texas A&M University and Kelly L. Haws of Vanderbilt found that men who made decisions together deepened their friendship over time. If they made a good decision together, they bonded over their shared virtues. If they decided to participate in vice together, they bonded as partners in crime.

This study reveals an important truth about our decision-making process: whether our goal is virtue or vice, we'll feel better about our decisions when they are made with friends. As faithful men, it should be our goal to seek virtue, because the consequences of vice are always more severe than we think.

Proverbs 13:20 (NIV) says, "Walk with the wise and become wise, for a companion of fools suffers harm." And 1 Corinthians 15:33 (NIV) says, "Do not be misled: 'Bad company corrupts good character.'"

Our friends naturally influence us—for good or ill—so we must be wise in choosing them.

If you need to break off some old friendships that led you in the wrong direction, stop frequenting your old meeting places and look for better relationships elsewhere. Churches are a great place to find friends with common values. Alternatively, pick a wholesome activity you enjoy and introduce yourself to the guys who do the same.

Friends are important—but friends who push you toward wisdom are irreplaceable.

How do your friends inspire you to live? How can
you encourage your friends to be wise?

DAY 138

BE THE MAN WHO CELEBRATES DIFFERENCES

*Just as our bodies have many parts and each part has a
special function, so it is with Christ's body. We are many
parts of one body, and we all belong to each other.*
ROMANS 12:4–5 NLT

Have you ever wondered why humans were designed with two eyes?
Why wouldn't one be enough?

To answer this question, we need to understand *stereopsis*—the ability to perceive depth due to the slightly different viewpoints offered by
each eye. If we only had one eye, we'd forever be bumping our shins into
coffee tables and missing easy throws. We have two eyes because having
multiple viewpoints makes us safer and more efficient humans.

Now consider the body of Christ, the church. We as individuals
are united by Jesus' love, but we each have a different viewpoint. We
may never fully appreciate those whose viewpoints we don't understand,
but to ignore them because they are different—or worse, to try to force
them to see things from our viewpoint alone—is like covering one eye
while the world throws its problems at us. It's just not safe.

The best way for the body of Christ to live and efficiently interact is
to celebrate our differences. When we recognize and appreciate the ways
we contrast, we honor the God who uniquely designed us.

Have you ever denied someone else's viewpoint? How can
you celebrate someone who is different from you?

BE THE MAN WHO REMAINS CURIOUS

*There was a man named Nicodemus, a Jewish religious leader who
was a Pharisee. After dark one evening, he came to speak with Jesus.
"Rabbi," he said, "we all know that God has sent you to teach us. Your
miraculous signs are evidence that God is with you." Jesus replied, "I tell
you the truth, unless you are born again, you cannot see the Kingdom
of God." "What do you mean?" exclaimed Nicodemus. "How can an
old man go back into his mother's womb and be born again?"*

JOHN 3:1–4 NLT

Nicodemus knew a lot about God. He could tell you all the rules and
how many times he'd obeyed them since breakfast. Nicodemus was used
to seeing the Pharisees and religious leaders comparing their personal
perfection, but he knew something was missing. He began to feel like he
wasn't really living.

So Nicodemus took a courageous leap of faith by seeking Jesus out
at night and asking Him to explain what He'd been teaching. He knew
that if word got out about this secret meeting, he'd be both ridiculed
and rejected by his own people. On the other hand, Nicodemus' curiosity
had reached the boiling point, and the answers he received that night
would alter his life forever.

As Jesus talked, understanding dawned in the mind of one who
thought he knew it all. Suddenly, he became aware of the ineffective-
ness of his old practices. And this courageous meeting climaxed with
the greatest truth anyone had ever heard: "For this is how God loved the
world: He gave his one and only Son, so that everyone who believes in
him will not perish but have eternal life" (John 3:16 NLT).

Nicodemus met that Son, and you can meet Him too—every day.

Do you ever approach God with questions of your own? How does
God use your curiosity to lead you to a place of faith and courage?

BE THE MAN WHO REJOICES IN THE LORD

Nehemiah said, "Go and enjoy choice food and sweet drinks,
and send some to those who have nothing prepared. This day is holy
to our Lord. Do not grieve, for the joy of the LORD is your strength."
NEHEMIAH 8:10 NIV

The backstory to Nehemiah 8:10 is a thrilling adventure. After grieving the destruction of the walls in Jerusalem (which had been mostly abandoned nearly seven decades before, when God sent the people into exile), Nehemiah was sent to Jerusalem to rebuild. When he was finished, the people began to return. For many of them, this was a new experience—they'd not been born when their parents had been sent away.

Upon arriving in the city and hearing God's Word, the people were in a festive mood—boisterous, even. Yet the longer they listened, the quieter their cheering became. They were confronted with the decisions that had removed their families from the city, the sin the nation had embraced, and the judgment that had placed an exclamation point on their long rebellion.

The mood turned somber, and the celebration was nearly abandoned. The people seemed ready to go home and obsess over the sins of their fathers. That's when Nehemiah stepped in and reminded them that this was a time to honor the God who'd reestablished freedom, not to grieve an unchangeable past.

Nehemiah told these former captives that their grief would cause them to become weak, but the joy found in what God had done would infuse their hearts with new strength. And they'd need this strength as they brought the city, left to years of ruin, back to its former glory. Suddenly, the hearts of men, women, and children who were accustomed to the tragedy of ruin had been invited to new life.

What reminds you that your past is different from
your future? How does this change your present?

DAY 141

BE THE MAN WHO SHOWS HOSPITALITY

Do not forget to show hospitality to strangers, for by so doing some people have shown hospitality to angels without knowing it.
HEBREWS 13:2 NIV

Ovid was a Roman poet who lived in the time of Caesar Augustus, and his *Metamorphoses* is one of the most important sources of classical mythology. In book eight of the collection, we find the story of Baucis and Philemon.

In the tale, Jupiter and Mercury—the Roman counterparts to Zeus and Hermes—travel to the city of Tyana disguised as peasants. They are greeted only by locked doors and unkind words, coming at last to the cottage of Baucis and Philemon—a poor couple who treat their guests with respect and rich hospitality. When Baucis notices that her pitcher of wine gets no emptier when serving her guests and Philemon's attempt to kill the family goose results in the goose climbing into Jupiter's lap, the couple realize their guests are supernatural.

In a scene reminiscent of the biblical story of Lot, the gods inform Baucis and Philemon that Tyana is going to be destroyed for its lack of hospitality. The couple flee the town and watch from a safe distance as a flood washes it away.

Clearly, hospitality was important in antiquity. People genuinely believed they could be hosting supernatural guests, so they treated all guests well. In fact, Acts 14:8–18 tells the story of how the people of Lystra (not far from Tyana) mistook Paul and Barnabas for Hermes and Zeus and sought to honor them as such.

Even though we might shake our heads at the misunderstanding, the Bible encourages such hospitality. Hebrews 13:2 (NIV) says, "Do not forget to show hospitality to strangers, for by so doing some people have shown hospitality to angels without knowing it."

Being faithful men means welcoming others into our home and treating them with the same respect we would a supernatural guest.

How can you show hospitality to someone in need? When was the last time you hosted a stranger in your home?

BE THE MAN WHO STAYS CONTENT

Keep your lives free from the love of money and be content with what you have, because God has said, "Never will I leave you; never will I forsake you."
HEBREWS 13:5 NIV

Contentment means being satisfied with the knowledge that what you have is enough. The word *content* comes from the Latin *contentus*, which is a compound word that means "to hold together." The picture is one of hands already full, thus not reaching for more.

When it comes to money, human beings have a tough time being satisfied. After all, there are always people who have more than us. Money is useful because it can be exchanged for goods and services. And in a capitalist society, money is the scorecard by which we rate our success. But when one hand clutches a bank statement and the other reaches for more, neither will grasp the richness of God.

When you have the promise of God's presence and protection, wanting more sounds ridiculous. It's like living in a mansion and being upset that your neighbor has a nicer outhouse than you. Contentment is having your hands full of God and knowing that you are safe in God's hands.

God's promise to be there for you comes from Deuteronomy 31:6 (NIV): "Be strong and courageous. Do not be afraid or terrified because of them, for the LORD your God goes with you; he will never leave you nor forsake you." The presence and protection in this verse was originally meant in a military sense. Joshua was about to lead the children of Israel into the promised land, conquering the giants and fortified cities which had cultivated the ground. God was ushering His children into a rich land to take care of all their needs, but they first needed to trust Him.

God's promise—as well as His call for trust—still stands. When we are content in knowing God is enough, we won't struggle with loving money or seeking the protection it offers. We are held as dear children by the God who wants to give us good things, the best of which is His presence.

Are you content with God? How could you
better take hold of His presence in your life?

BE THE MAN WHO STOPS RUNNING TOWARD FEAR

We have known and believed the love that God hath to us. God is love; and he that dwelleth in love dwelleth in God, and God in him. Herein is our love made perfect, that we may have boldness in the day of judgment: because as he is, so are we in this world. There is no fear in love; but perfect love casteth out fear: because fear hath torment. He that feareth is not made perfect in love.

1 JOHN 4:16–18 KJV

Fear initiates a fight, flight, freeze, or fawn response, often producing a huge adrenaline rush. Fear struggles to sit still. It's erratic in its search for safety. But for the fearful, *nowhere* feels truly safe. Fear keeps you on the run, so the idea of putting down roots feels foreign and unacceptable.

Love, on the other hand, offers roots a chance to grow. Trust is welcome in this place, and courage finds a voice. Even if you experience a personal course correction, you'll never be rejected. When love moves in, fear is evicted. The two are not compatible.

A man of faith and courage accepts God's love, refuses the adversary's fear, and allows his roots to grow deep into the new life that God offers.

Your life is a race, and love is leading you toward the finish line. You'll never be able to move toward God and recognize His love and acceptance if you're moving toward fear.

So what will you choose—cowardice or courage?

How much do you struggle with worry or fear?
How does love transform your relationship with God?

BE THE MAN WHO AVOIDS
A STRENGTH DEFICIT

My soul melteth for heaviness: strengthen
thou me according unto thy word.
PSALM 119:28 KJV

Have you ever experienced a melted soul—the crushing feeling that all good things have come to an end? Your memories of good times fade, replaced by bitter regrets. Your heart is shattered, your mind is bruised, and it seems like your body is ready to self-destruct. This isn't an invitation to get depressed—it's just a relatable description of life's worst moments. Maybe you're even there right now.

Depression is a universal no-fun zone. It's what drives some people to make terrible long-term decisions that negatively affect everything.

If you weren't aware of a strengthening God, a melted soul could very well mean the end. But when you feel those emotions start rising, reread Psalm 119:28 and make it your prayer. You have a choice.

It's not foolish to admit you need help. Left to our own devices, we'd *all* make the wrong choice. You have a strength deficit, and you can't fool yourself. You might even admit the fact. . .but still wallow in your weakness instead of seeking God's strength. But all this does is eliminate your willingness to try. Pity becomes your new best friend, but the more time you spend with him, the more you'll hate him.

Leave this place. Look for the "God space" that can change your perspective, drive weakness away, and infuse your melted soul with fresh and reviving strength.

Why does a little weakness, left unchallenged, always lead to
more weakness? Why is pity detrimental to a melted heart?

BE THE MAN WHO ADMITS WHEN HE'S WRONG

If we say that we have no sin, we deceive ourselves, and the truth is not in us.
1 JOHN 1:8 KJV

Exodus 20:16 (NIV) says, "You shall not give false testimony against your neighbor." This commandment is pretty simple. While the specific wording applies narrowly to situations involving neighbors and courtroom-style testimony, the broader rule of "Thou shalt not lie" is easily remembered and more applicable to our lives. Lying is wrong.

Does it matter who we're lying to? Or about?

Self-deception is a perilous game that can take many forms:

- Simple denial: flatly saying something didn't happen or couldn't happen
- Reality distortion: remembering things differently than how they were
- Projection: attributing our feelings onto other people
- Idealization: downplaying the negatives and remembering the positives
- Rationalization: making excuses for our negative actions

Psychology reveals self-deception as a natural defense mechanism designed to keep us moving forward through life. The problem, however, is that it prevents us from truly experiencing God's love. We adopt a false identity, seeking love from the world instead of presenting our true selves before God and accepting His perfect love and forgiveness.

God's truth cannot dwell inside a false image of ourselves. The first step to recovery is admitting we have a problem. There's a reason the verse after 1 John 1:8 says: "If we confess our sins, he is faithful and just and will forgive us our sins and purify us from all unrighteousness."

When we do wrong, we need to admit it to ourselves, to God, and to others. Only by confessing our sins can we enjoy true healing.

Are you lying to yourself about anything? If so,
what might be holding you back from the truth?

BE THE MAN WHO FORGIVES BEFORE GETTING THE APOLOGY

But God commendeth his love toward us, in that,
while we were yet sinners, Christ died for us.
ROMANS 5:8 KJV

A parent's love is strong. It is willing to sacrifice anything for its children. News stories of parents who die to save their children from harm are sadly common.

In 2018, Georgia father Brandon Gamble died while saving his five children from a house fire. His widow, Tyeisha, said in an interview, "I love that man. I've been with that man since I was thirteen. My husband was a gift from God to my kids."

Andre Anchondo and his wife, Jordan, were shot in 2019 while protecting their two-month-old son when a gunman opened fire on a crowd in El Paso, Texas.

In 2021, Pete Rosengren gave his life to rescue his kids from a strong rip current while his family was vacationing off the Gulf of Mexico.

All of these parents died as heroes to save their children. They sacrificed themselves because of their familial love. How much greater, then, is the love of Christ, who sacrificed Himself for us while we were still His enemies?

Before we ever became His children, before we had even repented, God made His eternal, life-giving forgiveness available.

If we are to love others like God loves us, we are called to sacrifice as He does. We are to die, not only for our loved ones—as Brandon Gamble, Jordan and Andre Anchondo, and Pete Rosengren did—but for those who hate us. We are to die to our selfish desires, our indignation, and our personal preferences. We are called to forgive before ever hearing an apology because God has forgiven us for more.

Are you holding out for an apology before forgiving someone? How is forgiveness like self-sacrifice?

BE THE MAN WHO KNOWS JESUS IS BIGGER THAN WHAT'S WRITTEN

Jesus performed many other signs in the presence of his disciples,
which are not recorded in this book. But these are written that
you may believe that Jesus is the Messiah, the Son of God,
and that by believing you may have life in his name.
JOHN 20:30–31 NIV

There is always more to any story than a single person can share, but it's not always fruitful to try filling in the blanks. . .especially if the blank-filling contradicts what's already been established as truth.

The authors of the Gospels used personal observation and interviews to capture in print the things that Jesus did and taught. Some witnessed moments that others did not. No one wrote down *everything* about Jesus—that would be impossible. Yet what they did write was more than enough. Combined, their books form a love letter that clarifies the purpose of Jesus' arrival—you! The story of Jesus was written so that "you may believe that Jesus is the Messiah, the Son of God, and that by believing you may have life in his name."

Jesus brings new life to anyone who accepts His sacrifice. He didn't come to earth to do magic tricks. Nor did He come to demand His own desires and pleasure. Jesus came to rescue humanity, and He allowed enough of His story to be shared in order to show His purpose. Faithful men can say, "Count me in," as they study the written record of Jesus. . .and anticipate learning more in eternity.

What aspects of Jesus' story resonate the most with you?
What comfort do you find in knowing that you were
part of Jesus' purpose in coming to earth?

DAY 148

BE THE MAN WHO'S NOT AFRAID OF DOUBT

[The man implored Jesus,] "Have mercy on us and help us, if you can."
MARK 9:22 NLT

Imagine a guy meeting Elvis Presley back in the day. This person doesn't know him, but he's heard about Elvis' special gift. So he tells Elvis, "Sing, if you can."

Now imagine someone telling Thomas Edison to invent something, "if you can." Roger Staubach to throw a touchdown pass, "if you can." Patrick Henry to stand up for freedom, "if you can."

We look at these questions and laugh. Of course Thomas Edison could invent, Roger Staubach could throw a ball, and Patrick Henry could stand for freedom.

Keep that in mind when you read the story about a man who came to Jesus and said, "Help us, *if you can.*"

This was the Son of God! Nothing was impossible for Him. He would heal the sick, raise the dead, feed thousands with a little bread and fish, and even rise from the dead. Whom did this guy think he was talking to?

But Jesus didn't use this moment to highlight His résumé. He didn't get upset, chew the man out, or refuse to help. Instead, Jesus had mercy on this man and his family. He helped even when this man expressed doubt.

This man's lack of belief did not diminish Jesus' strength, nor did it dismiss the man's need. Jesus didn't have to set the man straight about His power. He just. . .helped.

When you need a strength you can't find on your own, come to God—even if all you have to offer is one request and a lot of doubts. Believe what you can and allow God's strength to increase your trust.

Why is it okay to express doubt when you pray? What might you learn from the experience when God proves faithful?

BE THE MAN WHO PERSEVERES

Consider it pure joy, my brothers and sisters, whenever you face trials of many kinds, because you know that the testing of your faith produces perseverance. Let perseverance finish its work so that you may be mature and complete, not lacking anything.

JAMES 1:2–4 NIV

There are thousands of reasons not to exercise. Weather isn't always conducive. Our schedules might not allow for it. We don't want to cramp up after eating and drown (sure, this only applies to swimming; it's best to play it safe).

And, according to a study that appears in *Men's Health* magazine, men who exercise rigorously even have a greater chance of dying!

But many of our "reasons" not to exercise are really excuses. Sure, we need to be careful not to overdo it, but many other studies have shown the greater danger lies in laziness and unhealthy diets.

The same is true with our spiritual health. We can think of many "reasons" why we shouldn't share our faith or why we don't have time to read our Bible, but these are really excuses. James 1:2–3 called them "trials" or "tests."

Refusing to give in to temptations makes perseverance easier in the future. When we pass up a candy bar in favor of a walk around the block, for instance, the candy bar holds less temptation to us in the future. In both spiritual and physical trials, the goal is maturity.

Immature people have no self-control, but faithful men see temptations as opportunities to overcome. In fact, choosing spiritual perseverance results in joy which no earthly reward could match.

Where do you fall on the maturity scale? What might you need to change about your exercise habits?

BE THE MAN WHO SPEAKS HIS MIND. . .IN LOVE

"And I tell you this, you must give an account on judgment day for every idle word you speak. The words you say will either acquit you or condemn you."
MATTHEW 12:36–37 NLT

The First Amendment to the United States Constitution prohibits Congress from making any law that abridges freedom of speech. This freedom includes Americans' right to speak their minds, hold their peace, protest a war, and so on.

Freedom of speech gives people the right to question and disagree with government leaders without the fear of legal repercussions. It's part of what makes America *America*. But while people have the right to speak their mind, many would be better served by exercising their right to stay silent.

Today's Bible passage tells us that there will be a reckoning for the words we speak, that our words will reveal whether we've been acquitted of God's wrath or condemned to it. Words, especially idle ones, reveal what's going on inside of us.

In Matthew 12:34–35 (NLT), Jesus rebukes a group of hypocritical religious experts by saying, "You brood of snakes! How could evil men like you speak what is good and right? For whatever is in your heart determines what you say. A good person produces good things from the treasury of a good heart, and an evil person produces evil things from the treasury of an evil heart."

If your heart is filled with God's love, you can speak your mind freely and the world will hear His love come through. But if you are bitter or angry or self-obsessed—if sin is hiding in your heart—your words will inevitably reveal the truth.

Take some time to listen to yourself today—to the things you say at church, the chats you have with your friends, and the words you mutter under your breath. Pray that God will reveal your state of heart and fill it so that His love overflows through your lips.

Are your words uplifting and reflective of the love inside you?
Or are they negative, pointing to your struggles with sin?

BE THE MAN WHO'S A COURAGEOUS FRIEND

Jesus climbed into a boat and went back across the lake to his own town. Some people brought to him a paralyzed man on a mat. Seeing their faith, Jesus said to the paralyzed man, "Be encouraged, my child! Your sins are forgiven." . . . And the man jumped up and went home! Fear swept through the crowd as they saw this happen. And they praised God for giving humans such authority.
MATTHEW 9:1–2, 7–8 NLT

There was a healing in Israel, and Jesus was the healer. If there had been news media at the time, the story would've been front and center in the papers the next morning. Yet behind the sensational headline, there was another story too easy to ignore. Don't forget that a group of people had brought their paralyzed man to Jesus.

Where's the story in that? This whole account is about the paralyzed man, right? Not entirely. Consider that the man's friends loved him enough to band together and try to bring him out of his dark desperation. They were bold enough bring this man to Jesus, believing they would receive an answer.

Jesus performed two miracles that day: forgiving the man's sin and healing his body. Yet behind the miracles lay the courageous faith of friends. These individuals went the extra mile, confident that they had come to the right source. And Jesus met the paralyzed man's need on behalf of the faith of his friends.

You can be that kind of friend. You can carry your loved ones' pain to a God who can intervene in their lives—and loves to do so!

Do you believe God can do anything for your friends? If so, will you ask?

BE THE MAN WHO DOESN'T MIND LOOKING FOOLISH

God chose the foolish things of the world to shame the wise;
God chose the weak things of the world to shame the strong.
1 CORINTHIANS 1:27 NIV

Some guys are brilliant and have multiple degrees, and some look like they could bench press an SUV. Even if they don't announce it, the way they speak and conduct themselves can make other men feel insignificant.

If you are relying on your popularity or your ability to impress, you're in for a rude surprise: public opinion changes. God, however, uses a different metric. In the hands of God, weak people can become undeniable tools of strength and tenacity. Wisdom doesn't always come from a school, nor strength from a gym.

God takes what others consider deficits and uses them to make a huge impact in your world. He uses what some call foolish and weak to do things the smart and strong can only dream of accomplishing.

Maybe the reason for this lies behind the differences between weak and strong, foolish and smart. Intelligence and muscles tend to build pride, which clouds a man's ability to recognize his need for God to work in his life.

To be clear, there's nothing wrong with being strong or smart. . .but neither of them will get you where God needs you to be.

Does the idea of being weak and foolish sound undesirable
to you? In what ways can it be a good thing?

BE THE MAN WHO VALUES TEAMWORK

I appeal to you, brothers and sisters, in the name of our Lord Jesus Christ, that all of you agree with one another in what you say and that there be no divisions among you, but that you be perfectly united in mind and thought.
1 CORINTHIANS 1:10 NIV

Think of the last great team you were on. Everyone got along, pulled their weight, and supported each other. Now think of the opposite kind of team—constant fighting, unequal workloads, and members constantly throwing each other under the bus. What sets these two types apart?

James Folkman, founder of two leadership development firms, once wrote an article for *Forbes* on what sets highly effective teams apart. According to Folkman, these team leaders inspire more than they drive; help resolve conflicts quickly; set stretch goals—audacious goals which can only be accomplished by the specific team in question; communicate vision and direction; are trusted.

These team leadership tips can all be found in the apostle Paul's example to the church of Corinth. After opening with inspiration (1 Corinthians 1:4–9), he moves on to an appeal for unity (1:10). His stretch goal is for church members to love each other perfectly (chapter 13). His vision is to clearly communicate the resurrection of Christ (15:1–5). And his trustworthiness lies in his own experience with Jesus (15:8–11).

Being a faithful man means valuing teamwork and leading by example. You have the ability to make your team (your family, your workplace, your church) more dream than scream by following Paul's example.

Inspire others by praying for them and praising them. Address conflicts calmly yet openly, not allowing them to fester into behind-the-back bickering. Set a stretch goal for your team to achieve with you. Communicate your vision continuously. And be trustworthy in all your dealings.

What are some of your best moments of teamwork?
How can you avoid bad team experiences?

BE THE MAN WHO AVOIDS PRETENSE

Each year Solomon received about 25 tons of gold. . . .
King Solomon made 200 large shields of hammered gold,
each weighing more than fifteen pounds. He also made 300 smaller
shields of hammered gold, each weighing nearly four pounds.
The king placed these shields in the Palace of the Forest of Lebanon.
1 KINGS 10:14, 16–17 NLT

When Solomon's reign over Israel was established, God offered him anything he might ask for. Solomon requested the wisdom to lead God's people well, and God granted it. . .along with the wealth and fame Solomon could have requested but didn't. Unfortunately, Solomon's heart was divided, so his reign didn't reflect the wisdom he'd been given.

Solomon loved God, but he also loved himself. He built a temple for God, but he spent more time and money furnishing his own palace. Today's Bible passage reflects only a portion of the riches Solomon placed in his opulent home. In fact, Solomon did all the things the Bible said a king of Israel should not do if his heart is fully devoted to God.

Deuteronomy 17:16–17 (NLT) says, "The king must not build up a large stable of horses for himself or send his people to Egypt to buy horses, for the LORD has told you, 'You must never return to Egypt.' The king must not take many wives for himself, because they will turn his heart away from the LORD. And he must not accumulate large amounts of wealth in silver and gold for himself."

Of course, Solomon amassed wealth for himself, filled his stables with Egyptian horses, and married an Egyptian princess. . .along with a whole troop of other wives. He was always more concerned with appearing like a king than acting like a king of Israel ought to. Because his heart was far from God, Solomon's downfall was all but assured.

Is your heart divided between how others view you and what God calls you to do? Are you acting exactly how the Bible tells you not to? Perhaps the wisdom of Solomon's story is this: don't follow his example. Instead, follow God with your whole heart, today and every day.

Do you ever try to impress those around you? Do those actions honor God?

BE THE MAN WHO BELIEVES IN A MIRACLE

Whom have I in heaven but thee? and there is none upon earth
that I desire beside thee. My flesh and my heart faileth: but
God is the strength of my heart, and my portion for ever.
PSALM 73:25–26 KJV

The low fuel light was blazing the entire drive to work, and the commuter didn't have a single penny left. There was no way to get the fuel needed to return home. The driver searched frantically under the car seats but found very little spare change. Suddenly, a gentleman working at the gas station knocked on the car window and told the driver that while he had no idea why, he had put a few dollars' worth of fuel on the pump for the customer. No charge. He hoped it helped.

Needless to say, the trip home was very emotional.

You live in a place where desperation lives. Circumstances leave you trembling, and you are certain that if God doesn't show up, you'll never make it through. But take heart: God is at work, and He brings to reality things that live above your wildest dreams. When He shows up in your life, the only word that can describe it is *miracle*.

Faithful men understand that any successful outcome comes from God's grace. Kids have broken toys, teens have broken hearts, and men sometimes struggle to hold onto the fragments of a broken life. But thankfully, God can take brokenness and work a restoration miracle.

Do you (or someone you know) have a story of brokenness? When was the last time you asked God for help only He could provide?

BE THE MAN WHO INTERACTS DIFFERENTLY WITH GOD

[Peter] took [the lame man] by the right hand, and lifted him up: and immediately his feet and ankle bones received strength.
ACTS 3:7 KJV

You are fragile. Your body can break, and so can your mind. Age has a way of cruelly reminding you of your younger days, when personal strength seemed abundant. Failure and weakness can sneak into your life, and you won't even realize they exist until you reach for your strength and discover there's not enough for the trouble at hand.

On your own, there's no way to escape the despair.

In Acts 3, Peter and John encountered a crippled beggar. . .and quickly perceived he wanted something much more than money. So they gave the man an unexpected prize: they "lifted him up: and immediately his feet and ankle bones received strength." Afterward, this man went into the temple with Peter and John and had his own worship service.

As you age, it's tempting to embrace bitterness and anger. But God's strength offers a better way. It doesn't just make you a nicer person—it keeps you fit for lifelong duty. A broken body might require you to perform your duty in a different way, but God never sets you aside. He won't ask you to do anything that He hasn't given you the strength to do. This may not be physical strength but an inner strength that's rooted in the goodness of God. Either way, it'll make a difference.

The strength God offers changes not only you but the way you interact with Him.

How can God's strength bring you to a place of worship?
Are you using God's help to honor Him?

BE THE MAN WHO WORKS HARD

Whatever you do, work at it with all your heart,
as working for the Lord, not for human masters.
COLOSSIANS 3:23 NIV

Slavery was common in ancient Colossae. Unlike slavery in the American South—in which skin color was the deciding factor—Roman slaves might have entered servitude as a result of war. Or they might have sold themselves into slavery to pay off a debt.

The terms *slave*, *servant*, and *bondservant* all refer to individuals who are owned by their master, and Jesus used this form of servitude as an illustration of how Christians should live.

"Sitting down, Jesus called the Twelve and said, 'Anyone who wants to be first must be the very last, and the servant of all'" (Mark 9:35 NIV).

Far from endorsing slavery, Jesus was encouraging believers to recognize their relationship to God the Father as their owner. Since God owns us, we are to love Him above all else and love our neighbors as ourselves (see Mark 12:30–31). How do we love our neighbors? By becoming a servant to all.

Paul carries the image further in Colossians 3, where he lays out instructions for members of a Christian household: "Slaves, obey your earthly masters in everything; and do it, not only when their eye is on you and to curry their favor, but with sincerity of heart and reverence for the Lord. Whatever you do, work at it with all your heart, as working for the Lord, not for human masters, since you know that you will receive an inheritance from the Lord as a reward. It is the Lord Christ you are serving" (verses 22–24 NIV).

Being a faithful man means purposefully recognizing your true master and working accordingly.

Are you a hard worker? Are you working for yourself or your Father in Heaven?

BE THE MAN WHO IS WISE WITH HIS EYES

*"But I say, anyone who even looks at a woman with lust
has already committed adultery with her in his heart."*
MATTHEW 5:28 NLT

As official crime statistics continue to tick downward, the world should be safer than ever. In reality, the dangers are getting more subversive. Things that were once morally reprehensible are now shrugged off as normal parts of life. Sin is not frowned upon; it is winked at.

The Internet has changed the way the world works. Businesses are global, meetings can be performed remotely, relationships begin on apps before people ever meet in person. And pornography is only a click away.

What used to be a private sin has become a public joke. Mainstream films and television shows use pornography as a punchline. According to a Gallup poll from 2018, 43 percent of Americans view pornography as morally acceptable, a figure 7 percent higher than the same poll from 2017. Is pornography really a big deal?

Jesus says it is.

In Matthew 5:27–29 (NLT), Jesus says, "You have heard the commandment that says, 'You must not commit adultery.' But I say, anyone who even looks at a woman with lust has already committed adultery with her in his heart. So if your eye—even your good eye—causes you to lust, gouge it out and throw it away. It is better for you to lose one part of your body than for your whole body to be thrown into hell."

Lust is the intentional viewing of someone else for the purpose of arousal, and Jesus makes it abundantly clear that it's a big deal. An eyeball-gouge-worthy big deal. Why? Because lust is a form of idolatry. Pornography twists God's design for sexuality into an object of worship, an outlet for our selfish desires.

Becoming a faithful man means recognizing pornography as sin and treating it as such.

Do you see pornography as acceptable? How can
you make sure you don't fall into its trap?

BE THE MAN WHO FINISHES THE RACE

*For I am already being poured out like a drink offering,
and the time for my departure is near. I have fought the good
fight, I have finished the race, I have kept the faith. Now there
is in store for me the crown of righteousness, which the Lord,
the righteous Judge, will award to me on that day—and not only
to me, but also to all who have longed for his appearing.*
2 TIMOTHY 4:6–8 NIV

Many men start the new year with vigor. They invest in a gym membership and tell themselves—and anyone willing to listen—that they'll be rising each morning before the crack of dawn, lifting weights until sweat breaks out, and buffing up so much that everyone will notice.

Then day two arrives. Suddenly, all motivation fades into a mirage, the body screams for relief, and any semblance of courage collapses into a small, discouraged whimper.

The pace God sets for your life is neither fast nor slow. It is, however, a relentless pursuit—a continual willingness to put one foot in front of the other. The satisfaction that comes at the end of this endurance race will be unmatched by any workout routine.

Fight hard, run well, and prove faithful. Show rare courage by asking God to show you the way. Ask Him, who knows that trouble is common, to also show compassion and give you determination on your journey.

Life isn't just about where you are in this moment—it's about where you find yourself at the end.

What are you doing today to move closer to God's finish line? Do you see following God's leadership as necessary for completing life's race?

BE THE MAN WHO SHARES HIS STRENGTH

*I long to visit you so I can bring you some spiritual gift
that will help you grow strong in the Lord. When we
get together, I want to encourage you in your faith,
but I also want to be encouraged by yours.*

ROMANS 1:11–12 NLT

Housewarming gifts may not be as popular today, but they were once a way to show friendship and hospitality—to congratulate people on their important decision.

Today, most people live by the motto "Let your presence be your gift." Consequently, gifts are no longer required or expected. But Romans 1 reminds us that the best housewarming gifts are the ones that come from *God*.

These gifts are spiritual in nature, and they come from the hand of someone who recognizes their value. They include things like strength, hope, forgiveness, love, kindness, mercy, and compassion. These gifts are priceless.

When God gives you strength, take it with you. Every gift He shares is a gift you can share as well. Even if others refuse it, the importance of this gift can never be diminished. God gave it to you, so you can keep giving it and never run out.

God's strength can be passed along, and you have the opportunity to make that happen. Encourage and be encouraged—that's the cycle of sharing.

Are you intentional about sharing the strength God's
given you? What are some ways you can do it today?

BE THE MAN WHO ALLOWS GOD TO REDIRECT HIS LIFE

So you must live as God's obedient children. Don't slip back into your old ways of living to satisfy your own desires. You didn't know any better then.

1 PETER 1:14 NLT

Imagine your life as a river moving through the landscape of time. This moment right now is at the head of the flow, questing naturally forward along the path. Unless some obstacle impedes its flow, the water will continue in this direction until it comes to the sea.

When you accepted Christ, you became connected to the one who can move mountains and redirect the flow of any river. Without His power, your river wouldn't stand a chance of permanently changing its direction. But when His power is coupled with your humble request for His help, your river will flow where He desires.

You'll still feel the natural inclination toward your old path, but you no longer need to follow it. You are a new creation, and God's Spirit inside you can help you live obediently to His call.

How can you keep from slipping back into your old riverbed?

First, look honestly at your life through the lens of God's holiness. Which habits might not be pleasing to Him? Is there anything preventing you from changing? Pray for God's clarity in your life then write out a list of the changes you'd like to make with His help.

When you find yourself veering toward old habits, ask why. Every habit has a trigger, a routine, and a reward. What triggered you? What new routines can you put in place? And how can you strive toward a more lasting reward?

Take a moment to write out your new routines and rewards. Pray over each statement and ask God to help you stay obedient to His call. Ask Him to direct your river toward *His* ocean, not your own.

When you think of bad habits, is there anything in your life that comes to mind? With whom might you share your new goals in order to have an accountability partner?

BE THE MAN WHO LEADS THE BATTLE

In the spring, at the time when kings go off to war, David sent Joab out
with the king's men and the whole Israelite army. They destroyed the
Ammonites and besieged Rabbah. But David remained in Jerusalem.

2 SAMUEL 11:1 NIV

At the time when kings went off to war, David remained in Jerusalem. The king's men and the whole Israelite army besieged Rabbah, but the king didn't join them. If David had been where he should have been, the following disaster wouldn't have happened.

As David lingered on the rooftop one day, he happened to see Bathsheba—the wife of Uriah, one of his most loyal warriors—bathing. Instead of averting his eyes and heading indoors to attend to matters of state or visit one of his other wives, David stayed and watched. Then he took matters a step further and inquired after her, sending multiple messengers to invite her to his chambers for a private audience. As the king was unaccustomed to hearing no, he convinced Bathsheba to lay with him, impregnating her. Afterward, David concocted an elaborate scheme to cover his sin, resulting in his murder by proxy of Uriah and his marriage to Bathsheba.

There were so many places in this story where David could have chosen differently. If he hadn't tried to cover his tracks, Uriah would have lived. If he hadn't forced Bathsheba to lay with him, she wouldn't have gotten pregnant. If he hadn't sent messengers to get her, she would have been spared entirely. If David had looked away when he first noticed her bathing, he wouldn't have been tempted to do more. If he had been leading the battle in the fields with his men, he would have avoided the whole thing.

When you get caught up in sin, the consequences—and your desire to hide from them—will always escalate with time. The best thing to do is to be where you are meant to be in the first place.

Where are you meant to be at this moment? How might
you prevent yourself from being where you shouldn't?

BE THE MAN WHO ISN'T SHAKEN

*I know the LORD is always with me. I will
not be shaken, for he is right beside me.*
PSALM 16:8 NLT

God was offering Moses an opportunity to deliver God's people from
the oppression they'd endured at the hands of Pharaoh in Egypt. Moses,
however, felt it was the perfect moment for full disclosure: he'd never
done well in public speaking, he'd lived practically as a hermit for forty
years, and. . .well. . .he was old. Moses was hunting for disqualification
points, and he hoped his excuses were on point enough for God. *Surely*,
he thought, *God has other, more qualified candidates!*

But Moses wasn't thinking about the people—he was thinking only
about himself. Courage wasn't found in his response. His initial statement was essentially, "Not me! Not now!"

God gave His counteroffer in Exodus 3:12 (NLT): "I will be with
you." What kind of argument can refute the help of the living God? Even
with this perfect answer, Moses still seemed interested in loopholes and
excuses.

King David, who wrote today's scripture, had a different response
to God. To this king, God wasn't unreasonable. If God requested him to
follow, then God must know the way. Even more, he knew God would
share all the tools he needed for the job.

God is right beside you, helping in ways you don't always understand. You could make excuses, but why? He can do so much more with
your willingness instead. God has secured your future, so if He asks you
to follow, His plan can never fail.

In God, you can refuse to be shaken.

How can your comfort zone negatively affect your willingness to obey God?
Do you find it easier to make excuses than to believe God is right beside you?

BE THE MAN WHO PROCLAIMS FUTURE STRENGTH

Do not gloat over me, my enemy! Though I have fallen, I will rise. Though I sit in darkness, the LORD will be my light.
MICAH 7:8 NIV

Today's verse is the proclamation of an entire nation. Israel had been so bad that God was about to place them in a timeout, and their enemies would no doubt find it amusing that God was treating them like children. How weak and helpless Israel must've appeared! Of course, the enemy was right. On their own, the Israelites had been weak and ineffective. But God's goodness simply wouldn't allow them to stay in this weakened state. The people needed to understand that this was a corrective action designed to improve their strength. They would need to feel confident in following God once more.

Micah's proclamation was clear—the people had fumbled in darkness and fallen, not knowing where to go. But as bad as this proclamation seemed to be, it wasn't the end. Hope, assurance, and victory waited on the other side of their timeout. The people could say in unison that even though they had fallen, their story would end in victory. Despite the present abundance of darkness and despair, God Himself would be their light—their only source of rescue and clarity.

That's why strength could be found in the hearts of the fallen, hope in the minds of those living in darkness, and endurance in the souls who recognized God's plan. Through their new commitment to the God whom they'd once abandoned, they would begin their journey back to good health. He was waiting for their return—all they needed was His strength.

How long does God wait for the fallen to seek Him? Why is correction sometimes necessary to remind us of the source of true strength?

BE THE MAN WHO DOES GOD'S WILL

Rejoice always, pray continually, give thanks in all circumstances; for this is God's will for you in Christ Jesus.
1 THESSALONIANS 5:16–18 NIV

The will of God is perfect. His plans cannot be thwarted. Nothing can happen without His approval. If only we could be that certain about our own desires and plans. Or if only we knew for sure what He wants for us.

Should we find a new job or stick with the one we have? Do we take our relationship to the next level or cool things off for a bit? What should we make for dinner? Do we invest in the market or pay down our mortgage?

When faced with too many options, we quickly fall victim to decision fatigue. Scientists have discovered a correlation between the number of decisions a person makes and that person's likelihood of making poor or uninformed decisions. After a certain number of choices, we become incapable of wise decisions.

While we might ponder what to make for dinner, we don't need to waste any mental energy figuring out God's will for our lives. He tells us exactly what to do in 1 Thessalonians 5:16–18 NIV: "Rejoice always, pray continually, give thanks in all circumstances; for this is God's will for you in Christ Jesus."

Joy, prayer, and thanksgiving are to be the hallmarks of our lives. Being a faithful man means actively choosing to rejoice in God's goodness, praying for God's wisdom, and giving thanks regardless of the circumstances.

When we trust God, joyfully putting our lives in His hands and thanking Him for whatever happens, He is free to perform His will through us. No decision fatigue required.

How can you rearrange your schedule so that your biggest decisions are made early in the day? Do you tend to make bad choices late at night when your willpower is low?

BE THE MAN WHO USES HIS SHIELD

*Above all, taking the shield of faith, wherewith ye shall
be able to quench all the fiery darts of the wicked.*
EPHESIANS 6:16 KJV

The Roman scutum—a large, rectangular curved shield made of wood
and leather—was a soldier's best friend in Paul's day. Although it weighed
around twenty-two pounds and might have been a pain to carry, you
wouldn't want to be caught dead without one (which is probably just
what would happen). Scutums were large enough to hide your whole
body behind and were sometimes used to conceal an army's numbers
from an enemy.

When Paul uses the imagery of the scutum to describe faith, he's
specifically referring to the practice of soaking the shield's exterior in
water. These wet shields would be able to douse flaming arrows, which
might otherwise pose a threat to men hiding behind flammable chunks
of wood.

Our faith in God is designed to protect every part of us. The enemy
cannot harm us, even with flaming arrows, because we are soaked in the
living water.

One other detail about the scutum: it was often painted with the
soldier's unit, rank, and name. It was identifiable on the battlefield so
that your allies would know to help you and your enemies would know
to run away from you.

Today, make sure you have your shield of faith prepared when you
engage the enemy. Make it identifiable to others, and may God give you
victory in the battles ahead!

Are you living fully behind your shield, or are you dangling body
parts for the enemy to aim at? Do others know which side of
the battle you're on just by looking at your faith?

BE THE MAN WHO KNOWS GOD IS FOR US

What shall we then say to these things? If God be for us, who can be against us? He that spared not his own Son, but delivered him up for us all, how shall he not with him also freely give us all things? Who shall lay any thing to the charge of God's elect? It is God that justifieth.
ROMANS 8:31–33 KJV

The Philistines were a violent people prone to waging war and conquering lands. They seemed to think that if the giant Goliath was for them, who could be against them? Day after day, the giant would boisterously taunt the army of Israel.

Their tactic was working—no one wanted to fight them.

But these warriors got one crucial thing wrong: they put their trust in someone other than God. That meant their army was ripe for the picking.

When young David (the future king of Israel) walked onto the battlefield dressed like a shepherd, everyone laughed him to scorn. When he pulled out a sling and stone, nobody championed young David's cause. Yet David stuck to three undisputable facts: he was for God, God was with him, and no one could stand against God. That day, the armies of Philistia and Israel witnessed just how big God is.

If you start believing that God is smaller than your problems, your thinking needs realigned. When you make anything bigger than God, you stand against the one who wants to stand for *you*.

With whom are you standing today?

How does this reminder of God's power challenge your fears? How will you live out your belief that God is bigger than anything you face?

BE THE MAN WHO OVERCOMES

*Whatsoever is born of God overcometh the world: and this
is the victory that overcometh the world, even our faith.*
1 JOHN 5:4 KJV

Whenever you do something you thought you could never do—whether it's swimming, going to the dentist, or giving a speech—you are an overcomer. Everyone overcomes something. When you're very young, you might have a fear of the dark, spiders, or certain people. But when you beat back the challenge of coexisting with these things, you embrace the role of an overcomer.

Sometimes, overcoming comes naturally, like the process of growing up. But other times, you'll encounter things you can't overcome on your own. This might include trauma from childhood, ethnic prejudice, or memories of a violent encounter. The struggle can be debilitating—and even worse, no one else may understand. They might think it's silly, like a fear of the dark. But each tide of fear leaves you feeling overwhelmed and powerless—the furthest thing from an overcomer.

You start believing you'll never conquer this inexplicable fear. You come to hate this place, and you'd love nothing more than to toss this pain in the garbage bin.

First John 5:4 declares that it's faith in God alone that allows you to overcome the tough stuff. That's why God can wisely ask you to do what you think is impossible—to forgive those who hurt you, love those who hate you, and pray for those who fight against you. If God's commands can make *these* actions possible, there's *nothing* you can't overcome!

What's the most appealing thing about becoming an overcomer?
How can you use God's Word to overcome?

BE THE MAN WHO LEAVES SIN IN THE TOMB

Knowing this, that our old man is crucified with him,
that the body of sin might be destroyed, that henceforth we
should not serve sin. For he that is dead is freed from sin.
ROMANS 6:6–7 KJV

What goes into a tomb should stay in a tomb. Jesus is the only notable exception to this rule—everything else is the stuff of horror movies. Even worse are the true stories of people exhuming bodies for nefarious purposes—laws and common sense both tell us to leave dead bodies alone.

According to Numbers 19, anyone who touched or was in the same room as a dead body was ceremonially unclean for seven days. If the unclean person didn't partake in specific purification rituals, they were to be cut off from the rest of the community. That's a pretty serious punishment!

And yet Christians, who are dead to sin through Jesus' sacrifice, still occasionally creep into sin's tomb. If the thought of playing around with your decomposing sin doesn't gross you out, then you aren't taking redemption seriously enough.

Jesus died and rose again to give us new life, declaring us pure and freeing us from our tombs! Why on earth would we ever go back in?

Because just like in a horror movie, sin's dead body doesn't want to release its hold on life. It calls to us, reminds us of the "fun" we used to have, and lies about the consequences. We have been rescued from ultimate destruction, but we lose our close community with God and His church when we return to the tomb of our sin.

It's time to step out and stay out. Ask God to help you roll a stone over the opening. Allow the Spirit to renew your mind and help you live a pure life for Him.

What sin still calls to you from the tomb? What stone
can God help you roll in front of the opening?

BE THE MAN WHO SEEKS WISDOM

*If any of you lacks wisdom, you should ask God, who gives generously
to all without finding fault, and it will be given to you.*
JAMES 1:5 NIV

There's an old anecdote about a man of faith trapped on his roof during a flood. The man is fervently praying for God to deliver him when a guy in a rowboat floats by and asks if he needs help. "No thanks," the trapped man says. "God will deliver me." So the rowboat rows away.

The floodwaters continue to rise, and the man on the roof continues to pray for God's deliverance. Just then, a man in a speedboat motors up, asking if the man on the roof needs help. "No thanks," the trapped man repeats. "God will deliver me." So the speedboat speeds away.

The incident happens again, this time with a helicopter, and the conversation repeats itself once more. Eventually, the flood rises over his house, and he dies. When he gets to heaven, the man complains to God about his lack of deliverance, but God replies that He sent a rowboat, a speedboat, and a helicopter. What more could the man expect?

It is a wise man who realizes his need for—as well as the source of—greater wisdom. But praying for wisdom without listening to the people God has placed in your life is like sitting on a roof during a flood and refusing earthly rescue attempts.

Proverbs 19:20 (NLT) says, "Get all the advice and instruction you can, so you will be wise the rest of your life." God has given us loving friends and family who can be His physical presence in this world. Of course, we should cross-reference their wisdom with the Bible to make sure it is actually wise.

So pray for wisdom. Read your Bible. Listen to loved ones. And make sure that the counsel you listen to is wise because it accords with God's Word.

Have you ever ignored good advice because it wasn't what you wanted to hear? How might you be a source of wisdom for the loved ones in your life?

DAY 171

BE THE MAN WHO GROWS THROUGH INSECURITY

"I know the LORD has given you this land," she told them. "We are all afraid of you. Everyone in the land is living in terror. For we have heard how the LORD made a dry path for you through the Red Sea when you left Egypt. And we know what you did to Sihon and Og, the two Amorite kings east of the Jordan River, whose people you completely destroyed. No wonder our hearts have melted in fear! No one has the courage to fight after hearing such things. For the LORD your God is the supreme God of the heavens above and the earth below."

JOSHUA 2:9–11 NLT

There is a whole lot of bluff in people who don't know God. Their insecurity shows up in false confidence. None of us know the future, but Christians know the God who does.

The Bible tells of two men who went to the walled city of Jericho. Joshua, having heard God's promise that the city would be overthrown, had sent these men to scout it out.

While in the city, a woman named Rahab recognized that something new was happening and that the God of this advanced scouting team was supreme. So she sheltered the two men, knowing that if God wanted Jericho, nothing would stop Him. The only way of life she'd ever known was coming to a resounding end.

Although Rahab didn't know God, she had a willingness to admit her insecurity: "No wonder our hearts have melted in fear!" Rahab had little courage, but she had hope—hope that perhaps God would be gracious to her for not exposing the Hebrew scouting party.

Sometimes, courage begins with hope. Insecurity doesn't preclude you from the benefits of courage; instead, it could be the motivator that inspires you to let God fill in your gaps in knowledge, leading you to the life you've always needed.

> When do you feel the most insecure? How can you
> let God use this insecurity to inspire courage?

DAY 172

BE THE MAN WHO RECOGNIZES DECEPTION

You belong to God, my dear children. You have already won a victory over those people, because the Spirit who lives in you is greater than the spirit who lives in the world. Those people belong to this world, so they speak from the world's viewpoint, and the world listens to them. But we belong to God, and those who know God listen to us. If they do not belong to God, they do not listen to us.

1 JOHN 4:4–6 NLT

Sometimes, leftovers are better than the freshly served meal. Why? Because time has allowed the flavors to seep into every morsel. It gets richer the more you come back.

The Bible can be the same way. Take a familiar verse like 1 John 4:4–6, for example: "You have already won a victory over those people." Yes, that's comforting. . .but have you ever asked yourself, "Who are *those people*"?

The first three verses of this chapter speak of people who shared popular spiritual philosophy without welcoming God into their thinking. These unwise preachers had a following, which made life difficult for Christians who understood that God's truth contradicted such guesswork. So whom did people believe? The men who learned from Jesus or the men who accepted only what they wanted to believe and then added their own teachings?

If some people won't listen to Jesus, they certainly won't listen to you. But their faulty reasoning is no match for God's strength, which makes even the best of human wisdom look foolish.

God 1—deception 0.

Do you get upset when you hear people encouraging others
to believe lies about God? How can you gain strength
from knowing God has overcome faulty thinking?

BE THE MAN WHO AVOIDS RIVALRIES

In your relationships with one another, have the same mindset as Christ Jesus: Who, being in very nature God, did not consider equality with God something to be used to his own advantage; rather, he made himself nothing by taking the very nature of a servant, being made in human likeness.

PHILIPPIANS 2:5–7 NIV

The word *rivalry* comes from the Latin *rivus*, which means "brook," and stems from the idea of sharing a brook or stream with a neighbor. The rivalry part comes in when our neighbors across the brook begin to compete with us in terms of status, achievements, or belongings. Haven't we all looked at a neighbor's lawn a bit jealously when it is greener than ours?

But Christians aren't to fall into the trap of rivalry. The only thing in which we should try to outdo each other is kindness. And that only happens when we stop obsessing over our own accomplishments and start focusing on the grace God has given us.

In his letter to the Philippians, Paul wanted church members to rise above rivalries. Using Jesus' relationship with God as the ultimate example, Paul says the Lord "did not consider equality with God something to be used to his own advantage; rather, he made himself nothing by taking the very nature of a servant, being made in human likeness" (Philippians 2:6–7 NIV).

If Jesus, who could have made Himself as glorious on earth as He is in heaven, restrained Himself to become a servant of humanity, we can stop trying to outshine our neighbors. Faithful men choose neighborly love over neighborhood rivalries.

Instead of looking at our neighbors' lawns, we should be looking for our neighbors' needs. How can we show them God's presence if we're hoping they'll see our new boat? Philippians 2:3 (NIV) says, "Do nothing out of selfish ambition or vain conceit. Rather, in humility value others above yourselves."

Are there any rivalries in your life right now? How can you serve your neighbor today?

BE THE MAN WHO DOESN'T CONFUSE FALSE MODESTY WITH HUMILITY

Humble yourselves in the sight of the Lord, and he shall lift you up.
JAMES 4:10 KJV

Are you familiar with the "humblebrag"? It's when a boastful comment is hidden inside either a complaint or a seemingly humble, self-deprecating statement:

- "Don't you hate it when some bozo scratches your new convertible with a shopping cart? I mean, I parked a mile away from the store for a reason!" (Complaint)
- "I had to work late every night this week. I don't know why my boss keeps giving me the most important clients. I'm just honored to be part of the team, ya know?" (Humble)

These are both classic humblebrags, but there's a newer one made possible by social media:

- "What a beautiful sunrise!" written above a picture of someone's large house on the lake, an expensive boat floating in the background.

The whole point of a humblebrag is to impress others with one's talents, wealth, or even humility. But true humility doesn't call attention to itself in any way. True humility places trust in God's goodness and looks to impress Him alone. The only accolades that matter are the ones that come from God.

If you want to be lifted up by Him, humble yourself before Him and everyone else. Don't dwell on your accomplishments here on earth. When your efforts are recognized here—because you drew attention to them through humblebragging—you will have already received your reward. Don't settle for that. Work for the goal of God Himself saying, "Well done, my good and faithful servant," when you see Him face to face.

Have you been guilty of humblebragging in the past? How can a man avoid settling for human praise instead of God's praise?

BE THE MAN WHO TRUSTS
THE DEPENDABLE GOD

*Be of good courage, and let us behave ourselves valiantly
for our people, and for the cities of our God: and let
the LORD do that which is good in his sight.*

1 CHRONICLES 19:13 KJV

Joab thought like a warrior, acted like a warrior, and exuded the courage of a warrior in the face of any challenge. He worked to inspire his soldiers, and they fought hard for him. His warrior heart, however, must have been tinged with pride. Joab's strategies often replaced God's will. He often traded trust for deception. But one speech that he gave to his men seems to suggest that a kernel of truth remained lodged deep within his warring spirit.

Joab's words above presaged by centuries a quote attributed to Saint Ignatius: "Act as if everything depended on you; trust as if everything depended on God." Joab was very willing to go to war, but he concluded that in the end, God would do what God would do—even if Joab didn't like the outcome.

In the New Testament, another man was confronted with a similar struggle. He was a part of a group of religious leaders who had no use for the gospel. The group collectively sought to silence any talk about Jesus. But then this teacher, Gamaliel, said, "Let them alone: for if this counsel or this work be of men, it will come to nought: But if it be of God, ye cannot overthrow it" (Acts 5:38–39 KJV).

Faithful men know that their best plans may be in vain, but God's plans are always right. Be willing to set your plans aside when God reveals His better plan.

Have you ever refused to let God control your plans? If so, how did that turn out?

BE THE MAN WHO OVERCOMES THE WORLD

*Who is it that overcomes the world? Only the
one who believes that Jesus is the Son of God.*

1 JOHN 5:5 NIV

There are lots of things you can overcome—faulty thinking, unproductive habits, addictions, you name it. Success in these struggles can improve your life and strengthen your relationships.

"The world," in 1 John 5:5, is presented as something to be overcome. But what exactly is "the world"? The earth itself? While God gave humanity the responsibility to "rule over" creation (Genesis 1:26 NIV), that's not what 1 John 5 is describing. So what is this "world" that John mentions? Who does the overcoming, and where do they get their strength?

Back in Genesis, God created a "very good" world (1:31 NIV). The only thing the first man and woman were told to avoid was the very thing that created our need to overcome: sin. Once sin arrived on earth, it never left. We can't remove it, pay the price for it, or make it go away. But Jesus can.

Overcoming the world takes something bigger than our own personal effort. It takes an admittance of personal failure, a restoration of forgiveness, and an acceptance of rescue. When a man does these things, his faith in an overcoming God allows him to overcome "the world"— specifically, the sin that made this world such a sorry place.

Overcoming the world. . .what could be stronger than that?

What personal challenges are you struggling to overcome?
How can the message of 1 John 5:5 encourage you in the battle?

DAY 177

BE THE MAN WHO GUARDS HIS TONGUE

If you claim to be religious but don't control your tongue,
you are fooling yourself, and your religion is worthless.
JAMES 1:26 NLT

When you squeeze a tube of toothpaste, toothpaste comes out. If you squeeze out too much, too bad. It's not going back in.

When life squeezes you—when you hit your thumb with a hammer, when you get cut off in traffic, when your boss tells you to dust off your résumé because your position is gone—what's inside is what comes out. Jesus said in Luke 6:45 (NLT), "A good person produces good things from the treasury of a good heart, and an evil person produces evil things from the treasury of an evil heart. What you say flows from what is in your heart."

Like toothpaste, words that spurt from your mouth are never going back in.

Being a faithful man means both guarding your tongue and filling your mind with good things so that the words that do escape aren't bad.

If you want good things to flow from the treasury of your heart, you need to make sure your treasury is well-stocked. For this, Paul's prayer for the Ephesian church applies to you too: "May you experience the love of Christ, though it is too great to understand fully. Then you will be made complete with all the fullness of life and power that comes from God" (Ephesians 3:19 NLT).

The last similarity between using toothpaste and guarding your tongue is that both should be part of a regular routine. It's a cavity-filled mouth that uses toothpaste only before seeing the dentist; likewise, it's a sin-filled life that asks to be filled with God's power only before going to church.

What words come out when life squeezes you?
How often do you pray to be filled with God's goodness?

BE THE MAN WHO SEES WEAKNESS AS STRENGTH

Each time he said, "My grace is all you need. My power works best in weakness." So now I am glad to boast about my weaknesses, so that the power of Christ can work through me.
2 CORINTHIANS 12:9 NLT

What is weakness? The origin of the word *weak* goes back through Old Norse (*veikr*) or Old English (*wac*) to a Proto-Germanic word (*waika-*) which means "to yield, or to bend." Weakness, then, is to yield to a greater power, to change a plan in favor of something new.

Is weakness bad? Well, it can be, depending on what a man yields to. If an alcoholic has a weak moment, he yields to old habits by having a drink. If a guy gives a weak response to a question, we know he doesn't really know the answer. There are plenty of situations in which bending toward something is wrong, but the reverse can be true as well. Weakness, when applied toward something better, is a virtue.

Read today's verse again. God's power works best in our weakness because that is when we are willing to yield our lives to Him. The apostle Paul even boasted about his weakness, because it meant he was ready to change his plans in favor of whatever would honor God most. Once we allow God to work through us, our own desires take second place. God is most evident in us when we are most yielding to Him.

Like the proverbial contest between the reed and the oak tree, we must be willing to bend with God's will lest we break because of our own stubbornness or pride. And we must be rooted in God's love so that we don't simply blow away when the storms come.

Are you a weak man? If you want to witness God's power in your life, be willing to yield to Him alone.

Do you know any areas of weakness you can give to God so that His power can shine through? Is God asking you to change something in your life today?

BE THE MAN WHO CHOOSES TO ENCOURAGE

*Now I want you to know, brothers and sisters, that what has
happened to me has actually served to advance the gospel. As a
result, it has become clear throughout the whole palace guard and
to everyone else that I am in chains for Christ. And because of my
chains, most of the brothers and sisters have become confident in the
Lord and dare all the more to proclaim the gospel without fear.*

PHILIPPIANS 1:12–14 NIV

Madagascar is a great place, known for its wide variety of exotic creatures
and an animated movie that bears its name. The island's past, however,
was much darker.

In the mid-1800s, Christianity was outlawed in Madagascar. In the
beginning of the purge, missionaries were targeted and made to leave.
When Christianity didn't seem deterred, the queen resorted to confis-
cating land, forcing Christians into hard labor, and, finally, enacting the
tangena ordeal. This "ordeal" involved the harvesting of a poisonous nut
from the tangena tree and forcing a suspected Christian to consume it.
Whoever lived through the experience was considered innocent; whoever died was declared guilty. It's been estimated that 20 percent of the
total population died, but Christianity still continued to grow.

Sometimes, other Christians are emboldened by your struggles. It
isn't that they want to see you struggle; rather, the example you set by
trusting God encourages others to trust Him with their own struggles.

Be this kind of encourager.

Do you feel encouraged when you hear stories of brave
Christian men who remained faithful? What part of your
story could be an encouragement to others?

BE THE MAN WHO'S A GOOD NEIGHBOR

Be not overcome of evil, but overcome evil with good.
ROMANS 12:21 KJV

God's strength can do what you can't. It can help when you won't and love when you'd rather not. God's strength welcomes the good choice—a kind word and a willingness to help. It opens closed doors, puts caution tape around your old stomping grounds, and lays out a welcome mat for others who don't know the source of your new strength.

Fred was a man whose approach to life displayed the fruits of God's strength. He was uniquely gifted in making both adults and children feel accepted. He encouraged people even when they didn't understand his motives. He loved people even when they made fun of him. He could've been overcome by evil, but Fred consistently chose to distribute good. And people noticed.

You might know this man as Fred Rogers (or perhaps "Mr. Rogers"). He was a pastor who was commissioned to share his faith through children's television. Many people still remember and celebrate him and his neighborhood—that's how different his life was.

It can be easy to trade love for a gavel—to become so bent on exacting justice that you forget all about forgiveness. Or you might do the opposite: forsake justice and not care enough to offer the other person help when it's needed the most.

Be a man who uses God's strength to make a difference.

Why might it seem intimidating to make good your natural response?
What is one way you can choose good over the next seven days?

BE THE MAN WHO THINKS ABOUT GOOD THINGS

Finally, brothers and sisters, whatever is true, whatever is noble, whatever is right, whatever is pure, whatever is lovely, whatever is admirable—if anything is excellent or praiseworthy—think about such things.
PHILIPPIANS 4:8 NIV

Pathways in the brain are like dirt roads. When we dwell on certain things, we create ruts in the road, making it hard to change course. So the longer we dwell on negative things, the less likely we are to see the positive. But when we focus on the positive, we actually reward our brains with chemicals that reinforce our happiness.

According to an article from Harvard Medical School, an optimistic mindset can help "people cope with disease and recover from surgery. Even more impressive is the impact of a positive outlook on overall health and longevity. Research tells us that an optimistic outlook early in life can predict better health and a lower rate of death during follow-up periods of 15 to 40 years."

These "glass half full" studies are nothing new, however; the Bible has prescribed positive thinking for nearly two thousand years. Philippians 4:8 provides a whole list of things to think about: whatever is true, noble, right, pure, lovely, admirable, excellent, or praiseworthy.

Why? Because our thought process influences our attitudes and actions. Just a few verses earlier, Paul told the Philippians (and all of us) to let go of anxiety and rejoice in all circumstances, because this will lead to peace: "And the peace of God, which transcends all understanding, will guard your hearts and your minds in Christ Jesus" (4:7 NIV).

To get started, we need to retrain our brains to dwell on praiseworthy things, to see the world through the lens of God's goodness. Not only will we reap physical benefits, we'll experience the peace of God which exceeds all understanding.

What do you dwell on the most? How can you
retrain your brain to see more of God's goodness?

BE THE MAN WHO BREAKS UP WITH PHOBIA

So you have not received a spirit that makes you fearful slaves.
Instead, you received God's Spirit when he adopted you as
his own children. Now we call him, "Abba, Father."
ROMANS 8:15 NLT

Did you know there are around four hundred named phobias? Even the ones that don't have a name are covered by an umbrella term. That word is *panophobia*—the fear of everything.

Fear comes in three main categories: social, specific, and crowds. You can be afraid to speak in public. You can be afraid of clowns. You can be afraid of people who are popular.

Some fears affect only a small number of people. For instance, *arachibutyrophobia* is the fear of peanut butter sticking to the roof of your mouth, and *xanthophobia* is the fear of the color yellow. You may think it's funny that someone could be afraid of either, but for someone who has these fears, it's no laughing matter.

Fear makes you weak. It keeps you from making positive decisions. It causes you to retreat before you can even choose to move forward. It locks you in a place of danger instead of leading you to safety.

But God sympathizes with us. That's why He made a habit of telling His people that fear is unnecessary. The choice to believe Him is yours—and He wants you to make it. To make positive decisions, move forward, and seek help.

A strong, faithful man breaks up with fear and refuses to treat it like an old flame. There's no good reason to re-engage with the fear that made you ineffective. God has called you to a life of adventure—are you ready to receive His strength?

Why does God want you to trust Him over your fears? How can God's
"Fear not" reminders make a difference in your decisions today?

BE THE MAN WHO IS SOBER MINDED

In the same way, deacons must be well respected and have integrity.
They must not be heavy drinkers or dishonest with money.
1 TIMOTHY 3:8 NLT

Before they could become leaders in the early church, men were called to show their integrity by being sober minded and trustworthy with finances. Today's verse specifically calls out the practice of heavy drinking, but being sober minded applies to all forms of intoxication.

The US National Library of Medicine has identified four groups of consumable intoxicants: hallucinogens (substances causing visual, auditory, and other hallucinations); inebriants (things like alcohol, chloroform, and other solvents and volatile chemicals); hypnotics (substances causing states of sleep, stupor, or calm, such as tranquilizers and narcotics); and stimulants (things like tea, coffee, cocoa, tobacco, cocaine, and amphetamines).

One of the dangers of such substances—aside from the stresses they can put upon the body or the way they might induce one to act—is their addictive nature. To what lengths might an addict go to support an addiction?

And addiction doesn't stop at drugs and alcohol; it can also take the form of gambling, pornography, and cutting. These may seem extreme and obviously wrong, but what about eating, working, shopping, and playing video games? Anything that draws your attention away from God's priorities has the potential to derail your effectiveness as His follower. When you are chasing a high, you are not chasing God.

Addictions of any kind are not broken overnight, but they require constant brokenness in order to be overcome. If you want to be a sober-minded follower of Christ and an upstanding leader in the church, you must allow yourself, your desires, and your pride to be broken in order to be wholly God's.

Are any of the addictions listed above clouding your ability to
follow God? Are you using your money to support any habits
that would be better entrusted to the Lord's work?

BE THE MAN WHO UNDERSTANDS VICTORY

When our dying bodies have been transformed into bodies that will never die, this Scripture will be fulfilled: "Death is swallowed up in victory. O death, where is your victory? O death, where is your sting?" For sin is the sting that results in death, and the law gives sin its power. But thank God! He gives us victory over sin and death through our Lord Jesus Christ.

1 CORINTHIANS 15:54–57 NLT

You've probably heard the phrase, "Are you in it to win it?" This saying has a lot to unpack. If you really want to answer this question, a host of other questions arise. What are you in? Are you present? Are you engaged? Motivated? Do you believe your struggle is winnable? Do you need to do it all yourself, or will there be help? Is your opponent too big to conquer? What does *victory* mean? How will you know if you've won?

For the apostle Paul, his opponents were sin and death. Both separated men from God. But Paul clarified that God alone delivers victory. It wasn't by Paul's hard work, determination, or great personality.

You can never claim victory over sin and death alone. If you're in it to win it, then make sure you bring Jesus with you. He's the one who orchestrated salvation—and He didn't need your help. In fact, God made it clear His standard is perfection, and you have nothing to offer (see Romans 3:23). This isn't a solo competition—you need God on your side if you ever hope to win.

God has always been in it to win it. Go with team God.

Do you ever struggle with the same sin repeatedly?
Why is victory impossible when you try to go it alone?

BE THE MAN WHO PLEASES HIS FATHER

*Since we are surrounded by such a huge crowd of witnesses
to the life of faith, let us strip off every weight that slows us
down, especially the sin that so easily trips us up. And let
us run with endurance the race God has set before us.*

HEBREWS 12:1 NLT

If you watch enough movies about father-son relationships, you'll notice a common trope: dads are exceptionally busy. And because of their busy schedules, their seat is empty at sporting events, ballet recitals, and play performances. Their kids usually respond with dejection and frustration, to which the dads respond with a laundry list of excuses.

This is a relatable situation. Many men have disappointed their kids with unkept promises. Even if the situation is unavoidable, the sting remains long after the event was over. Even worse are the promises that some men never intend to keep. In these cases, a mere apology and a nice gift can never cover their failure.

Thankfully, there's a big difference between human fathers and Father God, the promise keeper. He not only shows up—He brings His own cheer squad! Every day is race day, and you never have to wonder if God is up there watching you run. He joyously pays attention as you use what you've learned from Him to run the race and bound over hurdles.

Your life is an endurance race, and God notices and rejoices when you persevere. So be a man of strength, endurance, and joy. Your momentum is growing.

Why do boys want their dads to be present for important moments?
Does it encourage you to know God does this for you?

BE THE MAN WHO LIVES SACRIFICIALLY

*Greater love hath no man than this, that a man
lay down his life for his friends.*
JOHN 15:13 KJV

Animal altruism—the tendency for animals to sacrifice themselves for the good of their offspring or group—has always been a thorn in the side of Darwinism. As a real but puzzling natural phenomenon, altruism has been the subject of many scientific theories.

The spider *Stegodyphus lineatus*, after delivering a small clutch of young, feeds them with regurgitated food. After a couple weeks, when the little spiders are strong enough, they kill and consume her, leaving an empty exoskeleton behind. Throughout the process, the mother spider does nothing to protect herself from her fate. Talk about a mother's love!

While it is instinctual for some animals to sacrifice for their offspring, humanity's strongest instinct is self-preservation. Yes, people are often willing to die for their own kids, but what about for friends? What about for strangers? What about for enemies?

Jesus says in John 15:13 (KJV), "Greater love hath no man than this, that a man lay down his life for his friends." Romans 5:8 (KJV), however, says, "But God commendeth his love toward us, in that, while we were yet sinners, Christ died for us."

Whether we are friends of Jesus or enemies of God, Christ laid down His life for us. Like the altruistic spider, Jesus died to give us life. So what are we to do with that information? Jesus tells us in John 15:12 (KJV): "This is my commandment, That ye love one another, as I have loved you."

We should sacrifice our desires, our preferences, and our lives to share Christ's love with others. Self-preservation has no place here. Faithful men seek out opportunities to lay down everything for Christ's sake.

Have you ever been the recipient of someone else's sacrifice?
What desires could you renounce to show love to someone else?

BE THE MAN WHO LIVES BY THE GOLDEN RULE

*"So in everything, do to others what you would have them
do to you, for this sums up the Law and the Prophets."*
MATTHEW 7:12 NIV

The "golden rule" isn't a secret. We've heard it from parents, teachers, and just about everyone else since the time we were old enough to treat someone else poorly. But there's a reason why it's so familiar: we need to be constantly reminded not to live only for ourselves.

It would be nice if there was some hidden secret to mastering the "golden rule" lifestyle. But in reality, we mostly live with our desires at the forefront of our minds, not considering how our actions affect other people. We have the first step down, at least: we intuitively know how we like to be treated!

We want to go first in line. We want the biggest piece of the pie. We want others to compliment us for everything we do. We want to put off the difficult tasks for someone else to take care of. We want the benefit of the doubt if someone takes our words or actions out of context. We want, we want, we want.

This is why the "golden rule" is so revolutionary. We take all our wants and we put them into practice, not for ourselves, but for others. There's no trick to getting started. Simply remind yourself often that God has summed up His entire Law by reminding us to live for the good of others, to consider their desires before our own.

Let this be your challenge for today. Forget the familiarity of the rule and live it out afresh. Look for ways to build others up, to help them with the things you know they don't enjoy, to give them the benefit of the doubt. Do it all day, with everyone, in every way.

How has someone else been kind to you in a way you would like to employ
for others? How can you live out the "golden rule" with your words today?

BE THE MAN WHO ISN'T JUST BEHAVIOR MODIFIED

Finally, my brethren, be strong in the Lord, and in the power of his might. Put on the whole armour of God, that ye may be able to stand against the wiles of the devil. For we wrestle not against flesh and blood, but against principalities, against powers, against the rulers of the darkness of this world, against spiritual wickedness in high places. Wherefore take unto you the whole armour of God.
EPHESIANS 6:10–13 KJV

God must have known that people would try to make salvation something they could do on their own. This is why "good" people often have a hard time accepting Christ. Because they strive to be good neighbors, don't cheat on their taxes, and love animals, they conclude that there isn't much God needs to save them from. After all, they're doing just fine on their own. They might even think that God should be happy that someone so good exists in a such a rotten world.

Good choices, however, should be an indication of something bigger happening in your life. God gave His commands to inspire a relationship and instill a willingness to obey, and He wants you to trust Him, not yourself, for the strength to follow what He says.

A faithful man admits that he can't do good apart from God. He is willing to ask for and accept God's help to achieve something more than behavior modification. This man gets wiser with every choice as his personal relationship with his Maker transforms him from a lone wolf to a child of God.

Have you ever believed that good Christians never make mistakes? How does a relationship with God change the reason for obedience?

DAY 189

BE THE MAN WHO PURSUES STRENGTH IN TRUTH

"You will know the truth, and the truth will set you free."
JOHN 8:32 NIV

Do you live with God's impressive strength? You can.

It may not even seem like a strength at first. You may want to dismiss the idea as odd, maybe even a bit insane. But here's the scoop: you will grow stronger when you know and accept God's truth. How does that make you strong? It sets you *free*.

When you are free, you become more confident in your choices. Now, we're not discussing a permission to do whatever you want to do, whenever you want to do it. No—this freedom means you're no longer prevented from doing what God designed you to do. You become confident in following Him, listening to His whispered guidance, and then doing what you know is right. And you understand this because you have encountered truth, accepted it, believed it.

You become God's faithful man of strength when you have fewer questions about your path and greater trust in your guide. Your growing confidence may feel a bit like working for one employer for a long time. At some point, because you've been paying attention to how your boss wants things done, you just know what you need to do. You begin to understand why things are done the way they are. You trust the boss enough to do things just the way he asks.

Those things make a difference in your occupation. They also make a difference when you're pursuing God's truth. It leads to freedom—the freedom to be His representative among everyone you meet.

What do you think of the equation Truth + Freedom = Strength?
In what ways is confidence necessary to improve strength?

BE THE MAN WHO DOESN'T ABUSE HIS AUTHORITY

*But Jesus called them together and said, "You know that the rulers
in this world lord it over their people, and officials flaunt their
authority over those under them. But among you it will be different.
Whoever wants to be a leader among you must be your servant, and
whoever wants to be first among you must become your slave."*
MATTHEW 20:25–27 NLT

Power does strange things to people. Studies show that, while people in power are more likely to see the big picture, they are also more likely to engage in risky behavior. Another study showed a correlation between power and rude behavior. While the connection may seem obvious to some, science has confirmed that drivers of high-end vehicles are more likely to cut off other drivers.

These problems may stem from how authority affects the brain. MRI scans reveal that motor resonance—a brain function responsible for allowing us to see things from other perspectives—is lower in powerful people than in the powerless. Whatever the reason, however, people in power shouldn't be excused for acting like jerks.

As the ultimate authority, Jesus knows how humans behave when given a taste of power. That's why He specifically instructed His followers to serve one another. Faithful men, whether they possess authority or not, must strive for empathy.

Jesus is our perfect example. He spoke the world into being then took on human form to save us. The world is His footstool, but He bent down and washed His disciples' filthy feet. He could have claimed His rightful throne in heaven at any time, but He chose a crown of thorns and a sinner's cross instead.

We must be leaders who serve because we are servants of the ultimate authority.

Have you ever been affected by power? How can you mix empathy with authority?

BE THE MAN WHO WASHES FEET

Jesus knew that the Father had put all things under his power, and that he had come from God and was returning to God; so he got up from the meal, took off his outer clothing, and wrapped a towel around his waist. After that, he poured water into a basin and began to wash his disciples' feet, drying them with the towel that was wrapped around him.

JOHN 13:3–5 NIV

Today's passage doesn't follow human expectations. "Jesus knew that the Father had put all things under his power, and that he had come from God and was returning to God." How would you handle such knowledge? If you knew God had given you the power to do anything in the world, what would you do?

In that moment, Jesus could have used His power to perform some amazing miracle, removing any lingering doubts about who He was—even for Thomas. Jesus could have called out Judas before the betrayal ever took place. He could have flown around the room just for the joy of seeing His disciples' jaws drop. But what did He do?

Jesus got up from the meal, humbled Himself, and washed His disciples' feet. The God of the universe who had the power to do anything got up from dinner and did the work of the lowest servant.

You may be rich and powerful, well-liked and respected, but you're no Jesus. If no job was too lowly for Him, you have no excuse for wriggling out of unpleasant tasks. Jesus could have done anything, and He washed feet. He deserved every ounce of praise the world could muster, and He humbled Himself instead.

If you ever think some task is beneath you, remember today's scripture. Jesus used His power to serve. Go and do likewise.

> Do you sometimes avoid tasks because you feel they are beneath you? How would you feel if Jesus wanted to wash your feet?

BE THE MAN WHO IS MORE
THAN A CONQUEROR

In all these things we are more than
conquerors through him who loved us.
ROMANS 8:37 NIV

Romans 8:37 feels like a bold, encouraging start to a pep rally or inspirational social media post. However, it's simply a summary of the more complex passage that precedes it.

When Paul wrote the words, "All these things," what was he talking about? To answer that question, go back a few verses and read about the adversity Christians faced. They were being charged with religious crimes, but God was defending them (verse 33). People were trying to condemn them, but God embraced them (verse 34). Paul challenged his readers to think, "Who shall separate us from the love of Christ?" The answer is *nothing*—not even "trouble or hardship or persecution or famine or nakedness or danger or sword" (verse 35 NIV).

Need proof? "I am convinced that neither death nor life, neither angels nor demons, neither the present nor the future, nor any powers, neither height nor depth, nor anything else in all creation, will be able to separate us from the love of God that is in Christ Jesus our Lord" (verses 38–39 NIV).

What a powerful encouragement! You are more than a conqueror because of Jesus, His love, and the friendship He wants with you. Don't run away, hide, or seek another choice—God has already proven He will do anything to reach you. His love is yours, and no one can take it away from you.

Do you feel like a conqueror in matters of faith? Does the
pursuit of God bring courage when your spirit is weak?

BE THE MAN WHO ALWAYS CARRIES LIGHT

*The light shines in the darkness, and the
darkness can never extinguish it.*
JOHN 1:5 NLT

Call it illumination, perspective, or even a front row seat to God's work. You are welcome to a world of light that God makes available to you. You can use that light to gain a clearer picture of where God is working. . .and go there!

Here's the truth about light—as long as it exists, darkness can never be complete. Even a small amount of light displaces the surrounding darkness. When light shines in darkness, this light can prevent others from stumbling in the dark.

This is important for when you're tempted to leave your light behind when you go out in public. Doing so only achieves two negative outcomes: (1) it makes you confused about where to go next, and (2) it removes the incentive for anyone else to follow God's light.

This is why God's strength is hard to find among those who refuse to name God as their source of strength. It's difficult to discover God's love among people who are always trying to hide His light. Concealing God's light can also make a man appear arrogant—it gives the impression that he doesn't think he needs help. While the people in darkness struggle to find their way, the last thing they need is someone who pretends the darkness doesn't exist.

God doesn't ask you to do anything He won't do, but He neither does He ask you to do things He doesn't equip you to do. So when He asks you to carry His light into a spiritually dark world, it isn't to draw attention to you—it's to draw attention to the light-giver.

When have you failed to take God's light with you? How did that go?
How might God's light change the way you interact with others?

BE THE MAN WHO TAKES
RESPONSIBILITY FOR HIS ACTIONS

Do not be deceived: God cannot be mocked. A man reaps what he sows.
Whoever sows to please their flesh, from the flesh will reap destruction;
whoever sows to please the Spirit, from the Spirit will reap eternal life.
GALATIANS 6:7–8 NIV

Actions have consequences. It's a fundamental rule of life, but in our broken world, it isn't always fairly applied. Speeding doesn't always result in a ticket, and innocent people are sometimes convicted for a crime.

Similarly, good deeds often go unrewarded. Our efforts at home are frequently ignored, and our safe driving doesn't mean a thing when someone rear-ends us.

While justice may be subjective here on earth, it won't be forever. We serve an eternal God who is perfectly just, so our present actions will be rewarded eventually. Galatians 6:7–8 (NIV) says, "Do not be deceived: God cannot be mocked. A man reaps what he sows. Whoever sows to please their flesh, from the flesh will reap destruction; whoever sows to please the Spirit, from the Spirit will reap eternal life."

We can't control the actions of others, but we can take responsibility for our own. As faithful men, we must admit when we've acted selfishly or wronged someone.

We must also accept our responsibility to do good. As bearers of God's image and adopted heirs of His kingdom, we are called to a higher level of accountability. Fortunately, He'll never give us more than we can handle.

Whether the world demands it or not, it's time to take responsibility for our actions. By doing so, we embrace God's love of justice and rely on His strength to help us succeed.

Do you take responsibility for your actions? Do you accept
the responsibility that comes with being a Christian?

BE THE MAN WHO CREDITS GOD

*Praise the LORD, the God of our ancestors, who made the king want
to beautify the Temple of the LORD in Jerusalem! And praise him for
demonstrating such unfailing love to me by honoring me before the
king, his council, and all his mighty nobles! I felt encouraged because
the gracious hand of the LORD my God was on me. And I gathered
some of the leaders of Israel to return with me to Jerusalem.*

EZRA 7:27–28 NLT

When Jerusalem fell to the Babylonian empire in 586 BC, the city was
ransacked, the temple burned, and the people exiled. About fifty years
later, the Babylonians fell to the Persian Empire, so Jerusalem's control
changed hands yet again. When the events of today's passage took place,
Ezra was a scribe in the court of King Artaxerxes, ruler of the Persian
empire from 464 to 424 BC.

Ezra was given Artaxerxes' blessing to return to Jerusalem and get
the temple up and running again. Ezra 7:6–7 (NLT) says, "This Ezra was
a scribe who was well versed in the Law of Moses, which the LORD, the
God of Israel, had given to the people of Israel. He came up to Jerusalem
from Babylon, and the king gave him everything he asked for, because
the gracious hand of the LORD his God was on him. Some of the people
of Israel, as well as some of the priests, Levites, singers, gatekeepers, and
Temple servants, traveled up to Jerusalem with him in the seventh year
of King Artaxerxes' reign."

Artaxerxes gave Ezra a blank check to repair the temple in Jerusalem. Ezra, however, didn't attribute this blessing to his own persuasive
skill; he knew God's hand was on him. Ezra, having been placed in a specific moment in history to return Jerusalem to the control of God's chosen people, honored God by recognizing where his blessings came from.

Let's be sure we always do the same.

How do you see God's hand on you? Have you
given Him the credit for the blessings you enjoy?

BE THE MAN WHO COURAGEOUSLY CONFESSES

*If we say that we have no sin, we deceive ourselves, and the truth
is not in us. If we confess our sins, he is faithful and just to forgive
us our sins, and to cleanse us from all unrighteousness.*

1 John 1:8–9 KJV

King Morty reigned over a faraway enchanted land. When one of his
subjects even thought about breaking his rules, King Morty somehow
knew. He would then bring those subjects before his throne and demand
an explanation. There were more prisoners than merchants in his kingdom because Morty prosecuted violators swiftly and to the full extent of
his law.

Did these lawbreakers love King Morty, or were they afraid of him?
He knew their most private thoughts but knew nothing of forgiveness,
grace, and mercy.

God also knows your every thought. He knows when you break His
law—but unlike Morty, He waits for you to come to Him. He wants you
to tell Him what you've done or even thought. You can't hide anything
from God, yet He's willing to forgive, wiping your criminal history clean
with His faithful love.

God isn't winking at your sin as if it's unimportant; He's holding out
a helping hand and is willing to walk with you toward obedience.

Under the tyranny of King Morty, who punishes every infraction
swiftly and mercilessly, courage would be impossible. God, however,
counts you as a friend, so you can come to Him and tell Him each time
you blow it. Give Him the details, experience His forgiveness, then remember Jesus' words: "Go, and sin no more" (John 8:11 KJV).

How is God's response to confession different than humanity's?
Why is forgiveness essential to trusting God?

BE THE MAN WHO ACCEPTS HELP

*By grace are ye saved through faith; and that not of yourselves:
it is the gift of God: not of works, lest any man should boast.*
EPHESIANS 2:8–9 KJV

To be saved is to be rescued from a perilous situation. Flood victims may be plucked from a roof by a helicopter or pulled by rope from a raging river. Tornado victims are saved by search teams sorting through debris or simply neighbors checking on neighbors. The need for rescue is never diminished by how well you prepare or how much you hate asking for help.

Your spiritual life is no different. You can't boast about not needing God, because you'll *always* need God. You can't rescue yourself, and you can't buy His help. Why? It's a gift. You can either accept a gift or reject it, but you can't buy it. That would make it no longer a gift but a purchase. God's rescue could never boil down to an exchange between bank accounts. No one could afford it.

You are strengthened when you acknowledge that God took you from a path of destruction and applied healing, light, and love to make you something more. Rejecting God's rescue won't make you stronger—it'll leave you as vulnerable as the man on a roof during a flood shouting at his rescuers, "Don't bother; I can make it!"

Don't tell God you just need to try a few more ideas on your own—embrace His rescue today.

Do you sometimes mistakenly believe you can rescue yourself?
How does being humble enough to ask God for help change a man?

BE THE MAN WHO STAYS SHARP

As iron sharpens iron, so a friend sharpens a friend.
PROVERBS 27:17 NLT

Weren't friendships easier as kids? It seemed like anyone could be friends on the playground. Friendships naturally formed around commonalities. If you watched the same television shows or liked the same sports or read the same books, you were friends.

Friendships don't come as easily for adults. Married guys with kids or full-time jobs—or both—have limited amounts of time to hang out with their buddies. Older guys whose kids have left the house have the time but maybe not the willpower, having fallen out of the practice of making friends long ago.

Yet, the Bible says friendship is important because it keeps us sharp. As one iron blade is used to hone another, so too can friends help us fulfill our intended purpose. This doesn't mean we sit around sharing our feelings all the time. It means sharing a common mission to follow Christ, glorify God, and live by the power of the Spirit. Our enemy wants us to think we're alone against the world, but our friends remind us we're in it together.

Not only do we share a mission, we share information. Friends talk about life! In John 15:15 (NLT), Jesus clarified His relationship with His disciples, saying "I no longer call you slaves, because a master doesn't confide in his slaves. Now you are my friends, since I have told you everything the Father told me."

So how do you make friends? Find some guys who share your interests and values and spend time with them. Church is a great place to start!

What interests do you have that could be the basis for a friendship?
How can you push yourself to make new friends?

BE THE MAN WHO GIVES HIS ANXIETIES TO GOD

Do not be anxious about anything, but in every situation, by prayer
and petition, with thanksgiving, present your requests to God.
PHILIPPIANS 4:6 NIV

If God's hand is on you in your blessings, it is there in your troubles as well. The trials we face are opportunities to trust God for our needs.

When the early church was under attack, Paul encouraged believers with this: "What, then, shall we say in response to these things? If God is for us, who can be against us? . . . No, in all these things we are more than conquerors through him who loved us. For I am convinced that neither death nor life, neither angels nor demons, neither the present nor the future, nor any powers, neither height nor depth, nor anything else in all creation, will be able to separate us from the love of God that is in Christ Jesus our Lord" (Romans 8:31, 37–39 NIV).

If nothing can separate us from God's love, if we are firmly held in His hand, then our biggest concerns have already been taken care of.

Of course, that doesn't stop us from having anxieties or troubles in this life. Losing a job, getting a frightening report from the doctor, being betrayed by loved ones—all these things happen, and God's love doesn't mean we won't feel the pain. Instead, God invites us to trust them to His care.

In every situation, by prayer and petition, with thanksgiving, we are to present our requests to the God who loves us enough to die for us. We are to recognize God's hand in each event in our lives and thank Him for our blessings, even when the rest of the world may call us cursed. When we come to God with thankful hearts, requesting His intervention in our troubles, we aren't assured that things will improve according to our standards, only that God will be honored by the trust we place in Him.

Has worrying about something ever produced a better outcome
than prayer? What does Jesus say about worry in Matthew 6?

BE THE MAN WHO IS
REDEEMED BY RELATIONSHIP

He asked them, "But who do you say I am?" Simon Peter answered,
"You are the Messiah, the Son of the living God." Jesus replied, "You are
blessed, Simon son of John, because my Father in heaven has revealed
this to you. You did not learn this from any human being. Now I say to
you that you are Peter (which means 'rock'), and upon this rock I will
build my church, and all the powers of hell will not conquer it."
MATTHEW 16:15–18 NLT

If anyone had a chronic case of foot-in-mouth disease, it was Peter. He
was a master at promise breaking, and he would often commit himself to
actions he wasn't prepared to take. This disciple was impulsive, yet Peter
likely mistook this flaw for boldness.

Jesus saw all of this, yet He still wanted Peter to realize an amazing
truth: the church would start with him! Peter would need to know that
even when the church was battered and bruised, it would not be conquered. . .and this promise-breaking disciple would be instrumental in
its success.

As Peter preached the good news, there had to be nights when he
remembered his betrayals and foolish promises. He now realized that
personal bravado could never replace God's strength.

Peter's story can encourage you, and not just because you can say, "I
did better than him." No, his story proves that new life is a growing, daily
process. You continuously learn to identify errors, speak life, and forgive,
leaving your sinful choices further behind and redeeming your relationships with imperfect people.

God works through forgiven, hopeful, and courageous men like you.

How does it feel to know that your greatest mistakes do nothing to stop God from
working in your life? What encouragement do you find in the life of Peter?

BE THE MAN WHO LOCKS FEAR OUT

*Even when I walk through the darkest valley, I will
not be afraid, for you are close beside me. Your rod
and your staff protect and comfort me.*
PSALM 23:4 NLT

If God wants you to be strong, that means He doesn't want you to be afraid. Fear tells strength there's no vacancy—it steals into each room and redecorates the place. Inside, it's dark and foreboding. Danger lurks in every shadow, making it impossible to find the exit.

When God leads you, however, He gives you the power to deny fear a place to stay. When He's beside and before you, your soul becomes a place of protection and reassurance.

Confidence doesn't mix well with anxiety. Courage is weakened by worry. Yet too often, it feels like anxiety and worry are all we've got. A man might try to shrug them off or boast of how well he's handling it all. But inside, when no one else is around, he feels like a scared boy dreading his next nightmare.

If a man were honest about his true inner state, he'd probably use words like *cowardice*, *frailty*, *distrust*, *uncertainty*, *humiliation*, and *timidity*. None are fair companions. No one wants them around, yet everyone knows who they are. No one pursues them, yet everyone spends time listening to them.

God wants you to spend time with Him instead—it's the only way to lock the door when anxiety comes knocking.

Why is it important to keep your life "fear-free"?
What is one way you can replace fear with faith today?

BE THE MAN WHO SHOWS COURTESY

They must not slander anyone and must avoid quarreling. Instead, they should be gentle and show true humility to everyone.
TITUS 3:2 NLT

Courtesy isn't commonly associated with manliness. The stereotypical man belches loudly then mutters, "Excuse me," but only in the presence of a female. He works hard, fights hard, and doesn't take guff from anyone. Courteous behavior—manners, gentle speech, genuine interest in others, a humble attitude, and so on—is considered old-fashioned. But it shouldn't be.

Christians are called to a higher, more difficult standard. Bodily functions come naturally, and while holding them in may not always be possible, we shouldn't glory in their expulsion. Rudeness doesn't help in drawing people to Christ. Respecting others with everything that comes out of us, burps included, will better allow them to see God's love in us since they won't be closing their eyes and shaking their heads.

While common courtesy is one aspect of our call as Christians, real courtesy begins in the heart and reveals itself in our attitude. Just like body functions, masculine pride comes naturally. Pride is born out of a selfish heart, while humility puts others before itself.

Humility doesn't try to convince the world we are weak. It restrains our strength like we are a muscle car driving slowly through a school zone. Sure, we could press the pedal to the metal and show those school kids what speed really means, but we should be more concerned with keeping them safe.

Philippians 2:3–4 (NLT) reminds us, "Don't be selfish; don't try to impress others. Be humble, thinking of others as better than yourselves. Don't look out only for your own interests, but take an interest in others, too."

It's time for men to accept the challenge of being courteous again. Are you in?

Do you struggle with rudeness? How might you convert pride into humility?

BE THE MAN WHO DOESN'T FALL FOR GET-RICH-QUICK SCHEMES

Better is a little with righteousness than great revenues without right.
PROVERBS 16:8 KJV

As the COVID-19 pandemic disrupted economies around the world throughout 2020, many people lost their jobs, worried about their health, and questioned their news sources. As the world struggled to stay afloat and hospitalization rates surged, peddlers of snake oil saw their chance.

People who lost their jobs during the pandemic were recruited into multilevel marketing schemes to sell products they believed would prevent, treat, or cure the rampant disease. Of course, the recruiting companies would never claim their products were advertised to address such health concerns, but they'd wink and nod and count their money while the people selling their goods make such statements.

In addition to believing the false health information these companies spread—either directly or tacitly—the newly-unemployed people who were recruited to sell such products were then gouged for money with the false promise of future wealth. According to a report prepared for the Federal Trade Commission, 99.25 percent of all people involved in multilevel marketing schemes either make nothing or lose money.

The remaining 0.75 percent want everyone to believe they can be rich too. They sell the promise that with little to no effort, you too can be fabulously wealthy. But that's not the system God designed.

We were made to work. God gave Adam a job in Eden before sin ever entered the world. When we try to get wealth without work, the first person we deceive is ourselves. Truly, it's better to be poor with a clean conscience than rich at another's expense.

Have you ever been tricked out of your hard-earned money?
How would tricking others reflect on God's righteousness?

BE THE MAN WHO ONLY SPEAKS WHEN NECESSARY

Is anyone among you in trouble? Let them pray.
Is anyone happy? Let them sing songs of praise.
JAMES 5:13 NIV

Sometimes, courage means realizing that some of your thoughts are better left unsaid. Other times, it means speaking the truth when every other mouth is shut. But it *always* takes wisdom to know which kind of courage you need to use in each situation.

Courageous silence often means checking God's Word before you speak. Then, if you've decided something needs to be said, courageous conversation will bring God into the subject even when others don't want to hear about Him.

Ecclesiastes 5:2 (NIV) helps clarify the idea of courageous silence: "Do not be quick with your mouth, do not be hasty in your heart to utter anything before God. God is in heaven and you are on earth, so let your words be few."

Proverbs 31:8–9 (NIV), however, tells when your words might prove helpful: "Speak up for those who cannot speak for themselves, for the rights of all who are destitute. Speak up and judge fairly; defend the rights of the poor and needy."

It's easy to share opinions about things you don't understand. And sometimes, you might even be able to speak the truth, but your timing may be horrible.

When you get into God's Word, however, you'll grow better at discerning when something is important enough to speak about. . .and when you should allow your jaw to rest.

Is it easier for you to speak up or keep silent? Why? How can you learn to tell when you should use your words to honor God and help others?

BE THE MAN WHO CHOOSES MEEKNESS

*A truly wise person uses few words; a person
with understanding is even-tempered.*
PROVERBS 17:27 NLT

No matter how strong he may be, a faithful man is also meek. This can confuse people, especially those who define *meek* as "timid, shy, and somewhat fearful." But Jesus had another definition in mind: "humble, gentle, and kind." None of those three words describe weakness.

Think of it this way—meek people don't brag about what they can do; they just do it. They're not rough in dealing with people, but they are strong enough to be patient. They're not bullies; instead, they're compassionate toward those who have struggles of their own.

A man who embraces true meekness is exceptionally strong because he strives to be the man God made him to be. He chooses silence over arguments—understanding over anger. He seeks to understand the situation before drawing a conclusion, so he's rarely the first to react. And when he does react, he does so to deescalate. He's also extremely trustworthy, never hesitating to allow God to work in his life.

Needless to say, being meek isn't easy. Is it any wonder that Jesus said in Matthew 5:5 (NLT), "God blesses those who are humble [meek], for they will inherit the whole earth"?

Do these thoughts challenge the way you view meekness? Why is it important to find the perfect balance between strength and meekness?

BE THE MAN WHO UNDERSTANDS CONSENT

"For this reason a man will leave his father and mother and be united to his wife, and the two will become one flesh." This is a profound mystery—but I am talking about Christ and the church.
EPHESIANS 5:31–32 NIV

Sex is incredible. God made it so that people could experience pleasure— physically, emotionally, and spiritually—as they join with Him in the act of creating new life. While Satan has twisted the goodness of sex to exclude the spiritual element, physical and emotional relationships cannot healthily exist without it. Paul recognized this in Ephesians 5:31–32 when he compared the physical aspect of a marriage to Christ's relationship to the church.

Every physical and emotional relationship should operate with spiritual sensitivity. It may be strange to consider, but every kiss and hand-hold, every caress and sexual act, has spiritual ramifications. This is obviously true with relationships outside of marriage. But even within a marriage, our sexual relationship won't reflect Christ's relationship with the church if it is marked by selfishness instead of joyful admiration and consensual enjoyment.

There's a reason God offers salvation as a gift instead of a command. He wants us to want Him, but He allows us to make that choice. In romantic relationships, consent is just as important. We want to be wanted, treating affection as a gift, not a command.

Consent isn't only important for choosing to be sexually active; it is important in choosing not to be. First Corinthians 7:5 (NIV) says, "Do not deprive each other except perhaps by mutual consent and for a time, so that you may devote yourselves to prayer. Then come together again so that Satan will not tempt you because of your lack of self-control."

When our relationship with God is pure, our relationships with others will be pure as well.

Is your sexual relationship a reflection of Christ and the church or an outlet for selfishness? How do you view consent in relationships?

BE THE MAN WHO SERVES SACRIFICIALLY

*And let us not be weary in well doing: for in
due season we shall reap, if we faint not.*
GALATIANS 6:9 KJV

The Hazda people in northern Tanzania are one of the last remaining hunter-gatherer societies in the world. They have no livestock, crops, or ways of storing food; instead, they rely on their weapon skills to obtain meat and their other senses to find wild fruits and vegetables. They live in the moment by necessity, not paycheck-to-paycheck but hunt-to-hunt and forage-to-forage.

Now consider an agrarian society with rotating crops and livestock for meat, milk, and wool. The work is no less difficult than the hunter-gatherer lifestyle, but the rewards are far greater. Farmers can grow food enough to store, sell, and eat throughout the year. There is safety in predictability. The food, however, takes time to grow, so unless you've already got a ready source of sustenance, you'll end up hunting and gathering in addition to working your crops.

In today's verse, Paul encourages the Galatian church to keep planting good seeds. They will be better off planting with the Spirit to reap an eternal harvest than drifting back into a hunter-gatherer lifestyle to live for themselves and their transient desires.

Yes, spiritual farming is difficult, but that's where we see the difference between simple subsistence and an abundant, sustainable commitment to God. How can we have enough to share when we are living from paycheck-to-paycheck spiritually?

In effect, Paul is encouraging all believers to serve sacrificially, to put in the long hours that will produce the biggest harvest in due season. The work will be difficult, and it may be hard to see the value when the growth is slow—but God is the Lord of the harvest, not us. It's our job to spread the seed and put in the long hours on His behalf.

Are you serving sacrificially or living to feed only yourself? How can
you add some spiritual farming to your hunter-gatherer lifestyle?

BE THE MAN WHO REFUSES TO LET SIN DOMINATE

Let not sin therefore reign in your mortal body, that ye should obey it in the lusts thereof. Neither yield ye your members as instruments of unrighteousness unto sin: but yield yourselves unto God, as those that are alive from the dead, and your members as instruments of righteousness unto God. For sin shall not have dominion over you: for ye are not under the law, but under grace.

ROMANS 6:12–14 KJV

Sin is bossy, but it's not your boss. It has power, but only the power you give it.

Your adversary will try his best to convince you that the choice to sin is natural and fun. If he can convince you that God has been holding out on you, the allure of sin in your life will be enhanced even more.

God's grace is more powerful than the laws you break, so your sins don't need to interfere with your relationship with Him. But does this mean you have a free pass to sin? The apostle Paul gave a simple, eloquent answer in Romans 6:2 (KJV): "God forbid. How shall we, that are dead to sin, live any longer therein?"

Sin can seem like a default response when you're at your weakest, but God gives the strength you need to resist. You don't need to live by the old adage that forgiveness is preferable to permission.

A faithful man refuses to dance on the edge of unrighteousness. He's not concerned about what he can get away with; rather, he wants only to do the right thing. He doesn't want to constantly wonder if he needs forgiveness—he's committed to learning what God wants. He stops chasing sin and continues his passionate pursuit of God.

> Does sin sometimes seem like the resident bully in your decision making? Why is it liberating to know that just because sin makes a suggestion, you don't have to take it?

BE THE MAN WHO LIVES IN GOD'S YOKE

[Jesus said,] "Take my yoke upon you and learn from me, for I am gentle and humble in heart, and you will find rest for your souls."
MATTHEW 11:29 NIV

Strength isn't a commodity that can be bought or sold. It's not a self-help program that assures success in three easy steps. It's not even something you are born with. Strength is a gift—someone has to give it. And this someone is God. Without Him, strength doesn't exist.

God can give you lessons in strength development. He wants you to watch Him work, personally observing His goodness, and then to join Him. Refusing to go where He's working will leave you uncertain about His strength. But participating—working right alongside Him—will teach you how to do things the way He wants.

Being meek means being humble, gentle, and kind. . .and God is your greatest example. It's His meekness that demonstrates His great strength. Reread Matthew 11:29 for a clearer picture of how God wants you to learn as you work with Him in His strength.

The "yoke" described in today's verse is the linking of God's heart, mind, and will with your own. This helps you move in God's direction. It enables you to see what He sees when He's at work in the world.

A faithful man lives in God's yoke.

What have you learned while working alongside God?
Do you find it odd to think of God as meek?

BE THE MAN WHO VALUES WISDOM

How much better to get wisdom than gold,
to get insight rather than silver!
PROVERBS 16:16 NIV

On October 23, 2018, an anonymous South Carolina resident became the sole winner of the $1.5 billion jackpot in the Mega Millions lottery. Choosing to stay anonymous, the winner received a one-time cash payment of $877,784,124—the largest jackpot payout to a single winner in United States history.

This resident was represented by self-proclaimed "Lottery Lawyer" Jason Kurland. He has advised many winners how to guard against people who would take advantage of them.

Then, on August 18, 2020, the US Department of Justice announced Kurland and three co-conspirators had been indicted in a $107 million scheme to defraud lottery-winning clients. Officials alleged that Kurland took advantage of his clients' trust and good fortune, pillaging their wealth.

Lottery winners may seem lucky to us, but most—not just those who were allegedly bilked by Kurland—end up with regrets. While such wealth may bring worldly goods, it can also devastate relationships, encourage recklessness, and draw the attention of violent people.

Money isn't bad, but people who don't use it wisely can harm both themselves and others. Wisdom prevents harm, which is why Proverbs 16:16 says it is better than gold.

Wise people typically don't play the lottery, because they know how likely they are to lose, even if they win. Wisdom is a much better investment! But how can you get it? James 1:5 (NIV) says, "If any of you lacks wisdom, you should ask God, who gives generously to all without finding fault, and it will be given to you." Just ask!

Have you ever dreamed about winning the lottery? If so,
how can you change that dream into a prayer for wisdom?

BE THE MAN WHO DEFERS TO GOD'S WILL

"Do you still want to argue with the Almighty?
You are God's critic, but do you have the answers?"
Job 40:2 NLT

By every human standard, Job got a raw deal. Here's how God described Job to Satan: "He is the finest man in all the earth. He is blameless—a man of complete integrity. He fears God and stays away from evil" (Job 1:8 NLT). And what did Job get for his integrity? His livestock were stolen and his farm hands were killed (verse 15); his camels were stolen and his servants were killed (verse 17); and his sons and daughters were killed when the house they were in collapsed (verse 19).

And yet Job deferred to God's will. He said, "I came naked from my mother's womb, and I will be naked when I leave. The LORD gave me what I had, and the LORD has taken it away. Praise the name of the LORD!" (1:21 NLT)

After God speaks to Job in chapters 38–41, explaining why created beings are not able to accurately judge their Creator, Job reiterates his position before the Almighty: "I know that you can do anything, and no one can stop you" (42:2 NLT).

Now, before anyone thinks that this is a matter of "might makes right"—that the biggest bully on the playground doesn't have to play by the rules—it would be wise to think about God's nature. God is love (see 1 John 4:16). He is the giver of good gifts (see James 1:17). He wants us to have the desires of our heart, and He knows that what we should desire most is Him (see Psalm 37:4).

That doesn't mean God won't allow us to suffer while serving Him. Job certainly did. Rather, it means that even in our suffering, God's plan for us outshines whatever plan we have for ourselves. As 1 Peter 3:17 (NLT) says, "Remember, it is better to suffer for doing good, if that is what God wants, than to suffer for doing wrong!"

When you feel like God is giving you a raw deal, remember whom you're accusing—and then praise the name of the Lord.

How did God treat Job after his tribulations (see Job 42:10-17)? Does knowing that God's will cannot be stopped bring comfort to you?

BE THE MAN WHO SETS COURAGEOUS BOUNDARIES

Shadrach, Meshach, and Abednego replied, "O Nebuchadnezzar, we do not need to defend ourselves before you. If we are thrown into the blazing furnace, the God whom we serve is able to save us. He will rescue us from your power, Your Majesty. But even if he doesn't, we want to make it clear to you, Your Majesty, that we will never serve your gods or worship the gold statue you have set up."
DANIEL 3:16–18 NLT

The value of well-chosen words should not be taken lightly.

When King Nebuchadnezzar required everyone to worship a statue, he may not have considered the implications of such a law (the idea that he could determine who was a god) nor the penalty for disobedience (death).

Three friends, however, refused to compromise. They knew their choice could result in death, but they didn't believe the king was equal with God. So these men brought truth to the king, choosing their words carefully.

They openly rejected the king's command, stating that they were committed to serving God instead. They knew the king couldn't decide their fate—only God could do that.

The angry Nebuchadnezzar pronounced a death sentence, but God enacted a rescue plan. The king brought heat, but God brought perspective. In the end, the brash king boldly declared, "Praise to the God of Shadrach, Meshach, and Abednego! He sent his angel to rescue his servants who trusted in him. They defied the king's command and were willing to die rather than serve or worship any god except their own God" Daniel 3:28 (NLT).

Courageous boundaries give the world an impressive example.

In the face of mounting pressure to comply with sin, are you courageous enough to resist? What can you do to establish visible, courageous boundaries?

DAY 213

BE THE MAN WHO FEELS VALUED

*I give each of you this warning: Don't think you are better
than you really are. Be honest in your evaluation of yourselves,
measuring yourselves by the faith God has given us.*

ROMANS 12:3 NLT

You've probably heard that God is strong while you are weak. This is true. And it's also true that recognizing your weakness invites God's strength to assist you. On the other hand, pretending to be strong only proves that you're weak.

God wants your personal evaluation to be accurate. He wants you to recognize who you are—no better, no worse. You are a sinner saved by grace. You are broken but being remade. You are a formerly-lost slave who's been made an heir to God's kingdom.

Yet many men love playing the comparison game. Eager to present themselves as better than their peers, they miss the honest evaluation God asks for.

Admitting you are weak shouldn't make you feel like a victim. Instead, God's empowering strength, love, and forgiveness should make you feel like a victor who is part of an amazing partnership—one that nobody deserves but any can enjoy.

Comparing yourself to other people will poison your soul, hijack your heart, and spill from your lips. It's a game in which nobody wins. All it does is cloud your perception of how much God values you.

Don't strive to be better than anyone else—simply ask God to help you be the best you possible.

Do you find it easy to compare yourself to others?
Why is this a poor evaluation method?

BE THE MAN WHO CHOOSES TO GATHER

*[Nehemiah prayed,] "We have acted very wickedly toward you.
We have not obeyed the commands, decrees and laws you gave your
servant Moses. Remember the instruction you gave your servant Moses,
saying, 'If you are unfaithful, I will scatter you among the nations, but
if you return to me and obey my commands, then even if your exiled
people are at the farthest horizon, I will gather them from there and
bring them to the place I have chosen as a dwelling for my Name.'"*
NEHEMIAH 1:7–9 NIV

During the divinely foretold scattering, the disobedience of sinners was
punished by a trustworthy God.

Nehemiah prayed that this scattering would one day turn into a
gathering, in which Nehemiah's family, neighbors, and friends would
return home. Home, however, wasn't what it once was. The temple sat
empty, the walls of the city lay in piles of rubble, and few people lived
there anymore. For God to bring Nehemiah's family home, they would
need something to come home to.

Nehemiah's courage started with a bold prayer, and then it led to a
conversation with the king who held the people of Israel captive. Surprisingly, the king granted him the privilege of rebuilding the city walls!

One courageous man thought mourning the state of affairs was not
enough—something had to be done, and he was willing to step up to
the plate. Consequently, God took this man's courage and displaced a
nation's collective despair.

Today, the rubble of your broken life can be reclaimed by God, and
the scattered parts can be gathered. All you must do is courageously cooperate with God's reclamation project for your life.

How do you react when the odds are against you? How will you trust God
to lead you away from fear and toward the fulfillment of His plan?

BE THE MAN WHO UPHOLDS HIS WEDDING VOWS

*Marriage should be honored by all, and the marriage bed kept pure,
for God will judge the adulterer and all the sexually immoral.*
HEBREWS 13:4 NIV

Marriage is a big deal. It may not seem like it these days, however, since weddings and marriages are common fodder for reality television shows. In *Married at First Sight*, for example, couples are paired up and have eight weeks to decide whether they'll stay married or divorce. In *Love Is Blind*, the only way to see your mate is through a proposal. And *90 Day Fiancé* matches U.S. citizens with non-citizens, the prize being the ability to stay in the country legally.

Even without considering the current divorce rates, it is easy to see that marriage doesn't hold the same sense of honor it used to. But marriage is still a big deal.

If you are married, there's a good chance you took a vow on your wedding day to be faithful to your wife "from this day forward, for better, for worse, for richer, for poorer, in sickness and in health, to love and to cherish, till death do us part." There were legal witnesses present who can testify that your marriage is legitimate, but they were only window dressing compared to God as witness.

Marriage is more than a legal arrangement where two households join as one. It has spiritual ramifications as well. And whether you are married or single, you have a responsibility to consider the consequences of actions that would affect your wife, whether you've met her or not. For the marriage bed to be pure, all forms of sexual immorality—including lust, pornography, and sexual acts outside of marriage—are off-limits, and for good reason.

Marriage is a human manifestation of our intimate relationship with a holy God. We cannot live for ourselves and for Him any more than a married couple could date other people and consider their marriage healthy.

Why do you think God takes marriage so seriously?
How seriously do you take marital vows?

BE THE MAN WHO IS GENEROUS

Yes, you will be enriched in every way so that you can always be generous.
And when we take your gifts to those who need them, they will thank God.
2 Corinthians 9:11 NLT

In a 2017 study, researchers from the University of Zurich in Switzerland studied the link between generosity and happiness. Participants were promised one hundred dollars over the course of a few weeks. Half of the participants were asked to think about spending the money on themselves. The other half were asked how they would use the money for someone else. In the following weeks, those who were generous reported having lower stress levels and higher degrees of happiness than those who were selfish.

As the giver of all good gifts, God not only loves generosity—He's the *embodiment* of generosity. And when He gives generously to you, He isn't doing it so that you'll keep His gifts to yourself. He's doing it so that you can be generous like Him.

In Luke 6:38 (NLT), Jesus says, "Give, and you will receive. Your gift will return to you in full—pressed down, shaken together to make room for more, running over, and poured into your lap. The amount you give will determine the amount you get back."

And in Acts 20:35 (NLT), Paul says, "I have been a constant example of how you can help those in need by working hard. You should remember the words of the Lord Jesus: 'It is more blessed to give than to receive.'"

God designed us to be happier when we are generous, but our sin nature encourages us to be selfish. Being a faithful man means looking beyond our wants and using our blessings to bless others. When we do, we get the benefit of happiness, knowing that God is being glorified through our actions.

How have you been blessed in a way you can share with others?
How can you thank God for others' generosity to you?

BE THE MAN WHO KNOWS HIS LIMITS

There is a way that appears to be right, but in the end it leads to death.
PROVERBS 14:12 NIV

How much alcohol is too much? It is illegal in every state to drive with a certain blood alcohol concentration, but the number of drinks that equates to depends on factors like metabolism, body weight, and the potency of the drink. Certainly, there is room to argue that one drink is rarely enough to push someone over the threshold, but to an alcoholic or someone who strives to be the safest driver on the road, the question of how much one can drink is unhelpful.

How close can you get to someone else's wife and not consider it cheating? Is the line drawn at sex? Holding hands? Flirting? How accepting would you be if your wife were doing any of these things? For marriage to be the impenetrable union of two souls united as one, no amount of questionable relationship behavior is acceptable.

You could probably think of more examples in which drawing a line in the sand between "permissible" and "not permissible" is unhelpful. Really, the line should be drawn between what is "God honoring" and what is not—with some extra boundaries established to prevent *that* line from being crossed.

If you have alcoholic tendencies, you should probably avoid alcohol altogether. If you're married, you shouldn't entertain interests in other prospects. You may think in each instance that you can handle things better than last time, but that is the way that appears right only to end in death.

Whatever your struggle is—and there are many common to humankind—ask God to help you resist temptation and set up strong boundaries. Recognize that the question is never "How much can I get away with?" but rather "How can I honor God with this area of my life?" Know your limits by letting God set them for you.

What questions have you been asking when it comes to setting your limits? What things might it be wiser for you to avoid altogether?

BE THE MAN WHO FOLLOWS THE KING OF COURAGE

"Do not let your hearts be troubled. You believe in God; believe also in me. My Father's house has many rooms; if that were not so, would I have told you that I am going there to prepare a place for you? And if I go and prepare a place for you, I will come back and take you to be with me that you also may be where I am. You know the way to the place where I am going. . . . I am the way and the truth and the life. No one comes to the Father except through me."

JOHN 14:1–4, 6 NIV

Can you name a person with more courage than Jesus? He left His glorious life in heaven, knowing He would be betrayed, disbelieved, mocked, and killed. Each day, He had the burden of knowing all that would happen. His life was a countdown toward intense pain and suffering.

Even more, Jesus knew that many would reject His message. Many didn't want to hear it, and they certainly didn't want to believe. The Jews vehemently opposed the idea that God would come for anyone who was not a Jew. The rest of the world struggled because of the many gods they worshipped. They would need an incredible amount of faith to believe in one God and follow Him alone.

Jesus showed courage in sharing such inconceivable truth. Consequently, people are following His example by sharing that same news today.

Remember: Jesus won't ask you to do something He hasn't done. The King of courage boldly proclaimed the good news, so feel free to repeat His message.

Have you ever tried to make excuses for not following Jesus' courageous example? If so, how can you learn to defeat these insecurities with the truth?

BE THE MAN WHO FOLLOWS
A DIFFERENT LIST

Therefore, as God's chosen people, holy and dearly loved,
clothe yourselves with compassion, kindness,
humility, gentleness and patience.
COLOSSIANS 3:12 NIV

There are a lot of words that people use to describe men. They include *arrogant, proud, powerful, tough,* and *aggressive.*

What a different world it would be if men presented themselves the way God wants. His Word offers a different list of words that describe a man who uses His strength. This list includes *compassion, kindness, humility, gentleness,* and *patience.*

Despite popular misconception, true strength isn't the ability to manipulate circumstances to conform to your plans. Instead, God's strength values personal relationships over personal agendas.

Christians are set aside for use by God. He loves and cherishes them more than any human can. And when a man like you clothes himself in God's attributes, the resulting impact in his culture will be more profound than a massive wave of arrogant, proud, powerful, tough, and aggressive men.

To be clear, God's not denying the benefits that come with physical strength. He's simply saying that true strength is more than you can find in the gym. And if you can't adjust your understanding of strength to fit God's definition, then you're actually settling for spiritual weakness. You're relying on your own power, thus missing out on a greater power you can never possess on your own.

If this challenges your thinking about strong men, then this may be just what God intended for you to read today.

Why might it be hard to accept God's description of a man? What's one tangible way you can incorporate some of the items on God's list in your choices today?

BE THE MAN WHO LETS GO OF ANGER

"In your anger do not sin": Do not let the sun go down while you are still angry, and do not give the devil a foothold.
EPHESIANS 4:26–27 NIV

Anger happens. In itself, anger isn't bad. Some things are worth getting angry about: sin, injustice, the perversion of goodness. But these are rarely the anger-causing issues men deal with.

Most of us get angry when we perceive a threat to ourselves or our comfort. A person sits in your favorite chair. Someone has taken food that clearly had your name on it from the work fridge. The guy in front of you is going ten miles under the speed limit, but you're in a no-passing zone. If just reading any of those things gets your blood boiling, you have some work to do.

Anger is a natural response to stress or frustration. As such, you can use it to identify areas in your life that need God's attention. Feel the anger. Don't stifle it or ignore it. Allow it to guide you in prayer.

Do people get on your nerves? Pray for them, leaving them in God's capable hands. Pray you'll learn to love and accept them despite the annoying things they do. Thank God for bringing this person into your life so that you can practice the patience He has shown to you.

Ignoring anger or allowing it to fester only hardens it into resentment. If the devil can get you to focus on yourself, how you've been wronged, and what kind of treatment you deserve, he's successfully distracted you from seeing the needs of others and from praising God for His goodness.

Is it hard to be angry without sinning? Of course! But you can do all things through Him who gives you strength (see Philippians 4:13).

What things make you angry? How can those things guide your prayers?

BE THE MAN WHO SEES THE WISDOM OF GENTLENESS

But the wisdom from above is first of all pure. It is also peace loving, gentle at all times, and willing to yield to others. It is full of mercy and the fruit of good deeds. It shows no favoritism and is always sincere.

JAMES 3:17 NLT

The wisdom of the world says, "Look out for number one; no one else has your interests at heart." This self-protectionist outlook may indeed seem like wisdom, but its message of egocentricity—or selfish ambition—is dangerous. James 3:16 (NLT) says, "For wherever there is jealousy and selfish ambition, there you will find disorder and evil of every kind."

But if putting your own interests first isn't the best way forward, what is? Today's verse spells it out. Beginning with purity and ending with fairness and sincerity, this verse calls us to rise above the petty squabbles and infighting that naturally accompany selfish ambition. Not only should our message be different—focused on the well-being of others, not just ourselves—but our tone should stand out as well.

It's hard to argue with people who remain calm, speak gently, and see both sides of an issue. These people want to talk things through, and their tone of voice makes others more inclined to listen. After all, when you are trustworthy and your life is full of mercy and good deeds, you don't need to shout to be heard.

Gentleness stems from the quiet confidence that God is in control. It seeks peaceful progress toward love as the world around you crumbles into the chaos of selfish ambition. Whenever you step into a situation in which someone is using the wisdom of the world, counter with the wisdom from above. You don't need to worry about whether your needs will be taken care of—God has already promised they will be. Besides, the things of this world are rarely worth squabbling about anyway.

Who would you be more likely to listen to: a gentle, well-respected person or a guy who insists on getting his own way? Which of these people do you resemble the most?

BE THE MAN WHO CHOOSES
A PAIN-FREE FUTURE

*And I heard a great voice out of heaven saying, Behold, the tabernacle
of God is with men, and he will dwell with them, and they shall
be his people, and God himself shall be with them, and be their
God. And God shall wipe away all tears from their eyes; and there
shall be no more death, neither sorrow, nor crying, neither shall
there be any more pain: for the former things are passed away.*
REVELATION 21:3–4 KJV

You've probably heard the expression, "If it seems too good to be true, it
probably is." A calorie-free cake, an unbreakable toy, a camera that takes
perfect selfies—all these miracle inventions get peddled by late night
infomercials and shady websites each day, so we've learned to keep our
suspicion antenna raised high.

In a world of high expectations and false promises, it's not surpris-
ing that some of God's promises seem unbelievable. It takes courage to
believe in a future in which no therapists, hospitals, or funeral homes are
needed. But that's just a sneak peek at heaven.

The courage you bring to this celestial view is faith—and this faith
will not disappoint. Jesus said, "In my Father's house are many mansions:
if it were not so, I would have told you. I go to prepare a place for you.
And if I go and prepare a place for you, I will come again, and receive you
unto myself; that where I am, there ye may be also" (John 14:2–3 KJV).

If this sounds too good to be true, just remember: God has never
broken a promise.

Do you find it hard to believe in a heaven you've never seen?
How does the hope of heaven renew your courage?

BE THE MAN WHO THINKS ABOUT THE FUTURE

We are citizens of heaven, where the Lord Jesus Christ lives.
And we are eagerly waiting for him to return as our Savior.
PHILIPPIANS 3:20 NLT

There's a compelling reason to accept God's strength—He gave you the body you have, and He'll give you a new one someday. Your future body will be designed to last forever. That's why God doesn't emphasize keeping your current body in shape. True, He does say your body is where He lives—but that's only to highlight the strength He brings to your relationship with Him.

When you start contrasting your temporary earthly existence to eternity, then this time and place suddenly seem pretty small. Why spend so much time trying to impress people when you won't be able to do it for long?

For Christians, life on this big blue marble is but a blip. Earth is merely the place where we choose what happens after our last breath.

God never intended for you to live forever in the "here and now," especially since a "then and there" awaits. While you're here, you're given an extraordinary opportunity to seek wisdom and discover what's really important. So your best course of action depends on what you should look forward to the most.

Your strength-giving God provides the strength for the body you have right now. . .and for the eternal one that's waiting for you.

How does knowing there's more beyond this life alter your view of the strength God offers? Do you think of this place as temporary housing or a permanent residence?

BE THE MAN WHO IS CREATED IN GOD'S IMAGE

*So God created man in his own image, in the image of
God created he him; male and female created he them.*
GENESIS 1:27 KJV

Have you ever seen a photo of your dad or grandpa when they were the age you are now? Sometimes, we look like them or sound like them or act like them. We bear their image because they helped make us. When others see you, they see the evidence of your ancestors.

The whole human race was created in the image of God. Some people think this means we physically resemble God (or, more accurately, Jesus, the second person of the Trinity). Some think we have God's capacity for morality and ethics in ways animals don't. The main point of bearing God's image is not *how* we resemble Him; the point is that we *do*.

Since we reflect God's image, our treatment of each other becomes a reflection of how we treat Him. That's why murder is such a big deal in God's book. Genesis 9:6 (NIV) says, "Whoever sheds human blood, by humans shall their blood be shed; for in the image of God has God made mankind."

We should always remember we were made in God's image, not the other way around. Anne Lamott wrote in her book *Bird by Bird*, "You can safely assume you've created God in your own image when it turns out that God hates all the same people you do."

Being a faithful man means not only recognizing God's image when you look in the mirror but seeing Him in every face you meet. It means loving others simply because they bear God's image too. It means using your hands for His work, your mind for His thoughts, and your gifts for His glory.

Do you see others as God's image bearers?
How can you help people see God's image in you?

BE THE MAN WHO CONFRONTS FRIENDS

Faithful are the wounds of a friend; but the kisses of an enemy are deceitful.
PROVERBS 27:6 KJV

"It'll be awkward."

"What if I'm just making a big deal out of nothing?"

"It's better to keep the peace and play nicely."

There is no end to the justifications for not confronting a friend over some issue. Unlike family, the nature of friendship is more transitory. The risk is greater that the offended party won't want to be friends anymore, so it can be harder to broach sensitive topics. But when a friend says or does something seriously wrong, finding the courage to address the issue can lead to a deeper, more satisfying friendship.

Restoring relationships is so important that Jesus said to take care of any confrontations before coming to God's altar (see Matthew 5:23–24).

There are a few things to keep in mind when preparing for friendly confrontation. Remember, the goal is to restore a broken relationship—the fewer people who get involved, the better. Matthew 18:15 (NIV) says, "If your brother or sister sins, go and point out their fault, just between the two of you. If they listen to you, you have won them over."

Be specific about what is bothering you and why. Address one issue at a time and avoid broad generalizations like "You always do this" or "You never remember. . ." Stick to the facts of what was said or done and calmly explain why it's an issue. In fact, it's a good idea to rehearse your words beforehand.

Lastly—yet this step should probably come first—be willing to forgive and move on. Colossians 3:13 (NIV) says, "Bear with each other and forgive one another if any of you has a grievance against someone. Forgive as the Lord forgave you."

No matter how awkward it gets, true friends will be honest with one another and handle confrontation with respect and forgiveness.

Do you pray before confronting friends? How might you apply the Bible's instructions whenever your friendship is in crisis?

BE THE MAN WHO LEAVES
THE FUNHOUSE BEHIND

*They stumble because they do not obey God's word, and so they meet
the fate that was planned for them. But you are not like that, for you
are a chosen people. You are royal priests, a holy nation, God's very
own possession. As a result, you can show others the goodness of God,
for he called you out of the darkness into his wonderful light.*

1 PETER 2:8–9 NLT

Have you ever been in a carnival funhouse? It was filled with darkness, trap doors, and mirrors that distorted your perception of who you really are. It was designed to be amusing, but soon, you started feeling lost and discombobulated (a fancy word that just means "confused"; look it up!). Slowly, your confusion turned to awkwardness and discomfort. You tried to leave, but you couldn't find the exit.

Finally stumbling out of the funhouse reintroduced you to reality. Darkness became light and distortion gave way to solid shape and substance.

You have been chosen by God, and you get to choose Him. He called you from life's funhouse, so you never need to experience discombobulation again. Grab hold of the courage you need to leave your old life's distortion behind in the adversary's funhouse. Discard the lies you accepted as truth. It will be hard, but the results will be liberating. You will come to love this new life. Any allure to the old funhouse will become more and more absurd.

People are leaving the devil's funhouse every day. If you haven't joined them yet, today is the perfect time to start.

Has the spiritual funhouse ever left you discombobulated? Do you choose
each day to reject the funhouse in favor of God's wonderful light?

BE THE MAN WHO BELIEVES
BEYOND THE IDEA

*For the Kingdom of God is not just a
lot of talk; it is living by God's power.*
1 CORINTHIANS 4:20 NLT

God isn't just an idea, concept, or fairy tale. Don't let anyone tell you
otherwise, even if that person attempts to make your faith seem foolish.

God's Word is the foundation of all truth, and it teaches that He
has always been and always will be. And since God created everything—
and since He remains your only hope for rescue—why would you ever
devalue or mock His name?

But even if you do, His response to you will be love; His gift, forgiveness. His kindness is the best antidote to rebellion. His power is greater
than the jeers of the disbelieving. His love is mightier than those who
want Him to leave. His open arms are more powerful than your ability
to run away.

If you believe that God is a concept, idea, or fairy tale, then you've
missed the point—this so-called fairy tale *created* you. His kingdom co-
exists with your rebellion, but He will work tirelessly to chip away the
defenses of your heart.

In the grand scheme of life, rebellion against God makes you weak.
Changing your address to God's kingdom, however, brings strength. If
rebellion is uncertainty and suspicion, then strength is assurance and
growing faith.

Why do some see rebellion as strength? Why will this
never be true? Have you invited rebellion to leave?

BE THE MAN WHO IS CREATIVE IN GOD'S IMAGE

In the beginning God created the heaven and the earth.
GENESIS 1:1 KJV

The first thing the Bible teaches us about God is how creative He is. He created light, darkness, land, water, plants, animals, and finally us. Psalm 104:24 (NLT) says, "O LORD, what a variety of things you have made! In wisdom you have made them all. The earth is full of your creatures." No two things are alike.

Consider beetles, a mere subgroup of insects in the animal kingdom. As of now, more than 350,000 different species of beetles have been discovered, and there may be even more.

God must like beetles! But only humans are made in His image, sharing some of His attributes and abilities. We convert our thoughts into art, music, and literature. We build skyscrapers, furniture, and fantastic meals with our hands. We invent and create, not exactly like God did in the beginning, but from the resources He has provided.

Although He has given us the tools for the job, we sometimes hesitate to be creative. Usually, it's because we are afraid our creation will merit rebuke instead of praise, or attention when we prefer not to be seen. But by neglecting this aspect of our identity, we miss out on part of God's goodness.

Creativity doesn't have to be seen or praised to be worthwhile. Even the simplest act of creation teaches us how difficult, as well as how rewarding, it can be.

So draw a picture. Write a story. Build a chair. Create something that didn't exist before, and discover the joy God had in making you.

Do you consider yourself creative? How will you express your creativity?

BE THE MAN WHO DISCERNS BETWEEN JOKES AND CRUELTY

Like a maniac shooting flaming arrows of death is one who deceives their neighbor and says, "I was only joking!"
PROVERBS 26:18–19 NIV

There's always that one guy who takes practical jokes too far. It's one thing to stuff a sock in your buddy's shoes so that his feet don't fit. It's another thing to put broken glass in there. Similarly, plugging a spare wireless mouse into someone's computer and occasionally moving the cursor is different from deleting that person's documents and setting fire to the keyboard.

There are rules to practical jokes. They shouldn't be destructive or harmful. They shouldn't have permanent consequences. They shouldn't be played on someone who doesn't appreciate them. And if you play jokes on people, you're inviting them to play some on you.

The phrase "I was only joking" isn't exclusive to April Fool's Day. People say it whenever they feel the need to justify actions or words that are unjustifiable. According to today's scripture, it is foolish to speak without thinking of the consequences and then pass your comment off as a joke.

Have you ever taken a joke too far? Or have you ever spouted angry thoughts that you tried to cover up as "only joking"? If so, you should know there is a better way.

If you act foolishly or speak before thinking, apologize. Repent of your actions and words. Seek to make the relationship right. If your joke had serious consequences, you have a responsibility to make amends. Never try to pass foolish behavior off as a joke. You messed up, pure and simple. The only way forward is honesty.

Save joking for April Fool's Day, and make sure your joke is funny and follows the rules.

How would you feel if a friend hurt you and passed it off as a joke? Have you ever tried to justify yourself when your actions were simply wrong?

BE THE MAN WHO BELIEVES IN HOPE

Isaiah says, "The Root of Jesse will spring up, one who will arise to rule over the nations; in him the Gentiles will hope." May the God of hope fill you with all joy and peace as you trust in him, so that you may overflow with hope by the power of the Holy Spirit.
ROMANS 15:12–13 NIV

In the movie *Pinocchio*, a small cricket urges the title character to find a star and make a wish. If only reality were that simple!

Sadly, there's no evidence that stars, which are just balls of hydrogen and helium, have ever been able to grant wishes. . .but they do recognize God as Creator. The Lord Himself said "the morning stars sang together" when He laid the earth's foundation (Job 38:7 NIV).

The God who made the stars wants you to put your hope in Him. The stars are His creation. He is the Creator. That's a huge difference. You shouldn't honor a piece of art and not the artist, celebrate a song over the songwriter, or praise a meal without acknowledging the cook.

The hope God gives isn't a wish-on-a-star kind of hope, and it's not something you can manufacture on your own. Rather, it's the assurance that all His promises will come to pass. When you accept His hope, you have access to joy and peace.

There's no downside to courageously consuming a full dose of God's hope.

Do you regularly access God's real hope? How is this hope different from a wish?

BE THE MAN WHO KNOCKS OFF THE PRETENDING

God is our refuge and strength, an ever-present help in trouble.
PSALM 46:1 NIV

Somehow, weakness has become taboo for men—something to avoid at all costs. But this attitude is as foolish as it is spiritually dangerous.

What would happen if you were able to handle every challenge and carry every burden without God's help? Would God mean more or less to you? If you knew you could solve every problem, wouldn't God start taking a back seat in your life?

The practical reason for weakness is that it proves how essential God is. When God shows up and saves the day, it removes all doubt about who's really in charge. He has always been able to do what you can't, to go where you won't, to love when you don't.

If you refuse to admit this truth, you're deceiving yourself. Instead of accepting God's help, you keep pretending that you're better than everyone else. This minimizes the needs of others and inhibits any growth in your friendship with God.

Weakness is simply a reminder that everything you lack is readily available through God. But this shouldn't lead you to self-pity; instead, it should be a profound reminder of your connection to an amazing God who loves you and wants to guide you through life's challenges.

The benefit of this arrangement is that you'll always have what you need because God replaces your weakness with His strong plan of action.

Is it hard for you to admit that you need God's help?
Why is there such a stigma attached to this admission?

BE THE MAN WHO DOESN'T FEAR TRANSITIONS

"Be strong and courageous. Do not be afraid or terrified because of them, for the LORD your God goes with you; he will never leave you nor forsake you."

DEUTERONOMY 31:6 NIV

Moses was eighty years old when he encountered God in the burning bush. Living peacefully as a shepherd, he may have thought his days in Egypt were long behind him. Then came the plagues, the miracles, the pillar of fire, the commandments, and, for forty long years, the wilderness.

Forty years is a long time to follow someone. Whole generations of Israelites grew up in the wilderness, having never experienced their nation's captivity in Egypt. But the time had come for a change in leadership. At age 120, Moses knew it was time for Joshua to lead the nation of Israel into the promised land.

Not only were the Israelites preparing to fight enemies in a foreign land, they were now facing a change in leadership—a transition just as daunting as the upcoming battles. However, Moses' advice to both Joshua and the Israelites was the same: "Be strong and courageous" (see Deuteronomy 31:6–7).

Moses wasn't telling them to simply "not fear" the upcoming changes; rather, he gave them a reason for courage: "For the LORD your God goes with you; He will never leave you nor forsake you."

No matter what transitions are taking place in your life, there is one thing that never changes: God is with you. He walks beside you in times of peace and fights on your behalf in times of trouble. Whether you are tackling new responsibilities, exploring a new relationship, or starting a new chapter of your life, God is there.

Our strength and courage are not in ourselves. They are in the Lord our God.

What transitions can you place into God's hands?
How can you combat fear with trust?

BE THE MAN WHO TRUSTS GOD IN TOUGH TIMES

O LORD, I give my life to you. I trust in you, my God! Do not let me be disgraced, or let my enemies rejoice in my defeat.
PSALM 25:1–2 NLT

There are rules to gifts.

It's in bad taste, for example, to give someone a toaster and then ask, "Can I borrow your toaster? Mine just broke and you have two now anyway." When you give a gift, the recipient alone decides how to use it.

But when we give our lives to God, we violate the rules all the time. We say we are His, but then we ignore His desires in favor of our own. We face a hardship and decide that God's way doesn't make sense—so we better take over for a while. This shows a lack of trust in God, the most trustworthy Being in the universe.

When times get tough, we must hand our control over to God more than ever. Let's pray as David did in Psalm 25, expressing our trust in God then making our requests known to Him.

We should ask God for wisdom when making decisions—"Show me the right path, O LORD; point out the road for me to follow. Lead me by your truth and teach me, for you are the God who saves me. All day long I put my hope in you" (Psalm 25:4–5 NLT). And we must rely on His forgiveness when we mess things up—"Do not remember the rebellious sins of my youth. Remember me in the light of your unfailing love, for you are merciful, O LORD" (Psalm 25:7 NLT).

Trust God. Stop trying to "take back the toaster." God will do amazing things with your life if you'll only let Him.

How well do your actions reflect your trust in God? How can you stop yourself from trying to take back the gift of your life?

BE THE MAN WHO HAS A SECOND WIND

No discipline is enjoyable while it is happening—it's painful! But afterward there will be a peaceful harvest of right living for those who are trained in this way. So take a new grip with your tired hands and strengthen your weak knees. Mark out a straight path for your feet so that those who are weak and lame will not fall but become strong.

HEBREWS 12:11–13 NLT

The term *second wind* originated in the 1830s and is used to describe an unexpected burst of strength in times of weariness.

A second wind inspires you to continue moving forward. It somehow turns exhaustion into energy, reigniting your passion. You've probably felt it while doing anything from cross country running to lawn care, and you might even encounter it on a recurring basis.

Galatians 6:9 (NLT) perfectly describes the idea behind a second wind: "So let's not get tired of doing what is good. At just the right time we will reap a harvest of blessing if we don't give up." Here, God provides the purpose (doing good) and the outcome (blessings).

You can walk even when the steps are hard and run even when your spiritual lungs are on fire—all you have to do is access the second wind that the Spirit offers. Then you can continue pursuing righteousness without the need to turn aside or take a break.

A faithful man moves past the desire to call it a day before his work is done. He presses on, even when he's certain he can't. He believes that a spiritual second wind will come soon.

Have you ever felt a second wind in your spiritual life? Why is it comforting to know God makes all things possible?

BE THE MAN WHO IDENTIFIES WITH JESUS

*The Word was made flesh, and dwelt among us,
(and we beheld his glory, the glory as of the only
begotten of the Father,) full of grace and truth.*
JOHN 1:14 KJV

There was a time when God's Son, Jesus, had a human body. He was still God, but His body would end in destruction. Jesus could be hurt, injured, and drained of health. He had the strength of God. . .coexisting with a weak body.

Jesus was beaten, bruised, and hung from a cross. People abused Him, pierced Him with thorns, and pulled the hair from His beard. He was subjected to more physical pain than most will ever experience.

If the Son of God experienced weakness in a human body—if He had to ask God to help Him—then why wouldn't you think it's the same with you?

When you refuse to ask God for help, you're saying you are superior to Jesus. That may not be your intention, but it's the message that's conveyed every time you turn down God's essential help.

Jesus recognized that the human body had limitations. He knew that sometimes, He just needed to talk to God about life's unrelenting waves of struggle.

All human bodies, including yours, have a shelf life. Your physical strength will decrease over time, but the strength God offers will last until the end of this life and throughout the eternal life that comes next.

So why settle for physical strength? There's more to life than this.

Does thinking about Jesus' struggles impact your
willingness to ask God for strength? Why or why not?

BE THE MAN WHO DOESN'T TRY TO IMPRESS

Obviously, I'm not trying to win the approval of people, but of God.
If pleasing people were my goal, I would not be Christ's servant.
GALATIANS 1:10 NLT

When it was initially published in 1936, Dale Carnegie's book *How to Win Friends and Influence People* was an instant success, requiring seventeen printings in its first year alone. The book's popularity has continued, and many consider it to be one of the most influential books of all time.

Carnegie's advice has been used by businesses to train leaders and improve employee communications. It's helped businessmen like Warren Buffett gain wealth, but it's also helped cult leaders like Charles Manson convince their followers to kill. While Carnegie's book contains many exemplary guidelines—be a good listener, give honest and sincere appreciation—some can be used for manipulation. In other words, the method may be good while the focus is all wrong.

Our goal in life should not be getting people to like us or convincing them to do what we want. Our goal should be pleasing God. Paul said as much in Galatians 1:10 (NLT): "Obviously, I'm not trying to win the approval of people, but of God. If pleasing people were my goal, I would not be Christ's servant."

The apostle John lamented those who recognized the Messiah privately but not in front of the human religious authorities of the day. He said, "For they loved the praise of men more than the praise of God" (John 12:43 KJV).

Pleasing people can be an addictive habit, giving us instant gratification in the form of smiles, thanks, and attaboys. When this becomes our focus, our actions—no matter how good they are—become expressions of selfishness, far removed from our ultimate goal of giving praise to God.

Have you ever been guilty of trying to please people rather
than God? How might you remove the focus from yourself
in order to better influence people for God?

BE THE MAN WHO TELLS THE TRUTH

An honest witness tells the truth; a false witness tells lies.
PROVERBS 12:17 NLT

Today's verse doesn't need much explanation. Honest people tell the truth. Liars don't. Simple.

Being a faithful man means being honest. In fact, the word *honest*, meaning "free from fraud," comes from the Latin *honestus*, which literally means "honorable, respected, or regarded with honor."

But why should we be honest? What's in it for us? Whoever said that liars never prosper hasn't been paying attention. Companies willing to cut corners to make their investors happy are better able to compete in today's economy. Politicians, while regularly caught in compromising situations, often live double lives unreported by the press.

The fact is that truth is its own reward. Even if deceit goes unpunished by human justice, God will mete out His own justice in time. Liars always live with some level of fear that they'll be found out. There's always the chance their stories won't match something they said earlier or that someone witnessed them doing what they said they didn't. But truthful people don't need to keep their stories straight—the facts speak for themselves.

Proverbs 12:20 (NLT) says, "Deceit fills hearts that are plotting evil; joy fills hearts that are planning peace!"

The joy of truthfulness is one reward. Being told by our Father that we've represented Him well to other people is another. So while liars do sometimes prosper according to the world's standards, honest men will prosper most after this world has ended.

Have you ever been caught in a lie? Are you carrying any
lies right now that should be confessed and released?

BE THE MAN WHO REFUSES TO LIMIT GOD

*Then they cried out with a loud voice, and stopped their ears,
and ran upon him with one accord, and cast [Stephen] out of
the city, and stoned him: and the witnesses laid down their
clothes at a young man's feet, whose name was Saul.*
ACTS 7:57–58 KJV

While reading a novel, you may have noticed that the author provided time-released information, slowly filling in the blanks but leaving you hungry for more. Often, such books will drop names and crucial bits of context like breadcrumbs before revealing the twist at the end.

Guess what? The Bible uses this strategy too. Acts 7:58, for instance, is about Stephen, a devout follower of Jesus who was "full of faith and power, [and] did great wonders and miracles among the people" (6:8 KJV). In this chapter, this strong and faithful follower was killed for his faith.

Maybe you noticed the name drop at the end of verse 58 (KJV): "Witnesses laid down their clothes at a young man's feet, whose name was Saul." Who was Saul? Why did he hate Christians? Is he important to the story?

Well, the author later reveals that Saul was a Pharisee who thought Christians were misguided at best and dangerous at worst. He was all for eradicating them, so he was probably thrilled to be in charge of the religious protesters' coats.

But soon, Saul would meet Jesus. Nothing—not even his name would remain the same. Jesus renamed him Paul, and he became an apostle.

In a single verse, we read of a courageous man who died for his faith as well as a man who would soon receive that faith. As Paul's story proves, we should never view anyone—even the worst of sinners—as beyond redemption.

No one is too bad for God to rescue.

Do you ever doubt that God is willing to save someone? How can
this story of Stephen and Saul help erase these doubts?

BE THE MAN WHO EMBRACES SPECIAL SKILLS

*Put on all of God's armor so that you will be able
to stand firm against all strategies of the devil.*
EPHESIANS 6:11 NLT

If you're asked in a job interview to share your personal strengths, you'll probably reply with something that's relevant to your desired position. If it's a desk job, you probably won't mention how great you are with disc golf, video games, or chainsaws. (And you definitely won't want to bring up the "Most Likely to Take a Nap" award your family gave you.)

But there's one set of skills that's useful for *every* task: the "armor of God" that's described in Ephesians 6. If you learn to use this armor effectively, you'll be remembered for believing in the truth, valuing the peace found in God's Word over the chaos found elsewhere, relying on faith to improve your responses and cut out distractions, and trusting God's salvation as the source of all these skills.

The more you learn from God, the greater your inner strength becomes. The armor of God makes you not only a better person but a better employee, a better friend, and a better husband. It places you shoulder to shoulder with God, who stands with you when you face the enemy's lies. And when you're tempted to brag, it encourages you to remember who did all the rescuing.

Do you strive to apply the armor of God to every area of
your life? How does this skill set add strength to life?

BE THE MAN WHO HAS SELF-CONTROL

If you find honey, eat just enough—too much of it, and you will vomit.
PROVERBS 25:16 NIV

Honey is pretty amazing. Here are a few fun facts about it:

- Made from plant nectar by bees, honey has antibacterial and antifungal properties and has been used as a medicine for thousands of years.
- Bees produce honey as a winter food source, but since they make two to three times as much as they need, humans reap the benefits.
- In its lifetime, a worker bee will only make one twelfth of a teaspoon of honey.
- Honeybees share information on food sources with each other by performing a "waggle dance."

As amazing as it is, too much honey can be awful. Think of the bees who spent their whole lives making a twelfth of a teaspoon of honey just for you to throw it up because you ate too much. They'd do a waggle dance of shame right in your face.

Of course, Proverbs 25:16 isn't talking only about honey. Too much of anything can lead to trouble. Too many donuts will add doughiness to your frame. Too much reading or screen time will steal time away from family and important projects. In each instance, self-control is vital.

Some people see self-control as refraining from doing bad things, but it applies to good things too. If self-control doesn't come naturally to you, don't worry. It's a supernatural gift of the Holy Spirit (see Galatians 5:22–23). All we need to do is ask for God's help.

When you indulge in something, are you tempted to overindulge?
How will you pray for self-control in every situation?

BE THE MAN WHO COMPETES TO SHOW HONOR

Be devoted to one another in love.
Honor one another above yourselves.
ROMANS 12:10 NIV

Studies have shown that men are naturally more competitive than women. Maybe you remember the games you played as a kid—or even the sporting events you attend now—and are thinking, *Well, duh*. Competition seems to be part of a man's identity.

Even when men are not equipped to succeed in a given task, they are more likely to desire competition than refuse a challenge. This means most men would rather look foolish for losing than look weak for backing down.

On the downside, this means men do a lot of foolish things for not-very-good reasons. Maybe you could think of a few you've done yourself. On the upside, this means men can channel their competitive spirit to achieve good things instead. What if men competed in showing honor to one another? What would that even look like?

It might mean you always try to be last in line. Or maybe you try to be the first one to see and meet the needs of others. It could mean always putting your hand up first when someone needs a volunteer for a difficult job. Or it could be as simple as trying to hand out the most genuine compliments.

When we use competition to spur each other on to good works, God is honored. Who cares who wins? Winning people for Christ is all that matters. When they see you volunteering, working hard, and meeting the needs of others, they'll see God working in and through you.

So go bring God glory today. I dare you.

With whom might you start a friendly competition in
order to honor God? What areas could you compete in?

BE THE MAN WHO IS CONTENT

Not that I was ever in need, for I have learned how to be content with whatever I have. I know how to live on almost nothing or with everything. I have learned the secret of living in every situation, whether it is with a full stomach or empty, with plenty or little.

PHILIPPIANS 4:11–12 NLT

Contentment flies in the face of the American Dream, in which citizens are encouraged to always want more. But with nearly 80 percent of American workers living paycheck-to-paycheck (according to a 2017 survey by CareerBuilder), contentment is a necessity.

In his letter to the Philippian church, the apostle Paul writes, "For I can do everything through Christ, who gives me strength" (Philippians 4:13 NLT). This verse is often misquoted as an inspirational saying by people reaching for some new dream; however, in its biblical context, it explains how we can be content.

A faithful man is satisfied living for God's glory, sustained by God's strength. God doesn't promise full stomachs, full wallets, or full health. Contentment has nothing to do with physical comforts; it has everything to do with spiritual reliance on the God who controls all things.

When Paul asked God to remove the thorn in the flesh that troubled him, God didn't do it. Second Corinthians 12:9 (NLT) says, "Each time he said, 'My grace is all you need. My power works best in weakness.' So now I am glad to boast about my weaknesses, so that the power of Christ can work through me."

Paul learned contentment in times of hardship, not in times of plenty. God has promised to give us strength and grace, not health and wealth, so our contentment and reliance on Him should never waver. When we do everything through Christ, we can boast in our weaknesses and be strong in God's power.

What are some of the blessings God's given you?
How content are you with your situation?

BE THE MAN WHO'S BRAVE FOR THE RIGHT REASONS

Teach those who are rich in this world not to be proud and not to trust in their money, which is so unreliable. Their trust should be in God, who richly gives us all we need for our enjoyment.
1 Timothy 6:17 NLT

You can't be courageous when the thing you trust the most is unreliable. You probably wouldn't be courageous enough to take a cross-country trip in a dilapidated car that just passed 350,000 miles. You wouldn't enter a weightlifting competition if the biggest thing you've lifted lately is a twin pack of snack cakes. You wouldn't suggest the help of a friend if that friend has never shown up to help you.

You either have courage or you don't. You are either confident in God's abilities or doubtful.

Before you form your opinion, look at the facts: God is supreme (Isaiah 44:6–8), eternal (Psalm 48:14), loving (John 3:16), perfect (Psalm 18:30), merciful (Ephesians 2:4–5), good (Psalm 100:5), forgiving (Daniel 9:9), and understanding (Psalm 139:1–6).

When you have God, you have every reason to be brave. God is not faulty, unreliable, or shifty. He never has to say, "Sorry I wasn't there for you today. I'll try harder tomorrow."

In other words, God's not just a nice little addition to your life—He's everything you need. God can do everything that you can't. That's why you come to Him, read His words, and ask for His help.

Today, refuse to trust the wrong thing. Let God give you courage instead.

What do you lack that God offers? Do you try finding courage in Him alone?

BE THE MAN WHO BELIEVES WITHOUT FEAR

Jesus told [Jairus], "Don't be afraid; just believe."
MARK 5:36 NIV

Jairus was a religious leader who believed in God, followed Him, and told other people about Him. But the religious leaders of his day didn't equate Jesus with God. That's why they stood tall and proud about their connection to God. . .while totally missing God's Truth, who stood before them day after day.

When his daughter became very sick, Jairus acted like a daddy. Hating to see his daughter so ill, he did something highly illogical—he sought Jesus to see if he could help. But just as he found Jesus, he received word that his little girl had died. Put yourself in his shoes for a second. All sounds blur into an odd, silent roar. Tears well up, ready to burst from their gates—hindered only by the watching eyes all around. You're a loose cannon, standing face to face with God.

That's when Jesus gave a command that broke the sound barrier, drove Jairus' tears back, and called forth a strength he didn't think was possible: "Don't be afraid; just believe."

Strength leaves when fear is allowed to stay. Weakness renews its contract when you fail to believe. But you can't believe in just anything— you must believe in a good God with a good plan. He can calm your darkest fears, but when you don't believe He can do it, then fear only tightens its grip on your heart.

Jesus gave this advice to Jairus. . .and that day, his daughter rose back to life.

When are you most likely to pray for God's help? Why is
belief in God's strength always the right call on a bad day?

BE THE MAN WHO HAS PEACE

*"Peace I leave with you; my peace I give you. I do
not give to you as the world gives. Do not let your
hearts be troubled and do not be afraid."*

John 14:27 NIV

This world has a lot to offer. God made it with beautiful sunrises, nourishing fruits and vegetables, and awe-inspiring thunderstorms. But when sin entered the world, things began breaking down. The sun still rises, but now it shines on war-torn lands. The earth still grows food, but the greedy hoard it up while others go hungry. Thunderstorms are still amazing, but they can and do sometimes kill.

The world holds many wonders, but lasting peace isn't one of them. The peace of this world is like the eye of a hurricane—a brief lull in the middle of destruction. Real peace is available, but it's not from this earth.

Jesus said in John 14:27 (NIV), "Peace I leave with you; my peace I give you. I do not give to you as the world gives. Do not let your hearts be troubled and do not be afraid." Our peace—a supernatural peace that doesn't depend on our circumstances—comes from Jesus. Bad days, pain, and earthly sorrows can never take away the peace Jesus gives.

Jesus' peace is found when God Almighty accepts us—despite our sins—into His family. He finds us faultless, seeking no payment beyond the one Jesus made on the cross. Jesus' peace is not simply the absence of punishment; it is rooted in His all-surpassing love which this world cannot take away.

When we as Christ's followers live in this peace, sinners will see our calm and know its source is supernatural. We are to spread Jesus' peace as we spread His gospel, knowing we can't have one without the other.

Are you a living example of Jesus' peace? How can
you shift your focus to be calm in a crisis?

BE THE MAN WHOSE CONDUCT REFLECTS HIS RELATIONSHIP WITH GOD

Be careful to live properly among your unbelieving neighbors. Then even if they accuse you of doing wrong, they will see your honorable behavior, and they will give honor to God when he judges the world.

1 PETER 2:12 NLT

On February 7, 2021, Christopher Spell claimed the world record for the highest standing jump—a whopping five feet seven inches straight up! Clearly, such a feat is well-nigh impossible for the average person. So what would you do if a friend claimed to be able to jump just as high? You'd want to see some evidence.

When you make fantastic claims, you need to back it up with fantastic evidence. If you claim to follow Christ but live just like everyone else, your evidence is lacking. That doesn't mean Christians can't mess up. God still loves us, even when we have reasons to repent. But it does mean that the evidence of our behavior should be a compelling argument that we live for someone greater than ourselves. It's hardly worthwhile to *say* Jesus changed our lives and took away our sins if we *live* like the world and still wallow in immorality.

In today's verse, Peter anticipates a time when those who follow Christ will be accused of criminal offenses. Indeed, when the passage was written, Peter knew that following Christ to the exclusion of all other gods would be problematic, given that the Roman emperor himself claimed to be one of the Roman deities. Yet Peter knew that when (not if) Christians are accused of misconduct, they can save themselves a lot of trouble if their conduct matches the life-giving message of the gospel.

Ultimately, it is God who will judge your actions. But if you want to bring others to the saving knowledge of the gospel, make sure your actions match your words.

Have you ever made a claim you couldn't back up?
Would others know you are a Christian by your lifestyle?

BE THE MAN WHO RETURNS AND RESTS

*For thus saith the Lord GOD, the Holy One of Israel; in returning
and rest shall ye be saved; in quietness and in confidence shall
be your strength: and ye would not. . . . And therefore will the
LORD wait, that he may be gracious unto you, and therefore will
he be exalted, that he may have mercy upon you: for the LORD is
a God of judgment: blessed are all they that wait for him.*

ISAIAH 30:15, 18 KJV

As life churns by at breakneck speeds, the gift of rest seems perfect.
Sometimes, this rest is a physical time-out—a welcome relief from the
mind-numbing, sickening effects of stress.

God offered the people of Israel this kind of rest, but they first had
to leave their fast-paced tilt-a-whirl of sinful choices and return to Him.
Their time-out came in the form of captivity, the horrors of which slowly
moved their hearts back to God. When they finally returned home, they
were changed.

Humanity is guilty of rejecting God's offer of heart recalibration.
Thinking you know more than God is a common condition. When God
says, "Come back to me," we look at our schedules and don't seem to find
an opening until the twelfth of Never.

Ask yourself: Is it wise to reject an offer from the only one who
knows how to fix you?

Do you routinely seek the rest God has for you? Whenever you stray,
how does coming back to God shorten any unwanted spiritual time-outs?

BE THE MAN WHO'S NOT INTIMIDATED

*Don't be intimidated in any way by your enemies. This will
be a sign to them that they are going to be destroyed, but
that you are going to be saved, even by God himself.*
PHILIPPIANS 1:28 NLT

Struggle is inevitable. And when it comes, it will prove beyond a shadow of a doubt that you have weaknesses. But whether you moan and bewail your situation or take practical steps toward victory is up to you.

Your enemy is God's enemy, and his primary goal is to prevent you from trusting. . .and thereby keep you weak. He's managed to keep some people in this sorry state for decades. But you can be different.

When you stand strong in the strength only God can supply, God's enemy has lost already. Even the devil's mightiest attacks are powerless in the face of God's strength.

You may have heard that we're supposed to resist the devil, not trash talk him. But the Bible clearly teaches that this isn't a conversation—it's a confrontation. As a soldier in God's army, you are to resist Satan's attack while God deals with Satan himself. God doesn't need your help to do that.

Your soul—the part of you that goes on after death—remains untouchable by the enemy when you accept God's rescue. Even when Satan does his worst, God has already given His best. . .so the outcome of this struggle should never be in doubt.

When is the best time to remind yourself that Satan loses in the end? How can this knowledge change the way you face him? Why is this sometimes so hard?

BE THE MAN WHO DOESN'T LET HIS PAST DICTATE HIS FUTURE

No, dear brothers and sisters, I have not achieved it, but I focus on this one thing: Forgetting the past and looking forward to what lies ahead, I press on to reach the end of the race and receive the heavenly prize for which God, through Christ Jesus, is calling us.
PHILIPPIANS 3:13–14 NLT

As a religious teacher, Jesus called some unlikely disciples. A bunch of them were fishermen, not known to be the best or brightest of their day, and one was a tax collector—basically a Jewish traitor who collected money for the Roman empire. Then there was Paul, a bloodthirsty Pharisee bent on snuffing out Christianity. Nothing about these men's questionable pasts qualified them for the honor of learning at the Son of God's feet or imparting God's wisdom to others.

Moses was raised by the oppressors of the Israelite nation and fled after committing murder. David was a murderer *and* an adulterer. Joseph was a tattletale whose brothers hated him for his pride.

The Bible overflows with stories of men whose pasts were redeemed by God for His glory. The same can be true for you.

Have you lived a sinful life? Sure. Who hasn't? Are you worried you're too old to change? Those worries are unfounded: Jesus' sacrifice has set us free from the sins of our past and set us apart for God's use. But when we keep fixating on our past, we can never move toward God's future for us.

If Paul had dwelled on his former misdeeds, we wouldn't have half of the New Testament. If Moses had let his fear stop him from calling on Pharaoh, he wouldn't have led the Israelites out of Egypt. If you let your past sins stop you from obeying God's call, you'll miss out on seeing Him act in and through you.

Does your past get in the way of following God? How can you thank Him for rescuing you and move on in grace?

BE THE MAN WHO STANDS FIRM

*Therefore, my dear brothers and sisters, stand firm. Let nothing
move you. Always give yourselves fully to the work of the Lord,
because you know that your labor in the Lord is not in vain.*

1 CORINTHIANS 15:58 NIV

There's a simple beauty in the process of putting pen to paper. It is evidence that you were here. You made your mark in the world. If you were writing a book, the words would remain until you scratched them out or burnt the paper.

Then computers came along. People started typing things in word processing programs. At last, people with bad penmanship could express themselves—and in less time than it took to write things out in longhand. But it took a few years for AutoSave to become a feature, so if you spent all afternoon writing only to have the power go out or your computer freeze, you lost everything. You might as well have gone to the beach instead of writing anything at all.

How frustrating it is to labor in vain! Thank goodness for the AutoSave feature and backup versions that exist in "the cloud." We can work hard, assured that our work won't suddenly disappear.

In today's verse, the apostle Paul encouraged the church of Corinth to live in light of God's AutoSave feature. When they were frustrated by persecution, a lack of personal growth, or the grief of lost loved ones, they weren't better off going to the beach and calling it a day. They could stand solid against disappointment and frustration, firm in the knowledge that their labor in the Lord was not in vain. And so can we. When your circumstances make Christianity seem less appealing than the world's easy (but false) offers, stand firm. Don't give up. Keep working for God's glory. All your progress has been saved, and God will reward you for keeping the faith.

Have you ever been tempted to give up
on Christianity? What helps you stand firm?

BE THE MAN WHO KEEPS
THE DIVIDING WALL BROKEN

Deceit fills hearts that are plotting evil; joy fills hearts that are planning peace! No harm comes to the godly, but the wicked have their fill of trouble. The LORD detests lying lips, but he delights in those who tell the truth.
PROVERBS 12:20–22 NLT

Why do you think God detests lying lips? Is "thou shalt not bear false witness" (or, in other words, *lie*) just an arbitrary command?

Probably not. Maybe the reason God hates lying is because of the effect it has on courage. Without courage, it's easy to believe that God is so harsh and cruel that you have to hide behind lies for safety. But do you honestly think God doesn't know. . .or couldn't find out?

The truth is, God forgives any sin you confess and then removes it from your record. He strongly desires to see you get back on the right path—*His* path. Manipulating the truth only leads to confusion and frustration. Lies require energy that could be diverted to God's plan for you.

Detesting lies seems more like a logical response now, doesn't it?

Truth tellers get God's approval. They advance His message, refuse to waste time, and recognize the absurdity of running from God. These people are courageous and confident, refusing to let lies erect a dividing wall between their heart and God's Spirit.

Each of God's rules has a purpose, and it often involves improving your relationship with Him—as well as with others.

Has lying ever affected your friendship with God? Have you ever considered that God detests lies because He knows they hurt you?

BE THE MAN WHO FINDS STRENGTH IN OBEDIENCE

*"Then you will have success if you are careful to observe
the decrees and laws that the LORD gave Moses for Israel.
Be strong and courageous. Do not be afraid or discouraged."*
1 CHRONICLES 22:13 NIV

King David, who was currently on the throne, gave instruction to his son Solomon, who'd soon take his place.

It wasn't strategy that David spoke of. It wasn't the cleaning schedule. It wasn't the intense demands Solomon might face. Instead, David knew that Solomon's relationship with God would make or break his leadership.

David knew how easy it was for a king's brain to grow discouraged and fearful after a full day of complicated decisions. Such a mindset leads to a place of weakness and vulnerability. No king wants that. So David told his son the key to his success: obeying God and gripping the strength and courage that He offered.

Solomon would have to trust when it was hard to trust, obey when God's commands contradicted his plans, and stay courageous when the storm clouds of fear started to gather. Is it any wonder that Solomon asked God for the wisdom to lead the people?

You need strength. That isn't a question—it's a fact. The two most famous kings of Israel admitted this, identified the source of their strength, and prioritized it in their administrations. They knew that unless they passionately pursued a strong and strength-sharing God, their power was really no power at all.

Do you strive to make your pursuit of strength a generational pursuit?
How might you pass along what you're learning to someone in your family?

BE THE MAN WHO KNOWS THE SOURCE OF SUCCESS

Uzziah sought God during the days of Zechariah,
who taught him to fear God. And as long as the king
sought guidance from the LORD, God gave him success.
2 CHRONICLES 26:5 NLT

Success is often associated with trailblazers who find wealth, power, or the mastery of some ability. We hear the rags-to-riches story of some leader and think, "They've sure made a success of themselves," or we assign success to star athletes on account of their winning.

The faithful man, however, forgoes such a definition, seeing it as rooted in selfishness. True success is found in the original meaning of the word *succeed*, which is "to follow after." At its root, success is simply the accomplishment of a desired end.

We need to think of success not in terms of trailblazing, but in terms of following. We can only be successful if we follow the trail marks and arrive at the proper destination. This can be a big mental shift for those of us who think asking for directions is an admission of failure.

Second Chronicles tells the story of Uzziah, the boy-king of Judah who had military success when he sought guidance from the Lord. "Uzziah provided the entire army with shields, spears, helmets, coats of mail, bows, and sling stones. And he built structures on the walls of Jerusalem, designed by experts to protect those who shot arrows and hurled large stones from the towers and the corners of the wall. His fame spread far and wide, for the LORD gave him marvelous help, and he became very powerful" (26:14–15 NLT).

But that power led Uzziah into self-reliance, bringing his success to an end (26:16). If we want success, we must seek God's guidance and run from self-reliance.

How do you define success? Why does
self-reliance lead to failure instead of success?

BE THE MAN WHO SEEKS THE KINGDOM

But seek ye first the kingdom of God, and his righteousness;
and all these things shall be added unto you.
MATTHEW 6:33 KJV

When you are hired for a job, your employer has a few responsibilities. Under the Occupational Safety and Health Act (OSHA) of 1970, employers are required to provide "a safe and healthful workplace."

For you to do your job, employers must provide you with adequate training and equipment and ensure safety regulations are being followed. Employers can't expect employees to succeed in the workplace if they don't equip them for success.

Today's verse is all about equipping kingdom seekers for success. While some people use Matthew 6:25–34 to say that Christians will always have enough food to eat and clothes to wear, that's not exactly the point. Instead, these verses teach that we don't need to worry about our food and clothes because God will make sure we have what we need to do His will. If God gets the most glory from your sharing food with neighbors, He'll supply the extra food for you. But if He gets the most glory from your remaining faithful to Him through hunger and cold, He'll provide those conditions as well.

Seeking the kingdom doesn't mean you'll always love what you are given—it means you'll be given what you need in order to share God's love. And if God cares more about His image-bearers than the birds and flowers, He'll go to greater lengths than OSHA to equip you for the job He's called you to do.

How does seeking God's kingdom differ from seeking your
own plans? What job has God called you to do for Him today?

BE THE MAN WHO WANTS TO KNOW MORE

As a dog returns to its vomit, so a fool repeats his foolishness.
There is more hope for fools than for people who think they are wise.
PROVERBS 26:11–12 NLT

Imagine this scenario: Alexander Graham Bell, Thomas Edison, Albert Einstein, and a host of the world's greatest minds are attending a party, demonstrating their inventions and formulas. Suddenly, a guy walks in and starts using big words and flowery speech. But it soon becomes evident to everyone that this man actually has no idea what he's talking about. He's just trying to fit in. The brilliant attendees could contradict the visitor quickly and easily—but they'd rather stand by and watch as the man digs himself deeper and deeper into humiliation.

When you think you know it all, you belittle everyone else. You feel certain no one can teach you anything. You might even tell God that His work in your life is no longer mysterious because you already understand it. God, however, takes greater delight in those who admit their thinking is foolish than those who believe they could teach Him a thing or two. No one can match wits with God.

It always takes courage to admit you could use some wisdom—to admit that you've played the critically acclaimed role of a fool. But such a confession will prove to everyone that you can listen without trying to impress.

Be a courageous fool who realizes that learning is the best part of knowing.

When you approach God, do you behave like a teachable fool or a
know-it-all? How wise do you think you are compared to God's knowledge?

BE THE MAN WHO ACCEPTS (AND LIVES) JESUS' RIGHTEOUSNESS

For Christ has already accomplished the purpose for which the law was given. As a result, all who believe in him are made right with God.

ROMANS 10:4 NLT

Being a faithful man means living in a right relationship with God. But what does that even mean?

The bad news is that there's nothing we can do to make things right with God. He's perfectly holy and we are anything but. The good news is that Jesus did all that work for us by becoming the perfect sacrifice. God has accepted Jesus' sacrifice and welcomed us into a right relationship through our faith in Jesus.

So trying to be righteous is useless, right? Paul writes in Philippians 3:8–9 (NLT), "Yes, everything else is worthless when compared with the infinite value of knowing Christ Jesus my Lord. For his sake I have discarded everything else, counting it all as garbage, so that I could gain Christ and become one with him. I no longer count on my own righteousness through obeying the law; rather, I become righteous through faith in Christ. For God's way of making us right with himself depends on faith."

Righteousness without faith is definitely worthless. But faith without righteousness is problematic too. First John 3:7 (NLT) says, "Dear children, don't let anyone deceive you about this: When people do what is right, it shows that they are righteous, even as Christ is righteous."

For righteousness to be present in our lives, we first need to accept Jesus' righteousness through faith in His sacrifice—then we must do what is right in order to show His righteousness to the world around us. To be righteous, we must realize that nothing we do is enough. . .yet do it anyway because we're grateful that Jesus has done it for us.

How does Jesus' righteousness inspire you to live more righteously? How do you know the right thing to do?

BE THE MAN WHO MINDS HIS MONEY

Dishonest money dwindles away, but whoever
gathers money little by little makes it grow.
PROVERBS 13:11 NIV

Get-rich-quick schemes are as old as the Garden of Eden. (What else could you call the serpent's promise of great reward in exchange for breaking one tiny rule?) The idea of getting rich with little effort is incredibly appealing. We can all think of good ways to use a windfall of cash.

The Nigerian prince email scam is one of the most infamous get-rich-quick schemes in recent history, not because of its ability to deceive but because of how laughably obvious and ill-conceived it is. And yet, there's a reason we still get those emails from time to time. The misspelled words and the nonsensical premise of sharing our bank account details to unlock a dead man's hidden millions are designed so that only the most foolish would fall for them.

Before we laugh at the ones who take the bait, however, we should examine how we mind our own money. The reason get-rich-quick schemes work is because they appeal to our desire for instant gratification. If you find yourself living paycheck to paycheck, never putting money into a savings account, you may be your own Nigerian prince.

If you think budgeting lacks spiritual importance, think again. Our approach to money reveals how we value the resources God has entrusted to us. If we spend our whole paycheck on gratifying our selfish desires, we've fallen into the devil's scam. But if we tithe and save little by little, we will be able to give freely whenever the Spirit prompts us.

Do you have a budget? How does your spending reflect your spiritual values?

BE THE MAN WHO PURSUES UNFAILING LOVE

*Whoever pursues righteousness and unfailing
love will find life, righteousness, and honor.*
PROVERBS 21:21 NLT

Think of an honorable man. Is he loud or quiet? Brash or considerate? Does he draw attention to his good deeds, or does he do good deeds when no one is looking?

Now think of a man seeking to honor himself. He loves the spotlight. He revels in the compliments of others. He wants to be loved but isn't motivated by a love for others.

People who live honorably rarely seek honor for themselves. People who seek honor for themselves rarely find it. Why? Because honor is the byproduct of a righteous life and unconditional love. You can't go straight for it because that's not how you get it. What you pursue instead is love.

As recipients of the greatest love ever given, we have an intimate understanding of what this looks like. First John 4:10–11 (NLT) says, "This is real love—not that we loved God, but that he loved us and sent his Son as a sacrifice to take away our sins. Dear friends, since God loved us that much, we surely ought to love each other."

Loving others naturally leads to a righteous life. First John 4:17 (NLT) continues, "And as we live in God, our love grows more perfect. So we will not be afraid on the day of judgment, but we can face him with confidence because we live like Jesus here in this world."

If you want to be an honorable, faithful man, you can't get better than living like Jesus. By pursuing His unfailing love that leads to righteousness, you'll get eternal life, righteousness, and honor. Other people may recognize your love and honor you, but that won't matter—the honor that comes from pleasing God is the only honor worth having.

Do you find yourself seeking honor sometimes? If so,
how might you pursue unfailing love instead?

BE THE MAN WHO ACCEPTS STRENGTH

*Then there came again and touched me one like the appearance
of a man, and he strengthened me, and said, O man greatly
beloved, fear not: peace be unto thee, be strong, yea, be strong.
And when he had spoken unto me, I was strengthened, and
said, Let my lord speak; for thou hast strengthened me.*
DANIEL 10:18–19 KJV

Telling yourself that you are strong is just wishful thinking. Lying to yourself will never make these whispers true.

Men have been lying to themselves since the beginning of time, telling themselves that they actually are whatever they want to be. And almost all of these things they tell themselves have one thing in common—courage. No man wants to be weak.

If God says you are strong, then you are strong—stronger than you could ever be on your own. You can't equate your workout at the gym with true strength. God doesn't care how much weight you can lift. Even if you could bench press a tractor, you'd never be as impressive as the Creator of the universe, the one who flung stars into space, carved out canyons, and still listens to your voice.

God gave Daniel strength, and Daniel knew it because he could pay attention to God without fear. When you think about how impressive God is—how far His power, creation, and love for us extends—it's easy to become overwhelmed. However, don't let this weakness replace the courage you need to approach Him. God gives us this courage because He always chooses friendship over intimidation.

How often do you dwell on how amazing God truly is?
How does your friendship with God give you strength?

BE THE MAN WHO DOESN'T PROCRASTINATE

*"You also must be ready all the time, for the
Son of Man will come when least expected."*
LUKE 12:40 NLT

Deadlines are important. If a book isn't delivered to the publisher on time, for instance, the publisher's production schedule suffers, throwing their budget out of whack. Some authors are better with deadlines than others. Douglas Adams, author of the comic sci-fi classic *The Hitchhiker's Guide to the Galaxy*, once said, "I love deadlines. I love the whooshing noise they make as they go by."

It's one thing to procrastinate when you know a project's due date, but what about when a task has no clear deadline? Jesus told this parable in Luke 12:35–38 (NLT):

"Be dressed for service and keep your lamps burning, as though you were waiting for your master to return from the wedding feast. Then you will be ready to open the door and let him in the moment he arrives and knocks. The servants who are ready and waiting for his return will be rewarded. I tell you the truth, he himself will seat them, put on an apron, and serve them as they sit and eat! He may come in the middle of the night or just before dawn. But whenever he comes, he will reward the servants who are ready."

When there is no clear due date, working hard is even *more* important! If we're found faithful, we'll be rewarded. If we aren't faithful, well. . . "The master will return unannounced and unexpected, and he will cut the servant in pieces and banish him with the unfaithful" (Luke 12:46 NLT).

These consequences won't be put off to accommodate our schedule, so we shouldn't put off our responsibilities either. Yes, this includes our work projects, but more importantly, it includes our spiritual responsibility to share the gospel.

*Are you known for missing deadlines? How can
you better prioritize your responsibilities?*

BE THE MAN WHO AVOIDS TIME THEFT

*Let him that stole steal no more: but rather let him labour,
working with his hands the thing which is good, that
he may have to give to him that needeth.*
Ephesians 4:28 kjv

Most people would agree that embezzlement is wrong. Whether you're working at a fast-food restaurant or as the CEO of a major corporation, swiping money from the cash register is a punishable crime. But it's possible to steal from the company, a little bit every day, and still avoid jail time. What's worse is that seemingly everyone does it. How? Time theft.

Time theft is getting paid for work you haven't done. It's the extra-long breaks and lunches that eat into your scheduled work time. It's when you show up late and say you just forgot to punch in. It's checking your personal email, scrolling through social media, playing online games, and simply messing around while you are on the clock. It's hard to track, but just about every business experiences the effects of time theft, and it adds up to billions of dollars in lost productivity.

While time theft isn't illegal, it is immoral. It is evidence of a selfish mind that justifies itself by saying, "My company doesn't pay me enough for what I'm worth, so this is what they get." It's evidence of a lazy attitude that thinks, *No one will notice if I slack off a bit. I'll fit right in.*

Time theft is unacceptable for a faithful man. Not only does it reflect poorly on the one we're truly working for (check out Colossians 3:23), it deprives us of the blessing of having enough to give to those who *can't* work. God wants us to be generous toward others, which is extremely difficult to do when we place our jobs at risk by stealing from our employers.

The next time you are tempted to take a long lunch or goof around at work, remember that your goal is to have enough to share with others—and that God is your true boss. Don't be selfish or lazy at work. Work hard for God.

How is your work ethic? How might you become more generous with your paycheck?

BE THE MAN WHO DISMISSES FOOLISHNESS

God has made the wisdom of this world look foolish. Since God in his wisdom saw to it that the world would never know him through human wisdom, he has used our foolish preaching to save those who believe. It is foolish to the Jews, who ask for signs from heaven. And it is foolish to the Greeks, who seek human wisdom. So when we preach that Christ was crucified, the Jews are offended and the Gentiles say it's all nonsense.

1 CORINTHIANS 1:20–23 NLT

You might've heard parents or grandparents tell you that if you swallow bubble gum, it won't digest for years. That cracking your knuckles when you're young will give you arthritis. That carrots make your eyesight better. That you shouldn't shave your hair because it makes it come back thicker.

It turns out, these bits of wisdom (and dozens like them) aren't true. You might have believed them because they were told to you by people you trust. You had no reason not to trust those people—they just had an incomplete picture of the truth about gum, knuckles, carrots, and hair.

When someone comes to you with statistics, scientific research, or even a parent's supposed wisdom, you expect facts from that person. But in the end, this wisdom might well prove to be no more than foolishness.

Many of those same people might dismiss statements like "God exists," "God loves people," and "Jesus offers forgiveness." They see these ideas as foolish and misguided, even though what they're hearing is *true* wisdom indeed!

A faithful man understands that guesses can't override what God says is true.

Why does disbelief in God make no sense? Which do you prioritize: God's truth or the daily news?

BE THE MAN WHO WELCOMES THE IMPOSSIBLE

Sing to the LORD with grateful praise; make music to our God on the harp. He covers the sky with clouds; he supplies the earth with rain and makes grass grow on the hills. . . . His pleasure is not in the strength of the horse, nor his delight in the legs of the warrior; the LORD delights in those who fear him, who put their hope in his unfailing love.

PSALM 147:7–8, 10–11 NIV

You are a warrior because God made you one. You can do nothing on your own. Without His help, even your best efforts look embarrassing and misguided.

If you're like most men, you probably like to show off your warrior identity. But looks can be deceiving. How often have you trembled beneath a confident pose? Felt your mouth turn dry as cotton while you spoke?

When you say you can handle anything but know deep down that you're bragging about the impossible, just remember that you serve the God of the impossible. In Jeremiah 32:27 (NIV), He asked, "I am the LORD, the God of all mankind. Is anything too hard for me?" The answer will always be no.

No amount of physical strength can compare to God's power. Working out doesn't hurt, but it's not what God delights in when He looks at you. Respect God and put every bit of trust you have in His love, which never quits, breaks, or stops reaching for you.

Life can seem like asking a five-year-old to complete a thousand-piece puzzle by lunchtime—impossible. Yet when God gives you an assignment, you must leave your insecurities behind, trusting that He'll provide the help you need.

How scared are you of failure? Does the word impossible inspire you to trust God even more?

BE THE MAN WHO SIMPLY STANDS FIRM

So, if you think you are standing firm,
be careful that you don't fall!
1 CORINTHIANS 10:12 NIV

Peter was a living example of the warning in today's verse. As soon as he thought he was standing firm, he fell. . .hard. No doubt thinking there was no other disciple as dedicated or brave as he was, he made brash promises and bold statements. He was a proverbial foam hand—Jesus' number one guy. But Jesus didn't buy it. And He certainly didn't celebrate it.

Peter was incapable of giving a fair and accurate self-evaluation. He must have thought he was top of the class and more reliable than most. Yet unlike Jesus, when Peter made a promise, he consistently broke it. His self-proclaimed strength was exposed as a profound blind spot of weakness.

If this happened to you, would you be able to sleep at night? Would you ask yourself why you had such trouble holding your tongue? Would you wonder why you were motivated to make promises you couldn't keep? Yes, you might have been trying to impress the Son of God, but maybe you overlooked the most obvious truth—it's not about what you *think* you can do but what God *absolutely* can do.

Peter refused to admit weakness, even after blowing it over and over again. He still thought he could master his impulsiveness without God's help.

When you stand firm, remember who is holding you up. You don't need to buy a T-shirt that says you are standing firm. You don't need to wave to the crowds. Pride has no place in standing firm. You stand with help.

Are you ever tempted to boast about your ability to stand strong?
How might this boasting turn people away from seeking God?

BE THE MAN WHO IS LOYAL

*A friend is always loyal, and a brother
is born to help in time of need.*
PROVERBS 17:17 NLT

The phrase "I've got your back," is probably a recent addition to the English language, dating back to World War II. As soldiers advanced on retreating armies, they used small squads of men to clear out enemy defensive positions. A soldier approaching these strongholds would turn to his buddy and say, "Watch my back," in the hopes that his comrade would defend him against enemies shooting from behind. The request would be answered with, "I've got your back."

Although our enemies remain unseen, we live in a spiritual warzone, and it is vital that we have a loyal squad of men watching our backs. Ephesians 6:12 (NLT) says, "For we are not fighting against flesh-and-blood enemies, but against evil rulers and authorities of the unseen world, against mighty powers in this dark world, and against evil spirits in the heavenly places."

The last thing we want is for one of our friends to turn us over to the enemy, which is exactly why we should be loyal to our friends. Our loyalty should not be the type that covers up sin or makes excuses for each other. Rather, we should commit first to following God and His commandments. Then we should commit to helping our brothers do likewise.

It isn't when things are going well that our loyalties will be tested, but when everything seems to be falling apart. When our first loyalty is to God, the Holy Spirit empowers us to be better friends and loyal brothers-in-arms. If our loyalty to God starts to crumble, our brothers will hopefully have our back, reminding us who the enemy really is.

Are you loyal to God first? How can you prove
your loyalty to your brothers-in-arms?

BE THE MAN WHO IS
WILLING TO BE VULNERABLE

*Therefore confess your sins to each other and pray for
each other so that you may be healed. The prayer of
a righteous person is powerful and effective.*
JAMES 5:16 NIV

A faithful man of honor is able in many ways. He's likeable (able to be liked) and reliable (able to be relied on). However, we don't often think of him as being vulnerable. What does that even mean? Able to be. . . *vulnered*?

The root of the word *vulnerable* implies being wounded. If you enter the battlefield without proper armor, you make yourself vulnerable to attack. That's a bad thing. The Bible is clear that a man of faith should be fully equipped to withstand such attacks, to be *invulnerable* to the enemy: "Put on the full armor of God, so that you can take your stand against the devil's schemes" (Ephesians 6:11 NIV).

But there's a good kind of vulnerability too. Undergoing surgery requires a patient to be wounded in order to be healed. Because we trust the intentions and skills of the surgeon, we make ourselves vulnerable.

In the same way, we make ourselves emotionally vulnerable to spouses, family, and friends. When we are experiencing some internal issue, it's healthy to open the wound and allow trusted people to pray for us, to help us put the issue in the hands of the greatest healer of all.

If you trust God's intentions and skills with whatever causes you pain, He will prove Himself faithful to you, even if He chooses not to relieve your suffering the way you desire. With each trusted companion who promises to pray for you, God's faithfulness is proven once more.

How did the apostle Paul react when his vulnerability didn't lead
to his desired healing (2 Corinthians 12:7-10)? With whom
can you be vulnerable about your struggles?

BE THE MAN WHO IS THIRSTY FOR MORE

O God, thou art my God; early will I seek thee: my soul thirsteth for thee,
my flesh longeth for thee in a dry and thirsty land, where no water is;
to see thy power and thy glory, so as I have seen thee in the sanctuary.
Because thy lovingkindness is better than life, my lips shall praise thee.
Thus will I bless thee while I live: I will lift up my hands in thy name.
PSALM 63:1–4 KJV

In the movie *Castaway*, Tom Hanks plays a survivor on a deserted island. He's surrounded by water but has little to drink. His lips are chapped, his voice is hoarse, and the appearance of his entire body screams that he needs to be refreshed.

Similarly, King David described what it was like to be on a proverbial desert island, far away from God. Everything about the experience filled the king with bold desperation to return to his source of nourishment. His spiritual tank was empty, and he knew God was the missing ingredient.

Do you want God that much? Or do you sometimes think of Him as a crutch—an item to pick up only after all other options have failed? Here's the catch: there never were any other options—you need His help for *everything*.

It's okay to recognize that you're thirsty for spiritual water that only God can offer. This, in fact, is the only good response. Being needy is great when it leads to the God who meets needs.

You seek God because God satisfies. Longing for His relief isn't a sign of weakness—it's the perfect approach for a faithful man who refuses to stay in the desert.

Do you find it hard to admit you can't do everything on your own?
Are you courageous enough to show your desperation to God?

BE THE MAN WHO PRAYS FOR WEAK MEN

*Epaphras, a member of your own fellowship and a servant of
Christ Jesus, sends you his greetings. He always prays earnestly
for you, asking God to make you strong and perfect, fully
confident that you are following the whole will of God.*
COLOSSIANS 4:12 NLT

What if you had the opportunity to petition the God of the universe to
step into someone's life and give that person a taste of divine strength?

Seeking strength doesn't have to be solely for yourself. Plenty of people are wallowing in the muddy pit of weakness right now, believing their
life will never be anything more. If you can't convince them on your own
to give God a try, ask God to pursue them and introduce them to real
strength.

You know weak men who live in the cycle of addiction, pornography, and failed relationships. They want to change, but they dismiss the
possibility as a mere fairy tale. *It'd be nice to have this kind of strength*, they
think. *If only it were real.* It may be so far from their experience that they
start viewing the strength they see in other people's lives as weakness.

Everyone's been there. It might happen when someone intentionally
rejects or walks away from God. Or it could be a knockout after a twelve-round bout with pride. It could even stem from the fear of walking away
from weakness.

Many people need to discover that the strength they need is the
strength God offers. Pray for these people today.

> When was the last time you prayed for God to strengthen
> someone you know? How might praying that kind of prayer
> today make an impact you've so far been unable to make?

BE THE MAN WHO RESPECTS HIS ELDERS

*Thou shalt rise up before the hoary head, and honour the
face of the old man, and fear thy God: I am the LORD.*
LEVITICUS 19:32 KJV

Old age is hard won but often ill rewarded. With experience and wisdom come aches, pains, and memory loss. Comedian George Burns once quipped, "By the time you're eighty years old you've learned everything. You only have to remember it."

Despite these issues, elderly folks have a lot to offer younger generations. The Bible has a few things to say about respecting and learning from our elders: "With the ancient is wisdom; and in length of days understanding" (Job 12:12 KJV); "Gray hair is a crown of splendor; it is attained in the way of righteousness" (Proverbs 16:31 NIV); "Rebuke not an elder, but intreat him as a father; and the younger men as brethren" (1 Timothy 5:1 KJV).

What can we learn? First, our elders could teach us to better value spiritual matters. According to a study by the Pew Research Center, "Religion is a far bigger part of the lives of older adults than younger adults. Two-thirds of adults ages 65 and older say religion is very important to them, compared with just over half of those ages 30 to 49 and just 44 percent of those ages 18 to 29."

What else could we learn? Today's elderly folks lived without how-to videos on YouTube, learning by experience the best ways to build, fix, budget, and plan.

Lastly, many elders are prayer warriors who would love to take your requests before God's throne. The first step in learning from their wisdom is starting a conversation. Honor them by listening and inviting them into our lives. Then, when it is our turn, we can impart their knowledge to the generations which follow us.

When was the last time you had a conversation with
an elderly person? How could you honor one today?

BE THE MAN WHO LIVES BY GOD'S PRINCIPLES

*At the end of the ten days, Daniel and his three friends
looked healthier and better nourished than the young men
who had been eating the food assigned by the king.*
DANIEL 1:15 NLT

Daniel, for whom the Old Testament book is named, lived through the overthrow of the kingdom of Judah by Nebuchadnezzar. As leader of Babylon, the dominant world power at the time, Nebuchadnezzar surrounded himself with slaves from his conquered foes. They were chosen for their looks, demeanor, and ability to learn (see Daniel 1:4), and given new names and reeducated in the Babylonian traditions to ensure their allegiance to their new ruler. And if they didn't pass the reeducation, they didn't get to serve in the king's court.

For Daniel, whose country had just been conquered, being chosen from among his peers to enjoy food and wine from the king's table might have seemed like a fortuitous turn of events. As long as he didn't cause trouble with his new overlord, he could enjoy a much easier life than his countrymen. But Daniel wasn't that kind of guy.

Daniel 1:8–20 tells us that Daniel and his friends politely refused to eat those things from the king's table that were unclean according to Hebrew law. In response to their loyalty to the true ruler of the world, "God gave these four young men an unusual aptitude for understanding every aspect of literature and wisdom. And God gave Daniel the special ability to interpret the meanings of visions and dreams" (1:17 NLT).

Daniel could have taken the easy route, but he chose to live according to God's principles instead. Today, you have the same choice. Regardless of your dietary situation, you can either live according to the world's standards and participate in their reeducation efforts, or you can choose to honor God and live by His principles. Which will it be?

How is the world trying to reeducate you? What would have happened
had Daniel and his friends eaten the king's food and wine?

BE THE MAN WHO SPEAKS UP

The sayings of King Lemuel contain this message, which his mother taught him. O my son, O son of my womb, O son of my vows. . . . Speak up for those who cannot speak for themselves; ensure justice for those being crushed. Yes, speak up for the poor and helpless, and see that they get justice.
Proverbs 31:1–2, 8–9 NLT

As Mr. Smith stood to speak about greed and corruption, some thought he was foolishly throwing away his political career. Others worked overtime to push him over the edge. A few, however, stood in his corner, knowing his efforts might prove futile yet strongly hoping his words would be heard. Perhaps Mr. Smith could do what no one had yet been able to do.

If this story sounds familiar, that's because it's the plot of the classic movie *Mr. Smith Goes to Washington*, starring Jimmy Stewart as the title character.

You too have a certain amount of influence, large or small, wherever you go. It takes guts to speak up for others, especially when you feel no one else is listening. It's always easier, after all, to just stay silent. However, for those misunderstood, mistreated, poverty-stricken souls, your voice may be the only hope in sight.

These opportunities aren't just limited to social programs—everyone, including you, has an opportunity to change a life. When you speak for those who lack a voice, new friendships start to form, leading to new opportunities to share God's life-changing message of salvation. That opportunity can change eternity for someone in need.

Maybe that's why you're here—people need to know that God has sent help.

Do you feel uncomfortable speaking up for those who have no voice? If so, how can you change your outlook by identifying with those in need?

BE THE MAN WHO'S NOT AFRAID OF STRENGTH

*The disciples were in trouble far away from land, for a strong
wind had risen, and they were fighting heavy waves.*
MATTHEW 14:24 NLT

Nature's strength—the kind found in tornadoes, hurricanes, earthquakes, tsunamis, and blizzards—can be impressive but frightening.

The disciples were in a boat in the middle of the lake when they witnessed the full extent of this power firsthand. On their own, they had little chance of battling the storm and reaching shore.

The closest most of us ever come to feeling the disciples' terror is when we're sitting in a storm shelter or waiting out a hailstorm in our car. We hear the earth rumbling, the dishes clattering. Fear creeps in as we imagine what the world will look like once the storm passes.

In Matthew 14, Jesus proved that even nature's strength is subject to God's. This storm wasn't over yet, but when Jesus spoke, the raging chaos stopped—no questions or delays.

The strength of a storm is a perfect image of chaos—of a frightening power far out of our control. But God has no problem controlling it. And since God has the strength to stop a storm, why shouldn't you believe He can calm the storm that rages in you? In fact, He can do even better— He can *give* you the strength to do the impossible.

Which type of strength seems the most overwhelming to you?
How can it help to know that even this power is subject to God?

BE THE MAN WHO DOESN'T GIVE IN TO PEER PRESSURE

Do not set foot on the path of the wicked or walk in the way of evildoers.
Avoid it, do not travel on it; turn from it and go on your way.
PROVERBS 4:14–15 NIV

It's nice to be included. We're wired to crave the safety and acceptance which comes from being part of the crowd. But when the crowd is going the wrong way, safety is the last thing we'll find.

As our culture drifts further from worshipping God and closer to self-deification, things once recognized as sin are becoming celebrated cultural icons. *Wickedness* is no longer a socially acceptable term because of the world's desire to define itself in its own terms.

We can either flow with the world's momentum or stand up for truth as defined in the Bible. Taking a stand won't be easy. We'll surely offend some and make enemies of others, but it is not for us to decide what happens to those who oppose God.

Second Thessalonians 1:6–9 (NIV) says, "God is just: He will pay back trouble to those who trouble you and give relief to you who are troubled, and to us as well. This will happen when the Lord Jesus is revealed from heaven in blazing fire with his powerful angels. He will punish those who do not know God and do not obey the gospel of our Lord Jesus. They will be punished with everlasting destruction and shut out from the presence of the Lord and from the glory of his might."

When it seems easier to just go along with the world, or when your friends try to convince you sin is no big deal, remember the big picture. Get out of there. Avoid the dangers. Move along toward righteousness.

Why do you think Proverbs 4:14-15 warns against wickedness in multiple ways? Are there any sins you are tempted to label as "no big deal"?

BE THE MAN WHO WALKS IN THE LIGHT

*When Jesus spoke again to the people, he said, "I am
the light of the world. Whoever follows me will never
walk in darkness, but will have the light of life."*
JOHN 8:12 NIV

The Jewish festival Sukkot—also called the Feast of Booths or the Feast
of Tabernacles—is celebrated yearly in September or October. The festival commemorates God's provision for the Israelites in the wilderness
after their exodus from Egypt.

In Jesus' time, the festival ended with the lighting of huge candelabras at the temple in Jerusalem. The candelabras could be seen from miles
around the city and called to mind the pillar of fire that led the Israelites
through the wilderness generations prior. "By day the LORD went ahead
of them in a pillar of cloud to guide them on their way and by night in a
pillar of fire to give them light, so that they could travel by day or night"
(Exodus 13:21 NIV).

This is the backdrop to today's verse. As Jesus stood with the crowds
at the lighting of the gigantic candelabras during Sukkot, He identified
Himself as the light who leads the world to the promised land. His audience would have understood the implication of this message: Jesus was
God in the flesh, and He came to lead them into the kingdom of heaven
just as the pillar of fire had led the Israelites to the promised land.

Jesus is still the light of the world. He is still the God whose flesh
was pierced so that we could be saved. When we follow Him, living according to the gospel and sharing His love with others, we are not walking in darkness. We are following the pillar of fire and reflecting His light
to the dark world around us.

Are you following Jesus' pillar of fire toward the promised land of His kingdom?
How are you reflecting His light into the darkness of this world?

BE THE MAN WHO STRIVES FOR PERFECTION

*"But you are to be perfect, even as
your Father in heaven is perfect."*
MATTHEW 5:48 NLT

In the Sermon on the Mount, Jesus set new guidelines for living holy lives. Instead of simply refraining from murder, for instance, we are to reject hate altogether. Likewise, we are to love our enemies, go the extra mile for others, and even gouge out our eyes if they tempt us to lust. Jesus wasn't messing around!

This section of the sermon concludes with a seemingly impossible task: "But you are to be perfect, even as your Father in heaven is perfect" (Matthew 5:48 NLT).

Faithful men don't get easy passes. Jesus was serious about perfection and, fortunately for us, explained exactly how to get there.

Matthew 19:16–30 tells the story of a rich man who claimed to have followed the Hebrew Law to the letter, yet knew he was still missing something. In Matthew 19:21 Jesus tells him, "If you want to be perfect, go and sell all your possessions and give the money to the poor, and you will have treasure in heaven. Then come, follow me."

By human standards, the rich man was pretty close to perfection. But Jesus revealed the one thing standing in the way: this man's wealth meant more to him than following Jesus.

The only way to be perfect is to give up whatever stands in the way of following Jesus—because Jesus is the only perfect sacrifice for our sins. If riches are holding you back, sell everything and give the money to God. If you're gripped by pride, humble yourself in your own eyes first, then crawl to Christ on your knees.

Perfection is possible only through Jesus. We are called to forsake everything that stands between us and Him.

Is anything standing between you and Christ?
If so, how can you lay it down at Jesus' feet?

BE THE MAN WHO ACCEPTS SUSTAINED STRENGTH

And the child grew and became strong in spirit; and he lived in the wilderness until he appeared publicly to Israel.
LUKE 1:80 NIV

John the Baptist was born with a purpose. He was a voice in the wilderness—a human megaphone that shouted, "Hey! Have you noticed Jesus?" And in doing so, John pointed others toward the same strength he himself possessed.

John was more than willing to look foolish and even weak to those who didn't understand. He was given a purpose—and then the strength—to do something God created him to do. John didn't care if people made fun of him or thought him strange. God's strength sustained this preacher, so when the time came to introduce Jesus to the world, John didn't hesitate. And once God's Son actually arrived, he began to quickly step back. Jesus had a much bigger job to do, and John was determined that he wouldn't stand in the way.

This man grew strong in spirit because he kept close to God. He chose obedience over recognition—and at the right time, he set the stage for God's main attraction. Jesus' message of salvation then grew in the void left behind by a vanishing wilderness preacher named John.

God gave you a purpose, and He can also give you every ounce of strength you'll need to fulfill it. But this requires your full cooperation—a willingness to step down when God wants another to rise. Do you have that kind of strength?

Does public opinion ever sway your willingness to use the unique gift God gave you? How does God's strength enhance your purpose?

BE THE MAN WHO'S EQUIPPED FOR EVERY GOOD WORK

*All Scripture is God-breathed and is useful for teaching, rebuking,
correcting and training in righteousness, so that the servant of
God may be thoroughly equipped for every good work.*
2 TIMOTHY 3:16–17 NIV

There are many screwdrivers in the world: flat head (slotted), Phillips, Torx (star), Hex, and Robertson (square), to name a few. Each screwdriver corresponds to a specific screw head design. Try to use a Phillips screwdriver on a slotted screw, and you'll run into trouble.

One of the lesser-known screwdrivers is the Birmingham screwdriver. . .which is actually a hammer. This joke is at the expense of Birmingham, England, implying its residents solve their problems with brute force rather than using the right tools.

How does this relate to our spiritual life? Some men treat the Bible like a Birmingham screwdriver when it's actually a well-stocked toolbox. Second Timothy 3:16–17 (NIV) says, "All Scripture is God-breathed and is useful for teaching, rebuking, correcting and training in righteousness, so that the servant of God may be thoroughly equipped for every good work."

When we need to open our minds, we can turn to James 1:5 (NIV): "If any of you lacks wisdom, you should ask God, who gives generously to all without finding fault, and it will be given to you."

When we need to be corrected, 1 John 1:9 (NIV) offers the solution: "If we confess our sins, he is faithful and just and will forgive us our sins and purify us from all unrighteousness."

Whatever our situation, the Bible has the right tool for the job. But to be better craftsmen, we need to familiarize ourselves with the whole toolbox.

Have you ever treated the Bible like a hammer? What are some verses you can memorize to deal with common issues you face?

BE THE MAN WHO LIVES AS A NEW CREATION

Therefore if any man be in Christ, he is a new creature:
old things are passed away; behold, all things are become new.
2 CORINTHIANS 5:17 KJV

Imagine you were told you've just won a new sports car. For now, forget about the taxes and the increased insurance costs—just focus on the joy of this unexpected news.

Now imagine going out to the parking lot only to see your old car with a new racing stripe painted on it. Same dents, same transmission issues, same loud muffler. You'd probably want a word or two with whoever ran this "contest" because the thing you won wasn't the thing that was promised.

For some guys, inviting Jesus into their lives means little more than slapping a paint job on their old lifestyle and calling it new. That isn't what Jesus promised or what He wants for you—not even close!

When you recognize your need for a Savior, you recognize that no amount of paint can cover the sins in your life. You don't need a repair job. You need to be made new in every way. And when the Holy Spirit comes in, you *are* made new. God isn't asking you to fix things on His behalf in your life. He's asking you to stay out of the garage while He's working and allow Him to replace every single area of your life with new parts that are dedicated to receiving His love and giving Him glory.

You are a new creation, designed to run on a brand-new source of fuel. God didn't paint a racing stripe on you and call it a day. You've got His Spirit inside you, just waiting to take you to the checkered flag with His power and guidance.

Are you allowing God to work in the garage of your heart, or are you standing over His shoulder and second-guessing His choices? What would it look like to truly live as a new creation today?

BE THE MAN WHO STANDS FOR TRUTH

The Jews took up stones again to stone him. Jesus answered them, Many good works have I shewed you from my Father; for which of those works do ye stone me? The Jews answered him, saying, For a good work we stone thee not; but for blasphemy; and because that thou, being a man, makest thyself God.

JOHN 10:31–33 KJV

Sometimes, the desire for privacy is understandable. A spy, after all, won't wear a T-shirt advertising his identity, and a member of the royal family won't wear a tiara to the shopping mall. Other times, however, a refusal to speak the truth is tantamount to lying.

When Jesus came to earth, He felt and experienced human emotions. Each day, He probably wrestled with the temptation to keep His divine identity silent. Yet Jesus was the supreme man of faith and courage—truth was consistent with Him, whether it made His audience uncomfortable or not. His words directly challenged the falsehoods of His day.

Many people struggled to accept the truth that Jesus spoke—even His own family. Others, such as the Pharisees, outright rejected it, hating it so much that they eventually killed Him. His kind of truth sounded so unbelievable that His enemies saw no other option than to forcibly silence it. Only a few saw the truth behind His message.

Today, strive to know, live, and share the truth. Jesus brought it, proved it, and left it for you to explore. Be faithfully courageous, and don't keep truth to yourself.

What can you do today to courageously share
the truth? With whom will you share it first?

BE THE MAN WHO SEES STRENGTH

Therefore, brothers and sisters, in all our distress and persecution
we were encouraged about you because of your faith.
1 THESSALONIANS 3:7 NIV

Your level of spiritual strength isn't just about you. It impacts your family, friends, neighbors, coworkers, clients, and even strangers. When people are in distress, they can be encouraged by your display of a strength that can only come from God. It can make onlookers consider the possibility that weakness can be overcome.

Perhaps that's one reason why God tells Christians to associate with Christians. None of us are perfect, but the more time you spend with God and His believers, the more likely you are to witness moments of strength. On the contrary, if you never observe strength, renewal, and growth in the lives of those around you, it might be hard to believe God's promise of strength.

Whether a man is the encourager or the encouraged will depend on where he's found in the weakness/strength cycle. The church is full of broken, hurting people. . .but perfection can be found in God and His Son, Jesus. Only He can inject new life into a body, mind, and soul defined by weakness.

Often, it takes a moment of desperation to make us reach out for God's strength. But God is not some miserly being who makes it hard for you to find His strength. You can look around at any time and witness the truth—there's strength in the body of Christ! Rejoice because this strength can also be yours.

Do you think it's important for you to see God's strength lived out in the lives of people around you? Why should you want to live life with other believers?

BE THE MAN WHO RESPECTS AUTHORITY

*Everyone must submit to governing authorities. For all
authority comes from God, and those in positions of
authority have been placed there by God.*
ROMANS 13:1 NLT

Americans are born with a confused sense of respect for authority. Our country was founded on rebellion against British rule. Our presidents are chosen by an electoral college, which sometimes goes against the majority of voters. It would be easy to say, "I didn't vote for them, so I don't need to respect them." But the easy way is rarely the biblical way.

Romans 13:1 says we must submit to governing authorities because all authority comes from God. This verse was written by Paul, who would eventually be martyred for his faith by Roman authorities. Paul didn't demand respect for these leaders because they were worthy of it in themselves but rather because they were subject to a greater authority.

Though earthly leaders are not always moral, they are placed in authority by the one who sees and controls the larger picture for His own purposes. Daniel 2:21 (NLT) says, "He controls the course of world events; he removes kings and sets up other kings. He gives wisdom to the wise and knowledge to the scholars."

The message is echoed in Psalm 75:7 (NLT): "It is God alone who judges; he decides who will rise and who will fall."

So how are we to show respect to authorities who prove themselves unworthy? Through prayer and blessing. When we pray for them, we place them under God's authority instead of ours. And we are to bless them, even when they oppose us and our values. Romans 12:14 (NLT) says, "Bless those who persecute you. Don't curse them; pray that God will bless them."

*Do you struggle to respect those in authority?
How can you pray for their blessing?*

BE THE MAN WHO ISN'T HYPOCRITICAL

Such people claim they know God, but they deny him by the way they live.
They are detestable and disobedient, worthless for doing anything good.
TITUS 1:16 NLT

In 2018, Joseph Langston, a researcher at the Atheist Research Collaborative, published a study in the journal *Religion, Brain & Behavior* that linked the age at which someone chose to become an atheist with the evidence of faith's importance in the person's childhood home. The study was conducted with input from over five thousand people who had abandoned their faith.

"At the beginning of this project, the thought process was that, perhaps a growing number of people are becoming non-believers because belief was not modelled to them in any appreciable or robust way during their upbringing," Langston said in an interview with *PsyPost*, but added that the end result of the study surprised him.

One of the project's takeaways, Langston noted, was this: "The extent to which parents faithfully model their own religious beliefs to their children, works in tandem with other processes to produce unique trajectories of the timing at which one becomes an atheist: being allowed greater religious choice seems to drive the age of atheism down, but so do elevated levels of religious conflict."

So if you claim to know Christ and want to bring others to Him, especially within your own household, it's vital to back up your claims with actions consistent with that relationship. This is why today's verse is followed by examples of what God-filled lives look like.

A faithful man must exercise self-control, earn his respect, and live wisely. He must have sound faith and be filled with love and patience. When your actions back up your claim to faith, the world—and your own family—will see it for the truth it is.

Do you model your faith in front of your family? How could you pray for those who turned away from the faith as a result of their parents' hypocrisy?

BE THE MAN WHO MOVES FROM QUESTIONS TO PRAISE

*The Sovereign LORD is my strength! He makes me as
surefooted as a deer, able to tread upon the heights.*
HABAKKUK 3:19 NLT

Many scholars believe that Habakkuk worked in the temple and composed worshipful songs, some of which are written down in his book.

But before the praise began, this songwriter was filled with questions and complaints: "How long, O LORD, must I call for help? But you do not listen! 'Violence is everywhere!' I cry, but you do not come to save" (Habakkuk 1:2 NLT). God, however, answered the songsmith: "I am doing something in your own day, something you wouldn't believe even if someone told you about it" (1:5 NLT).

These words rocked the prophet's world. God's plan, he discovered, *included* the Israelites' captivity. The end result would be much better than letting people continually break His laws.

As a result, this is what the prophet concluded: "Even though the fig trees have no blossoms, and there are no grapes on the vines; even though the olive crop fails, and the fields lie empty and barren; even though the flocks die in the fields, and the cattle barns are empty, yet I will rejoice in the LORD! I will be joyful in the God of my salvation! The Sovereign LORD is my strength!" (3:17–19 NLT)

Even in the face of total failure, Habakkuk knew that God could be trusted to bring joy and strength—and that the fruits of His plan were just around the corner.

Today, take comfort in this strengthening glimpse of God's goodness.

Has God ever used your questions and complaints to alter your opinion?
How can you turn bad news into an occasion for worship?

BE THE MAN WHO KNOWS EVERYTHING'S GONNA BE ALRIGHT

He shall be like a tree planted by the rivers of water,
that bringeth forth his fruit in his season; his leaf also
shall not wither; and whatsoever he doeth shall prosper.

PSALM 1:3 KJV

Some people seem to be born for greatness. You might have someone in mind right now. Such people make great choices and stand up for what's right at seemingly the perfect time. They are great examples who may even seem larger than life.

But these same people often don't think of themselves as worthy of any accolades. During their "moment of greatness," they might've been scared senseless and simply wanted to hide. But bravery isn't the absence of fear—bravery simply tells fear who's boss.

Each of the Bible's heroes lived in that place where fear meets faith—a place in which God's voice whispered in their ears, "Everything is going to be alright." At this intersection, you get to decide: Will you be the man God needs you to be, or will you shrink back and wonder if you'll ever have this chance again?

Psalm 1:3 describes the man who chooses the first option as a tree nourished by the perpetual flow of a river. His roots pull deep draughts of God's goodness, causing him to bear fruit that others see. Spiritual sap runs rich inside his limbs and inner rings, growing long-lasting leaves that provide shade to those around him.

Be the man who invites others to discover the shade, refreshment, and fertile soil of God's strength.

How does your strength depend on your placement?
Why must faith displace fear before strength can show up?

BE THE MAN WHO GETS BACK UP

The godly may trip seven times, but they will get up again.
But one disaster is enough to overthrow the wicked.
PROVERBS 24:16 NLT

Being a perfectly faithful man would require you to flawlessly follow God with heart, soul, and strength. But let's be honest—that's impossible for an imperfect man to do. At some point, you'll slip up. Your attention will waver, your focus will shift, and your feet will stumble.

In the Old Testament, there was no prophet like Elijah. Active during Ahab's reign over Israel, Elijah performed many miracles to show God's power. He multiplied food supplies for the widow of Zarephath and even brought her dead son back to life (see 1 Kings 17:8–24).

Elijah's most famous exploit, however, was his face-off against the prophets of Baal. The challenge took place on Mount Carmel, where each side called upon its own deity to send fire from the heavens. No torches allowed.

After watching Baal's prophets plead fruitlessly for hours, Elijah got bored. First Kings 18:27 (NLT) says "About noontime Elijah began mocking them. 'You'll have to shout louder,' he scoffed, 'for surely he is a god! Perhaps he is daydreaming, or is relieving himself. Or maybe he is away on a trip, or is asleep and needs to be wakened!'"

After Elijah's turn, God sent a fire that consumed the sacrifice *and* the altar, and the story ends with Baal's prophets being put to the sword. Elijah should have been the epitome of confidence at this point, but immediately following this encounter, he ran and hid from Ahab's wife, Jezebel.

That could have been the end of his story, but it wasn't. Elijah got back up and continued doing God's will until he finally boarded a chariot to heaven, bypassing death entirely. Whenever we fall, Elijah's story should inspire us to get back up and keep moving.

Have you ever slipped up after confidently proclaiming victory for God? What could you accomplish for God by getting back up?

BE THE MAN WHO TAKES
JOY IN STAYING ON COURSE

*Folly brings joy to one who has no sense, but whoever
has understanding keeps a straight course.*
PROVERBS 15:21 NIV

It isn't hard to take joy in distractions. When life gets stressful—not just a rough day, but a rough patch—we often seek release in the form of entertainment, junk food, or both. In fact, our brains are wired to crave empty calories when we're stressed.

During short bouts of worry, our nervous systems send messages to the adrenal glands to release adrenaline, which shuts down cravings to aid in the body's fight-or-flight response. In prolonged periods of stress, however, the adrenal glands release cortisol, which increases appetite, though rarely for the right things. Studies have shown that eating "comfort food"—foods high in fats and sugars—can dampen stress responses and emotions.

Hard day at work? A doughnut will help! Stressful time at home? Sit down! Turn on an action movie! Grab some buttery popcorn! Really helpful, brain.

The problem is that stress-eating and binge-watching do nothing to fix the problems that stressed us out in the first place! When you're working toward a goal, there's nothing more *unhelpful* than a distraction. What you really need is to finish the job. Then, when all the necessary things are finished, you can celebrate in style.

The faithful man takes joy in staying the course and making sure his job is done well. He denies the folly of distractions because he knows they won't help him reach his destination. It won't be easy fighting against your own brain's inclinations, but you aren't working alone. God is more powerful than your brain's natural response. Pray and ask for His help, not only to fight against folly but to stay the course He's planned for you.

What things are stressing you out right now? How might you
make it easier to deny distractions when you are tempted?

BE THE MAN WHO GIVES IT ALL HE'S GOT

He asked him, "Of all the commandments, which is the most important?"
"The most important one," answered Jesus, "is this: 'Hear, O Israel: The Lord
our God, the Lord is one. Love the Lord your God with all your heart and
with all your soul and with all your mind and with all your strength."
MARK 12:28–30 NIV

Who doesn't love a good circus act? There's just something so satisfying about seeing dangerous stunts and unusual sideshows—it's hard to find these experiences anywhere else.

Frank "Cannonball" Richards wasn't your typical penny carnival performer, however. He had a cannonball fired into his stomach. . .twice a day! He started by allowing spectators to punch him in the gut, worked his way up to having sledgehammers hurled at his stomach, and eventually upgraded to cannonballs.

Frank didn't start as strong as he finished. He just found something he was passionate about and applied everything he had to pursuing it.

Your Christian life takes a similar path. While no one is asking you to take a cannonball to the gut, God *is* asking you to pursue Him with your heart's emotions, your soul's conviction, your mind's intellect, and every ounce of your body's strength. Combining these four things in your life is guaranteed to strengthen your courage and faith.

A courageous Christian doesn't leave himself out of the running or set himself aside when God says, "Get going." God is the one who gave what you've got, and He wants you to make the most of it for Him today. So bring all the willingness you can, and allow God to make up for your personal deficits with His goodness.

Be a full-time follower.

Do you sometimes feel as if you don't have enough for God?
How can you increase your passion as you pursue Him?

BE THE MAN WHO SPENDS TIME WITH GOD'S SPIRIT

*They were all filled with the Holy Spirit
and spoke the word of God boldly.*
ACTS 4:31 NIV

God uses four terms to describe His Spirit: *counselor, guide, helper,* and *companion.* Doesn't that sound like the friend you've always needed?

It's easy to overlook the Holy Spirit. The Bible is full of stories about Jesus and God the Father but far less about His Spirit. And the few that do exist are easy to pass over because we don't quite know what to do with them.

But God's four terms give us some great information about His Spirit. Because He's a counselor, He'll have some great advice. Because He's a guide, He'll offer great direction. Because He's a helper, He won't leave you when you need Him. Because He's a companion, He'll share the journey with you.

The last six words of Acts 4:31 take this understanding even further: all this counseling, guiding, helping, and friendship should lead to improved strength. . .which in turn, keeps you walking with God and sharing His message with others.

When you allow God's Spirit to help you, you shouldn't be surprised when you obtain an unnatural boldness. Peter and John, the subjects of today's verse, had been taken captive, interrogated, and ultimately released. But instead of growing quiet and finding a place to hide, they experienced the boldness that came from God. When they made room for God's Spirit, God's Spirit made room for strength. Strength was just what they needed.

So do you.

Do you make full use of the strength God's Spirit gives?
How can you make it a priority to keep close to God's Spirit?

BE THE MAN WHO LOVES WITH WORD AND DEED

Whoever claims to love God yet hates a brother or sister is a liar.
For whoever does not love their brother and sister, whom they
have seen, cannot love God, whom they have not seen.

1 JOHN 4:20 NIV

Words are incredible communication tools. Some men can do amazing things with grunts and nods, but words are the best way to convey complex concepts. And yet, words will always fall short when they are not accompanied by deeds.

For instance, if a man claims to be a gourmand but weighs 80 pounds sopping wet, you'd wonder if he really loves food.

Similarly, when a man says he loves God, there should be some evidence to support his claim. First John 4:7–9 (NIV) says, "Dear friends, let us love one another, for love comes from God. Everyone who loves has been born of God and knows God. Whoever does not love does not know God, because God is love. This is how God showed his love among us: He sent his one and only Son into the world that we might live through him."

God authenticated His claim to love us by sending Jesus to rescue us from the penalty of sin. As saved men, we should then pass along God's love to others.

James 2:14–17 (NIV) puts it this way: "What good is it, my brothers and sisters, if someone claims to have faith but has no deeds? Can such faith save them? Suppose a brother or a sister is without clothes and daily food. If one of you says to them, 'Go in peace; keep warm and well fed,' but does nothing about their physical needs, what good is it? In the same way, faith by itself, if it is not accompanied by action, is dead."

If we claim to love God, we must reinforce our words with action. The actions don't save us; they are evidence of our salvation.

Do your words and deeds prove God's love is in you?
How can you show someone His love today?

BE THE MAN WHO WELCOMES SCRUTINY

Test me, LORD, and try me, examine my heart and my
mind; for I have always been mindful of your unfailing
love and have lived in reliance on your faithfulness.
PSALM 26:2–3 NIV

When learning a new skill from someone who's done it for years, the student expects some degree of judgment. In fact, such judgments are desirable—they help students learn from their mistakes and become better at avoiding them. People who fear their teachers' judgment are likely aware that they've been slacking off in honing their skills.

Today's passage, written by David and designed to be sung with other people, invites God to judge the hearts and minds of those who are singing. How could David, who was no stranger to serious sin (even adultery and murder), publicly call for such judgment? Didn't he know he was far from innocent?

David knew. He also knew that *everyone* is far from innocent. His invitation for God's heart and mind exam wasn't borne out of a sense of prideful perfection but of prayerful reliance on God's love and mercy.

How do you feel about asking God to examine your heart and mind? Are you afraid that He'll find some reason not to love you? Impossible! He already knows you better than you know yourself. Have you been slacking in your efforts to live for Him? Then you definitely need to ask for His help to make things right.

God loves everyone perfectly, even those who aren't perfect themselves. And this perfect love should result in sincere efforts to live perfectly for Him.

Are there any areas in which you've been slacking off? How
might you invite God into each area of your life so that you can
be confident when you open yourself to His scrutiny?

BE THE MAN WHO FINDS
REST WHEN HE'S WEARY

*Come unto me, all ye that labour and are heavy laden, and I
will give you rest. Take my yoke upon you, and learn of me;
for I am meek and lowly in heart: and ye shall find rest unto
your souls. For my yoke is easy, and my burden is light.*

MATTHEW 11:28–30 KJV

A team of eight strongmen gathered in Ukraine. Using nothing but ropes
and their muscles, they pulled the world's heaviest cargo plane—which
weighed a whopping 628,300 pounds—fourteen feet in just over a min-
ute. Talk about a group of modern-day Atlases!

Physical exertion can be tortuous, but believe it or not, emotional
or spiritual exhaustion is even worse. Whether your battles are public or
private, the outcome will be disastrous unless you let God step in. Contrary to popular belief, the Bible never says, "God helps those who help
themselves," and neither does it teach, "God never gives you more than
you can handle." God *absolutely* gives His people more than they can
handle! Often, God allows you to become overwhelmed so that you'll
run to Him for rest.

God wants you to learn endurance and perseverance, not to be broken by exhaustion. Believing otherwise is a surefire path to weariness
and fear.

Tug on the rope as long as you like, but by yourself, you'll never move
far enough to reach your goal—only God has the strength you need.

How does exhaustion negatively affect you? When you're overwhelmed,
what's your first instinct—to work harder or to give it to God?

BE THE MAN WHO RESPONDS IMMEDIATELY

*"I publicly proclaim bold promises. I do not whisper obscurities
in some dark corner. I would not have told the people of
Israel to seek me if I could not be found. I, the LORD, speak
only what is true and declare only what is right."*

ISAIAH 45:19 NLT

Every human has quirks. One person, for instance, may have a violently
emotional response to a remark others would see as innocent. The mind
of such people may seem like a confusing labyrinth. What you see isn't
always what you get.

Not so with God. If He makes a promise, He keeps it. If He says
something is true, it's always true. If He gives a roadmap, there's no need
to guess where this road leads. He's always right. No exceptions.

There is strength in God's consistency. Why? It eliminates the need
for hesitancy. If He can be trusted completely, then you don't need to
weigh the risks of following Him. For instance, when God said that you
shouldn't lie, you shouldn't start wondering, "Hmm. Is that *always* true?"
If you do, your chances of lying increase. This is true for any of God's
laws: the more time you take to believe them, the weaker you'll become.

A strong and faithful man saves time by immediately going where
God sends him. Once you remove your hesitation, you'll begin to see
time saved, trust extended, and hope realized.

Have you ever spent time pondering what God wants—
even when you knew the answer? How can decreasing
your obedience "reaction time" make you stronger?

BE THE MAN WHO IS HOLY

The Scriptures say, "You must be holy because I am holy."
1 PETER 1:16 NLT

Holiness is a high standard. It's the standard of God Himself. Pastor and theologian John Piper defined it like this: "God's holiness is His infinite value as the absolutely unique, morally perfect, permanent person that He is and who by grace made Himself accessible."

But if the value of God's holiness is infinite, how can we as mortals be holy? If it is absolutely unique, we cannot, by definition, hope to achieve the same level of holiness. If it is morally perfect, our first sin dooms any chance we had of reaching it. How can we be holy like God is holy?

Only by the gracious way God Himself provides.

By our own efforts, holiness is unachievable. But because He has redeemed us, He has forgiven our past sins and given us the goal of living pure lives. In order to work, the process requires effort on God's side as well as ours.

Leviticus 20:7–8 (NLT) says, "So set yourselves apart to be holy, for I am the LORD your God. Keep all my decrees by putting them into practice, for I am the LORD who makes you holy." Did you catch that? God calls His children to set themselves apart from the world, then He says *He's* the one who makes them holy.

If you are failing to live up to God's level of holiness, you're relying on your own efforts too much. Trying to be holy without God's interaction is a fool's endeavor. Your efforts will wane, and you'll fall into sin's trap. But the faithful man doesn't stay down. He accepts grace, learns from his mistake, and moves on with God's help and restoration.

If you know you are living in sin and unholiness today, pray for forgiveness, accept God's grace, and start living for Him again.

How can you continually work with God to be holy like Him?
When you fail, how does the devil try to prevent your restoration?

BE THE MAN WHO MOVES MOUNTAINS

"You don't have enough faith," Jesus told them. "I tell you the truth, if you had faith even as small as a mustard seed, you could say to this mountain, 'Move from here to there,' and it would move. Nothing would be impossible."
MATTHEW 17:20 NLT

The highest natural point in Florida is Britton Hill, which is located along the top of Florida's panhandle near the Alabama border. Standing at 345 feet above sea level, Britton Hill is the lowest of all fifty states' high points and is dwarfed by some of Miami's skyscrapers.

With a bulldozer, a dump truck, and time, it would not be difficult to add enough dirt to a nearby hill to top Britton Hill's height. Of course, whether this would be officially recognized as the highest natural point (as it would be artificially constructed) is a matter for summit enthusiasts and land surveyors to debate.

When Jesus spoke about moving mountains with our faith, He wasn't talking about Britton Hill. Mount Hermon, one of the highest mountains in Israel, stands at 6,690 feet above sea level. Jesus' Jewish audience would have understood His reference to moving a mountain like Mount Hermon as a way to describe an impossible task.

How much faith, according to Jesus, is needed to do the impossible? Not much. He compared the necessary faith to a mustard seed, 1 to 2 millimeters in size. When we have a little faith in a God who towers over mountains, anything is possible.

Whether the bumps you face in life are the size of Britton Hill, Mount Hermon, or Mount Everest, they become little more than mole hills when you fix your eyes on God. As Jeremiah 32:17 (NIV) says: "Ah, Sovereign LORD, you have made the heavens and the earth by your great power and outstretched arm. Nothing is too hard for you."

What mountains do you need God to move for you? How could you shift your focus to Him instead of your mountain?

BE THE MAN WHO DOESN'T FEAR BAD NEWS

They do not fear bad news; they confidently trust the LORD to care for them.
PSALM 112:7 NLT

The word *anxious* comes from the very similar Latin word *anxius*—to be uneasy or troubled in the mind—which came from the earlier root word *angh*—meaning tight, painfully constricted, or painful. That root shows up in other modern words like anguish, anger, and even hangnail (you know, those painful strips of skin that tear off near the edge of your fingernail).

When you feel anxious, your chest tightens, making it difficult to breathe. Your heart rate skyrockets and your mind fixates on whatever worries you the most.

Anxiety isn't a sin, but sin can definitely make a person anxious. The Bible has a lot to say about why God's children shouldn't be anxious or fearful (check out Matthew 6:25–34, John 14:27, 1 Peter 5:7, Philippians 4:6–7, and 2 Timothy 1:7, just to name a few). This isn't because bad things won't happen; in fact, Jesus promised in John 15:20 (NIV) that His followers would face persecution: "If they persecuted me, they will persecute you also."

What's the difference between knowing bad things will happen and worrying that they might? Understanding who's in charge. If anxiety results in a painful tightening of the chest, what we need is more breath.

In fact, the word *breath* is intimately related to the person of the Holy Spirit. It was God's breath in Genesis that brought Adam to life (2:7). When Jesus met with His disciples after His resurrection, He "breathed on them and said, 'Receive the Holy Spirit'" (John 20:22).

So when bad news—or the threat of bad news—constricts our airways, we need to breathe deeper through the Holy Spirit, filling our lungs and hearts with His presence and trusting that God cares about us, no matter our circumstances.

Do you sometimes find yourself dwelling on bad news?
How can you breathe deeper spiritually?

BE THE MAN WHO ACCEPTS GOD'S PROTECTION

Pray, too, that we will be rescued from wicked and evil people, for not everyone is a believer. The Lord is faithful; he will strengthen you and guard you from the evil one.
2 THESSALONIANS 3:2–3 NLT

Satan was nearly salivating at the opportunity to bring a faithful man, Job, to ruin. When God commended Job's faithfulness, Satan boldly jumped at the chance to prove how irresistible his corrupting power truly was. He came before God with one request: "You have always put a wall of protection around him and his home and his property. You have made him prosper in everything he does. Look how rich he is! But reach out and take away everything he has, and he will surely curse you to your face!" (Job 1:10–11 NLT).

If you're thinking that God would decline this request, think again! God actually allowed Satan to give Job more than he could handle. Satan sought out everything that he believed caused Job to trust God—and he destroyed it. But while Job struggled to understand, he still chose to trust God. And God guarded Job's life from the devil's influence.

God didn't abandon Job, and He will never abandon you. The trouble you face is not unusual—wherever sin exists, pain is never far behind. Think of it this way: even if only one person in the entire world were capable of sinning (which is impossible; see Romans 3:23), the sin of that single individual would still bring trouble to everyone else.

That's why we must trust God in order to gain courage: He, not any of us, is leading the way. All we need to do is follow Him and accept the protection He offers.

How often does "trying harder" actually work? Have you surrendered your struggles to God, knowing He can protect you from the "evil one"?

BE THE MAN WHO DOESN'T CARE WHO NOTICES

The fear of the LORD is the instruction of wisdom; and before honour is humility.

PROVERBS 15:33 KJV

Humility describes those who live without arrogance. They don't force people to pay attention to them. They don't have to be first. They don't chase publicity. So how does this relate to strength? Because God's strength is amplified in those who are humble.

A humble man won't tell you he's humble. He will simply show up with a strength that is greater than himself, whether you applaud or not.

Such men are wise because they learn from God. They are humble because they know God is greater than their weakness. God can use them because they are happy to let the credit fall to Him.

If there were a humility hall of fame, you'd probably find biblical men like Daniel, Joseph, Moses, and Job on the wall. But no such hall exists. Why? Because that would defeat the purpose of humility!

Humility recognizes the strength it takes to simply be awesome. . . without ever wishing for anyone to view you as awesome. You know that whatever awesome deeds you do stem from God, who doesn't need to brag.

A strong man doesn't need a publicist to send out a press release on how amazing he is. What he does need is the conviction that God alone is worth following 100 percent of the time—even when no one's watching.

How does God use humility to make you strong?
Why is humility so hard to choose?

BE THE MAN WHO HAS JOY AMIDST SUFFERING

*But rejoice, inasmuch as ye are partakers of Christ's sufferings; that,
when his glory shall be revealed, ye may be glad also with exceeding joy.*
1 PETER 4:13 KJV

Joy and suffering aren't typically marketed as a package deal. Joy is usually used to advertise amusement parks, candy, and sugary breakfast cereals. When you imagine joyful moments, things like weddings and birthday parties probably come to mind.

But joy isn't all lollipops and rainbows. Joy is like the finest dark chocolate—bittersweet, rich, and lingering. Best of all—unlike happiness, which is dependent on circumstances—joy is a choice. If it weren't, it would be daft for the Bible to repeatedly command us to rejoice in unhappy circumstances:

- "Consider it pure joy, my brothers and sisters, whenever you face trials of many kinds" (James 1:2 NIV).

- "In the midst of a very severe trial, their overflowing joy and their extreme poverty welled up in rich generosity" (2 Corinthians 8:2 NIV).

- "But let all who take refuge in you be glad; let them ever sing for joy. Spread your protection over them, that those who love your name may rejoice in you" (Psalm 5:11 NIV).

How can joy exist in trials, poverty, and persecution? Because joy isn't the absence of suffering, but the presence of God. Romans 15:13 (NIV) says, "May the God of hope fill you with all joy and peace as you trust in him, so that you may overflow with hope by the power of the Holy Spirit."

When trials come, we must be intentional about resting in the power of the Holy Spirit. When we do, suffering can reveal the presence of God better than the happiest times can. . .and within that presence is joy.

Do you sometimes avoid suffering, thereby avoiding a
chance for joy? Would others label you as a joyful person?

BE THE MAN WHO DOESN'T USE FOUL LANGUAGE

Do not let any unwholesome talk come out of your mouths,
but only what is helpful for building others up according
to their needs, that it may benefit those who listen.
EPHESIANS 4:29 NIV

The Gospel of John opens with a description of God as the Word: "In the beginning was the Word, and the Word was with God, and the Word was God" (1:1 NIV). With words, God spoke creation into existence. And with words, He conveyed His laws to His people.

Words are powerful. But for them to be useful, a few things must be understood:

- Words cannot be intrinsically good or bad, clean or dirty. It is only when culture gets involved and a community assigns such connotations that words take on these labels.
- Words, when combined with things like tone and body language, can easily change their meaning.
- Finally, words can be used to either build people up or tear them down, bring truth to light or obscure it, reflect God's love or display selfishness. Since words have such drastically different effects, caution is necessary.

Today's verse encourages us to consider our words—their meaning and the way in which they are delivered—and use only those that are helpful toward building others up. Foul language, by its shared cultural understanding, isn't helpful toward this end. The words themselves aren't sinful, but they make it easier for other people to ignore your message.

Listen carefully to the words that come out of your mouth today. Make sure they are working toward what you want to accomplish, which ultimately is to bring glory to the Word Himself.

Do you struggle to think before you speak?
How can you use your words to build others up?

BE THE MAN WHO KEEPS HIS EYES FOCUSED

Why take ye thought for raiment? Consider the lilies of the field,
how they grow; they toil not, neither do they spin: And yet I say unto
you, That even Solomon in all his glory was not arrayed like one of
these. Wherefore, if God so clothe the grass of the field, which to day
is, and to morrow is cast into the oven, shall he not much more clothe
you, O ye of little faith? Take no thought, saying, What shall we eat?
or, What shall we drink? or, Wherewithal shall we be clothed?
MATTHEW 6:28–31 KJV

Have you ever wondered where your rent money is going to come from?
If you have enough spare change for the dollar menu? If so, you're not
alone—hard times come to everyone.

Concern can etch lines into your features and disturb your sleep.
Worry balks at the idea of adventure. But if you live in the weeds, you'll
never have enough bravery to change direction, even when you secretly
want to.

God says you don't need to worry about these things. He's very aware
that people have needs (Matthew 6:32), so His command is not just
"Quit complaining"—it's a reminder to use your time more productively.
When you worry, you stop seeking God and your role in His plan. . .and
your adversary loves it.

Your spiritual eyes should be focused on God and the people He
loves instead of things like food, drink, and clothing. Each second you
spend dwelling on these things only derails your spiritual focus and am-
plifies your tunnel vision. You are missing out whenever you insist on
identifying with small things instead of God's big ideas.

Do small worries ever cause you to miss big opportunities? How might
you use your trust in God to have a freer, more fulfilling life?

BE THE MAN WHO KEEPS "GOD COMPANY"

*Because of Christ and our faith in him, we can now
come boldly and confidently into God's presence.*
EPHESIANS 3:12 NLT

A faithful man is bold, confident, and brave. He is nourished by someone greater than himself. This man finds it easy to come to God and speak his mind. He lays his concerns on the table. His heart is an open book. His dreams are transparent.

Does that describe you?

God invites this kind of conversation, and He'll strengthen you to begin it today. Talk—He's listening. Listen—He's got things to share.

Today's verse explains how this connection is possible. You can come to God with a boldness that exists "because of Christ and [your] faith in him." It isn't because you are naturally bold enough to bring your troubles to the Creator of life. You're not strong enough to stand in His presence and feel anything but overwhelmed, unworthy, and undone. But because of Christ, you have that strength. You've tapped into the nourishment that causes godly growth.

A faithful man refuses to treat God as a temporary solution. God isn't just reliable when you feel stumped. A friendship with Him shouldn't be like calling 911—He wants to be in contact with you at all times. Why would you settle for less?

How did Jesus' work make it possible for you to pray?
How does your prayer life grow stronger by following Jesus?

BE THE MAN WHO DOESN'T JUDGE BY APPEARANCES

"Stop judging by mere appearances, but instead judge correctly."
JOHN 7:24 NIV

The rule, "never judge a book by its cover," is somewhat misleading, originating at a time when all books were similarly bound and thus looked basically identical from the outside. As time progressed and marketing professionals got involved, book covers were designed to appeal to specific buyers. These days, books are practically the *only* things you can judge by their covers.

When it comes to people, however, judging by appearance alone has never been wise. Although our brains are wired to help us form first impressions, we should never presume to know a person's story or abilities based on these impressions.

By appearances alone, Saul, Israel's first king, should have been an amazing leader. He was tall, strong, and good-looking, but his dynasty died with him. God chose David—whose appearance was much less impressive—to be king after Saul.

At David's anointing, even the prophet Samuel questioned whether God had made a mistake. After Samuel suggested one of David's elder brothers might be better suited for kingship, the Lord responded in 1 Samuel 16:7 (NIV): "Do not consider his appearance or his height, for I have rejected him. The LORD does not look at the things people look at. People look at the outward appearance, but the LORD looks at the heart.'"

As people, we cannot see what's inside a person's heart, nor can we accurately judge a person based on their appearance. How are we to act then? Romans 12:10 (NIV) says, "Be devoted to one another in love. Honor one another above yourselves."

Have you ever had a wrong first impression of someone?
How might you better see people through God's eyes?

BE THE MAN WHO IS HOSPITABLE TO THOSE IN NEED

*Rather, he must be hospitable, one who loves what is good,
who is self-controlled, upright, holy and disciplined.*
TITUS 1:8 NIV

Hospitality was a big deal in ancient times. Guests could expect to receive food, safe lodging, and provisions for their journey, all without being required to reveal who they were or where they were going.

Showing hospitality to strangers wasn't just expensive—it was potentially dangerous. What if your guest turned out to be a violent maniac? On the flip side, however, what if the person you were hosting turned out to be an angel in disguise? (see Hebrews 13:2.)

In either situation, the host's responsibilities are the same: provide great hospitality, treat your guest with respect, and hope for the best. The safest way to ensure the protection of your home and village was to show all strangers that you were worthy of their respect. . .and therefore beneficial to keep alive. Of course, this also worked out well for strangers who were neither angels nor potential enemies.

But what does hospitality look like in modern times? Honestly, it's not much different. We are called to provide sacrificially for those who cannot repay us. God has been radically generous with us by accepting us into His family when we did nothing but earn His enmity.

In Luke 14:13–14 (NIV), Jesus says, "But when you give a banquet, invite the poor, the crippled, the lame, the blind, and you will be blessed. Although they cannot repay you, you will be repaid at the resurrection of the righteous."

So look for opportunities today to show hospitality. Buy a stranger lunch. Put up a guest for the night. Listen when someone wants to talk. The reward for such a gesture may not happen in your lifetime, but it will still be worthwhile.

What does Matthew 25:34-46 say about hospitality?
How have others been hospitable to you?

BE THE MAN WITH CORRECTED VISION

I pray that out of his glorious riches he may strengthen you with power through his Spirit in your inner being, so that Christ may dwell in your hearts through faith. And I pray that you, being rooted and established in love, may have power, together with all the Lord's holy people, to grasp how wide and long and high and deep is the love of Christ, and to know this love that surpasses knowledge— that you may be filled to the measure of all the fullness of God.

EPHESIANS 3:16–19 NIV

Glasses aren't just a fashion choice. When correctly used, they improve your vision, bringing clarity to your blurry world. Suddenly, you can better read and understand words, and you no longer mistake one object for another. Better eyesight helps you ignore the unimportant and focus on the valuable.

The Bible is instrumental in improving your spiritual vision. It offers clarity that changes perspective, helping you see what you could only guess at before. And once you see where you're going, you have the confidence to walk with improved purpose. The apostle Paul wrote, "In him and through faith in him we may approach God with freedom and confidence" (Ephesians 3:12).

Paul, who saw his faith as the means of approaching God, wanted readers to know that God's overflowing, abundant and unmatched riches could give them strength when they felt like the last dry leaves hanging onto a tree in early winter.

If you want better eyesight, you must believe glasses can help. Similarly, if you want better spiritual vision, you need to believe the Bible can help. Be a faithful man and read the words of God's great Book, expecting to see things like you never have before.

> Is improved spiritual vision important to you? Would a correct understanding of what you see help you make better choices?

BE THE MAN WHO IS NOT ASHAMED

*I eagerly expect and hope that I will in no way be ashamed,
but will have sufficient courage so that now as always Christ
will be exalted in my body, whether by life or by death.*
PHILIPPIANS 1:20 NIV

In pretty much any battle-scar-showing contest, Paul would win. He'd been shipwrecked, bitten by a snake, beaten, wrongly imprisoned, and betrayed by fellow workers.

But this great apostle hadn't always been an apostle. His career path did not lead to Jesus—Jesus' path led to Paul. And after that meeting (sometimes simply called "the Damascus Road Experience"—see Acts 9), Paul's life became more challenging.

Many in the church—remembering his believer-persecuting, Christ-hating past—didn't accept him. So instead of being a pharisaical enforcer, Paul became an outcast to both Pharisees and those who followed Jesus. He didn't seem to fit. So God sent him away from what he knew to tell complete strangers about Jesus. He would need to take a second job (making and repairing tents) to make ends meet. He would meet with resistance. He would feel the cold, hard stone of a dungeon prison.

Who chooses that kind of life? One who knows how little this temporary trouble matters in light of eternity with the faithful God. This scarred man knew that as long as Jesus was amplified in his choices, it didn't matter if he were killed. His courage proved to everyone he encountered that he was not ashamed of Jesus.

How often do you base your behavior on others' opinions? Why is it important to make decisions based on Paul's principles in Philippians 1:20?

BE THE MAN WHO ACTS AS CHRIST'S AMBASSADOR

So we are Christ's ambassadors; God is making his appeal through us. We speak for Christ when we plead, "Come back to God!"
2 CORINTHIANS 5:20 NLT

Ambassadors are the representatives of one country to another. They act as the eyes and ears of their nation, reporting back all they see in the host country. They are also their home country's mouthpiece, advocating for their nation's interests and negotiating on its behalf.

Successful ambassadors are gifted communicators, savvy problem solvers, and experts on both their home and host countries. All embassy employees take the Foreign Service Officers Test and are assigned to a specific track of employment. Some ambassadors are appointed to their posts by heads of state, but most rise through their embassy's ranks, distinguishing themselves by their effort and expertise.

As followers of Christ, we are ambassadors of God's kingdom. Our citizenship is in heaven, and we act as God's agents in a foreign (and sometimes hostile) land. We function as God's eyes and ears, bringing our observations to Him through prayer. We are His mouthpiece to the lost residents of this world, pleading for them to "Come back to God!"

Whether we entered God's service by appointment or choice, we are called to represent God through our actions. We are not representing ourselves; we are on a diplomatic mission for God, and our behavior reflects on His character. If we love as God loves, we perform our duties well; if we hate our neighbors, act selfishly, or show favoritism, we are poor ambassadors for God.

As a faithful man, it is your job to represent God to the world around you. Get to know Him well, so that you can be a good ambassador.

What would you think about a nation whose ambassadors were rude or unkind? How can you be a good ambassador for Christ?

BE THE MAN WHO DRIVES RESPECTFULLY

The lookout reported, "He has reached them,
but he isn't coming back either. The driving is like
that of Jehu son of Nimshi—he drives like a maniac."
2 KINGS 9:20 NIV

Jehu—whose reign is outlined in 2 Kings 9–10—was one of the most intense kings of the Old Testament. A military commander who was elevated to kingship by the prophet Elisha's orders, Jehu was a man of bloodshed, but he was rewarded with a dynasty which lasted four generations.

As a king, Jehu exacted brutal justice on God's behalf by putting an end to the wicked leadership of Ahab and Jezebel; as a man, he was known for another trait. While other kings are known for their wisdom or benevolence, Jehu will forever be remembered as the king who drove like a maniac.

When driving, are you a wild king of the road like Jehu, your progress marked by roadkill and the cries of bystanders? Or are you known for your safety and courtesy? Believe it or not, how you drive is as important to God as everything else you do.

Sometimes, we forget this fact, allowing our frustrations to bring out our inner demons. We curse. We shout. We forget other drivers are made in the image of God. And we justify our actions, reactions, and verbal atrocities with the consolation that no one can hear us from our own vehicles.

But God hears. And as a loving parent, God wants better for us. He wants us to drive respectfully. When other drivers get in our way, He wants us to pray a blessing over them. When we are driving on a stretch of highway all alone, He wants us to obey the speed limit, respecting the law of the land and the leaders He's placed in charge.

Whenever you find yourself driving like Jehu, slow down and ask if that's really something you want to be known for.

Are you a different man behind the wheel? How can you honor God with your driving?

BE THE MAN WHO HONORS GOD IN EVERYTHING

Whether therefore ye eat, or drink,
or whatsoever ye do, do all to the glory of God.
1 Corinthians 10:31 kjv

The church of Corinth was divided. Some folks were eating food that had been offered to idols (since idols don't eat much, the food was clearanced out quickly), while others, not wanting their money to support the idol-worshipping industry, were opposed to the practice. Was it better for Christians to be frugal and have more money to help the needy, or was it better to avoid dealing with idol-worshippers altogether?

Paul's response was simple. In 1 Corinthians 10:21 (NLT), Paul writes, "You cannot drink from the cup of the Lord and from the cup of demons, too. You cannot eat at the Lord's Table and at the table of demons, too."

An easy answer, right? Well. . .

Paul also writes in 1 Corinthians 10:25–26 (NLT), "So you may eat any meat that is sold in the marketplace without raising questions of conscience. For 'the earth is the Lord's, and everything in it.'"

This isn't so much a food issue, but a heart issue. If you believe it honors God to save money and use it to provide for His people, buy the meat. If you believe it honors God to avoid idol meat, avoid it. The point is to always honor God in our hearts, regardless of the action.

When our hearts are pointed to God's glory instead of our individual preferences, we won't get caught up in disagreements. We'll do everything—eating, drinking, fixing lawn mowers, washing our hands, blowing our noses, writing books, *everything*—to the glory of God.

How might you shift your focus to give God more glory in your activities?
Have you ever fought with other Christians over something trivial?

BE THE MAN WHO KEEPS HIS HEART FOCUSED ON GOD

Guard your heart above all else, for it determines the course of your life.
PROVERBS 4:23 NLT

The ancient Hebrew understanding of the heart had nothing to do with the blood-pumping organ in your chest. No, the heart was the core of someone's being. It was the soul, a person's conscience, and the storehouse of one's accumulated wisdom all rolled together as one.

When a man's heart is oriented toward God, it means his soul is pure, his conscience is clean, and the wisdom of his forefathers brings God glory. The problem, of course, is that no one starts out with a clean heart. Jeremiah 17:9 (NLT) says, "The human heart is the most deceitful of all things, and desperately wicked. Who really knows how bad it is?"

The truth is that we all start out in the same sorry condition. It is only when God exchanges our old heart (soul, conscience, and mind) with His own that we are able to serve Him. To have a heart worth guarding, we must pray as David did when his sins with Bathsheba were called out: "Create in me a clean heart, O God. Renew a loyal spirit within me" (Psalm 51:10 NLT).

And once our hearts are made new, once we've been transplanted into God's bloodline, we need to stay focused on Him. It is far too simple for men to treat salvation like a one-time-fixes-all inoculation against sin's long-term effects. Sure, having God's heart within us means we are saved, but if God's heart isn't redirecting the course of our life toward bringing Him glory, it's either because we don't actually have God's heart within us or because we've done a poor job of guarding our heart against our old ways of living.

So guard your heart. Put up boundaries against old temptations. Fill your mind with the wisdom of the Bible. If you want the course of your life to lead others to God, make sure your heart is purely devoted to following Him.

What is the state of your heart? Where is your life headed?

BE THE MAN WHO UNDERSTANDS SUFFICIENT

Do we begin again to commend ourselves? or need we, as some others, epistles of commendation to you, or letters of commendation from you? Ye are our epistle written in our hearts, known and read of all men: Forasmuch as ye are manifestly declared to be the epistle of Christ ministered by us, written not with ink, but with the Spirit of the living God; not in tables of stone, but in fleshy tables of the heart. And such trust have we through Christ to God-ward: Not that we are sufficient of ourselves to think any thing as of ourselves; but our sufficiency is of God.
2 CORINTHIANS 3:1–5 KJV

Can you will a heart to beat? Can you force a blind eye to see? Can you create something from absolutely nothing? God did. . .and He still does.

You've probably heard the word *insufficient* more often than "sufficient." If you have insufficient funds in the bank, you don't have enough money to cover your purchase. If you try to land a job with insufficient skills, you won't know how to do required tasks. If you ask a computer to solve a problem for you, it might display INSUFFICIENT DATA. Each of these examples involves a lack of something you need to achieve your goal.

On your own, you don't have enough to meet your every need. Some things are simply outside your wheelhouse of expertise. This is where God shows up and bridges the gap between your abilities and His. When you invite God into your every effort, He'll respond by offering the help you want and the companionship you need.

Only God can be your absolute sufficiency. Nothing else will do.

Does the fact that God is sufficient for you change your attitude toward new opportunities? How might it enhance your courage?

BE THE MAN WHO REJECTS FEAR

One thing have I desired of the LORD, that will I seek after;
that I may dwell in the house of the LORD all the days of my life,
to behold the beauty of the LORD, and to enquire in his temple.
PSALM 27:4 KJV

King David understood that life was unfair. He knew that people often seek to destroy what they fear. . .which often includes parts of God's plan. Their bad choices stem from a fear of God. This isn't a reverential fear—it's terror at the thought of standing in the presence of love.

Psalm 27 relates a time when the future king encountered countless roadblocks. Some suggest the psalm is about Doeg the Edomite, who'd hated David so much that he killed eighty-five priests because one of them had shown kindness to this soon-to-be-king.

If this is the incident Psalm 27 is about, then these words show David's strength of spirit that transcends fear: "Though an host should encamp against me, my heart shall not fear: though war should rise against me, in this will I be confident" (verse 3 KJV).

In other words, David was saying that even if it took years—even if he never saw it happen personally—God would win against his foes. They could rise against him all they wanted, but they could never defeat God.

David, a battle-weary man in dire circumstances, had every logical reason to be scared. . .but he still turned to the strength only God can provide.

Have you ever been really tempted to give up? What kind of courage
can you take from Psalm 27 in order to face your impossibilities?

BE THE MAN WHO ASKS FIRST

What causes fights and quarrels among you? Don't they come from
your desires that battle within you? You desire but do not have,
so you kill. You covet but you cannot get what you want, so you
quarrel and fight. You do not have because you do not ask God.
JAMES 4:1–2 NIV

In the film *Road to Perdition*, Tom Hanks stars as Mike Sullivan, a mob enforcer from the 1930s. After his own family becomes a mob target, Sullivan and his son, Mike Jr., team up against his former employer by robbing mob-owned banks.

There is a scene in which Mike Jr. asks his dad for a cut of the money they're stealing. His dad asks how much he wants, and the boy quickly replies, "Two hundred dollars," an astronomical amount for the time. After a moment of consideration, his dad agrees to the amount. A few more moments pass in silence. Then the boy asks, "Could I have had more?"

"You'll never know," his father responds.

Regardless of the circumstances, parents love giving good things to their children. Our Father in heaven is the same way.

In Matthew 7:9–11 (NIV), Jesus says, "Which of you, if your son asks for bread, will give him a stone? Or if he asks for a fish, will give him a snake? If you, then, though you are evil, know how to give good gifts to your children, how much more will your Father in heaven give good gifts to those who ask him!"

God wants to give His children good things, but He wants us to ask for them first. When God blesses us without being asked, we may not notice or feel the same sense of appreciation. When we request and He provides, we can more easily see the relationship between asking and receiving, thereby reinforcing our trust in Him.

God can provide more than we ask. It would be better for us to echo Mike Jr. in saying, "Could I have had more?" instead of never asking at all.

Do you take your requests to God, or do your desires lead you to confrontation
with people? How has God already proven His trustworthiness to you?

BE THE MAN WHO DOESN'T BLUFF GOD

Before a downfall the heart is haughty,
but humility comes before honor.
PROVERBS 18:12 NIV

In poker, players with poor hands will often "bluff," acting like they have a royal flush when, really, their hand should be flushed away. Bluffing requires both an understanding of what the opponent might be holding and significant acting skills. If it succeeds, the player with a better hand will fold.

Bluffing, however, isn't limited to poker. It happens whenever people seek to gain something by acting prouder than their situations should allow. People also bluff their way through conversations by pretending to be knowledgeable about a topic entirely foreign to them—the payoff being that other people think they're smart.

Sadly, some guys try to bluff their way through faith. They want to look good in front of other people in church. They might share religious memes on social media. They might even quote Bible passages to score a few points in an argument. Some may even raise the ante so far that they start preaching from the pulpit, despite never having a relationship with God in the first place.

Faith isn't a game. But even if it were, God is holding all the cards. Never bet your future on your ability to act proud in front of God. When He calls, your hand will be revealed. It's always better to approach faith with humility than to face humiliation because you tried to bluff the Almighty.

What motives might people have to bluff their way through faith?
How should you humble yourself before you are humbled?

BE THE MAN WHO MAKES CONTINGENCY PLANS

Now listen, you who say, "Today or tomorrow we will go to this or
that city, spend a year there, carry on business and make money." Why,
you do not even know what will happen tomorrow. What is your life?
You are a mist that appears for a little while and then vanishes. Instead,
you ought to say, "If it is the Lord's will, we will live and do this or that."
As it is, you boast in your arrogant schemes. All such boasting is evil.
JAMES 4:13–16 NIV

Walter had big dreams, and he wanted his family and friends to know about them. This man was going to make his mark in the world of newspapers. However, despite Walter's ambitions and skill, his boss turned him away from this path, believing that Walter's interest in creativity was misplaced.

Like the people mentioned in James 4, Walter's vision for his future was based on personal ambition. But when his self-confidence was shattered, he was humble enough to redirect his ambition elsewhere.

Today, you probably know this man as Walt. . .Disney. Could you imagine what the world would be like if this young man had channeled his creativity into writing bylines in a newspaper?

God wants to be your life consultant. He hates to see you waste your time. He knows you, and He knows what you should do. When you insist on bypassing God's plan in favor of yours, the tension between the two will never leave.

A faithful man doesn't hesitate to admit that all his plans are contingent on God's input and redirection.

How can self-confidence lead to pride? What can you do to ensure
that you never forsake God's plan and pursue your own?

BE THE MAN WHO WALKS WITH ASSURANCE

They are confident and fearless and can face their foes triumphantly.
PSALM 112:8 NLT

Bad news is simply a half-told story—but it's the news in the largest font. Bad headlines grab the eye, and tragic endings capture the heart. Any good in the middle gets squeezed out of memory, replaced by all the bad bits. . .which then get passed down from generation to generation.

Many men are barraged with the bad news of betrayal, job loss, health issues, relationship stress, conflicts, and gossip. Most see injustice in these issues, so they either look for the chance to leave the scene or offer the person who's suffering some magical three-step plan that can solve every woe. Neither response is helpful.

God knows that the sin lodged in the heart of mankind will hurt you, but He also knows how to take this hurt and somehow make it useful—either to you or anyone around you.

Your struggle is indisputably real—real enough to take your breath away and steal your strength. Yet God keeps supplying the oxygen you need and the help you can't find on your own. He invites you to trust, even when rage is striving to find a voice.

When you understand that trouble (and all its nasty cohorts) is a temporary guest, then you can see your predicament with new eyes. Trouble has come before, and it left. It will come again, but it'll never be the end.

> Why is it so hard to wait for good outcomes? When was the last time your story transformed from bad to good?

BE THE MAN WHO HAS A GOOD HEART

"A good person produces good things from the treasury of a good heart, and an evil person produces evil things from the treasury of an evil heart. What you say flows from what is in your heart."
LUKE 6:45 NLT

Have you ever heard someone talk about a terrible person and finish by saying, "But he has such a good heart"? You know the speaker is either woefully misinformed or has a huge blind spot for the person being described.

Good-hearted people are kind, thoughtful, and generous. They are not violent against others. They are not cruel to animals. They are not selfish in their attitudes or actions. It isn't difficult to recognize a good-hearted person. Usually, all it takes is a conversation.

Before we label people as good-hearted or evil, however, we need to understand the difference. It is tempting to think we have the power to change our own hearts, but we don't. We are the patients, not the doctor.

Jesus says in Luke 6:43-44 (NLT), "A good tree can't produce bad fruit, and a bad tree can't produce good fruit. A tree is identified by its fruit. Figs are never gathered from thornbushes, and grapes are not picked from bramble bushes." God is the one who plants, sends the sunshine and rain, and tends His garden with love. We are the trees who bear fruit. Does this mean we have no responsibilities? No. It means our good choices ultimately originate from a perfect and holy God.

None of us have the power to change our own hearts. Only God does. What we *can* do is give our hearts to Him so that He can change them for us. Similarly, we can't change the hearts of others. . .but we can introduce them to a God who can.

Can others tell what kind of tree you are by your fruit? Are you letting God control your whole heart to make it all good?

BE THE MAN WHO LETS GOD RENEW HIS MIND

And be not conformed to this world: but be ye transformed
by the renewing of your mind, that ye may prove what is
that good, and acceptable, and perfect, will of God.
ROMANS 12:2 KJV

Our brains are hard-wired to crave acceptance. There's safety in numbers, especially when the numbers are on your side. So we try—consciously or subconsciously—to fit in with those around us. We conform to the crowd because it's safer than standing out.

But when the crowd is living by the world's standards instead of God's, blending in is dangerous for a Christian. It's better to stand out while standing up for God than to suffer God's displeasure. We cannot conform to the world; we must allow God to transform every part of us, starting with our minds.

Like an old, overused dirt road, our brains develop deep ruts, rewarding us with happiness chemicals when we stay in bounds. Breaking out of these ruts and forming new pathways takes more than willpower; it takes the Holy Spirit's assistance. When we ask God to renew our minds, to remove the world's influence from our thinking, we are able to recognize His priorities.

As you allow God to rewire your mind to take pleasure in Him, you need to change your old habits to reinforce the new pathways. Stop hanging out with friends or frequenting places that might influence you in unhelpful ways. Create new routines where prayer keeps you focused on God's will.

We'll never stop craving acceptance, but we need to start craving it from the proper source. Today is the day to stop living for the world and start living to hear God say, "Well done, good and faithful servant."

Would you say your life is conformed to the world or transformed by God? What evidence can you provide to back up your claim?

BE THE MAN WHO KNOWS
YOUR OPPOSITION ISN'T GOD

If the LORD delight in us, then he will bring us into this land, and give it us; a land which floweth with milk and honey. Only rebel not ye against the LORD, neither fear ye the people of the land; for they are bread for us: their defence is departed from them, and the LORD is with us: fear them not.

NUMBERS 14:8–9 KJV

Imagine this scene: people are criticizing your personality, clothes, or skin color. They don't like your name, workplace, or opinions. And because they just don't like you much, they make life hard for you.

Those kinds of people have always been a part of life. Your parents, grandparents, and all your ancestors knew them long before you did.

The Bible is full of stories about opposition. David would one day be king, but before that happened, King Saul tried his best to kill him (1 Samuel 19). Nehemiah rebuilt the walls of Jerusalem, but his enemies showed up in force and tried to stop him (Nehemiah 4). John the Baptist was opposed by King Herod (Mark 6:14–29), and Stephen was opposed by the local religious elite of his day (Acts 7:54–60). In each case, the opposition sought the demise of good people.

God, however, told these men, "I am with you. Don't fear the opposition." Because no one had been able to oppose God and win, courage made more sense than fear. This message for the people of Israel is for you too. You don't need to fear anything that God is not afraid of.

Faithful men leave fear behind.

What are you afraid of? How can you use the courage that God provides to conquer this fear?

BE THE MAN WHO BEGINS WITH WEAKNESS

I had to feed you with milk, not with solid food, because you weren't ready for anything stronger. And you still aren't ready.
1 CORINTHIANS 3:2 NLT

Like it or not, weakness is a great launching pad for strength. But staying weak isn't what God has in mind. This would be like trying to prevent babies from growing up by treating them the same forever. In both our physical and spiritual lives, there's a growth pattern that changes our abilities, desires, and techniques.

Some men *choose* weakness over strength. Maybe the idea of strength overwhelms them or seems too good to be true. Maybe they know what God wants but refuse to act. Maybe they're afraid they'll miss the milk after they give solid spiritual food a try.

It's hard to grow strong when you're doing everything you can to stay weak. Admitting your weakness isn't enough—you must have the desire to change. This change doesn't depend on your abilities but on your willingness to be strengthened by God.

Once you see the futility of doing what you've always done and somehow expecting a different result—once you stop arguing with God or defending your lack of obedience—God will start making you a new creation.

You have a choice: will you stay weak. . .or find new strength?

Have you ever refused God's strength? What would be the outcome of continuing to do things your way?

BE THE MAN WHO FINDS STRENGTH IN WAITING

If we hope for what we do not yet have, we wait for it patiently.
ROMANS 8:25 NIV

Patience is a strength that most want but few are willing to learn. Why? Because you have to wait for it! It doesn't come in a package in the "Virtues" aisle. It must be learned.

Patience is a word that conjures up ideas of endurance and perseverance. . .which both ultimately lead to strength. Getting patience means willingly attending a master class in struggle. It means not only experiencing the struggle but taking notes through the pain. Then you can apply this knowledge to your future decisions. It also means waiting is easier, since you now know all struggles come to an end.

When you don't have clarity—when answers are hard to come by—you're faced with a choice: become frustrated or become patient. Give up or endure. Throw your hands in the air or persevere. Sometimes, this choice is a split-second decision, in which you hardly have the time to think of the consequences. You might give up without realizing what a disaster that will cause.

That's why possessing a strong faith is so important: it'll make you comfortable with waiting—for both physical things and spiritual. You don't have the best life yet, but being patient means you're certain there's a better day to come.

Don't give up.

Why is waiting so hard for most men? Has growing
in patience improved your trust in God? How?

BE THE MAN WHO SEES NEEDS AND FILLS THEM

For we are God's handiwork, created in Christ Jesus to do
good works, which God prepared in advance for us to do.
EPHESIANS 2:10 NIV

Which invention revolutionized a key aspect of warfare in the early nineteenth century? If you are thinking about weapons or vehicles, think again. The answer is canned food. Scientist Nicolas Appert developed a method for canning food in glass jars with metal lids, saving armies around the world from rotten rations on the battlefield.

Before long, metal cans replaced glass jars, but opening them required a hammer and chisel. Minor improvements were made over the years, but it wasn't until 1920 that the classic toothed-wheel crank can opener was patented by Charles Arthur Bunker.

Consider for a moment the time gap between the invention of tin cans and the invention of a convenient can opener. Cans around the world were stacking up or being opened in crude ways while much of the food inside went unused.

According to Ephesians 2:10, we are a bit like can openers. We've been designed for a specific purpose. The needs of the world have been stacking up like cans, waiting for us to come along. We ourselves are not the solution. We are simply tools in the hands of God. We cannot nourish any more than a can opener can create food, but we can be the instruments which make nourishment possible.

God has prepared good works specifically for you to do. What needs do you see around you? What cans of blessing will you open for others? What knowledge do you possess which someone else needs?

As a faithful man, you have been created for God's use. How will you let Him use you today?

> What gifts has God given you to use for Him? How can
> you encourage others to join you in being useful for God?

BE THE MAN WHO HEARS GOD'S CALL

By his divine power, God has given us everything we need for living a godly life. We have received all of this by coming to know him, the one who called us to himself by means of his marvelous glory and excellence.
2 PETER 1:3 NLT

Imagine this scene: All the kids are lined up in gym class. It's kickball day. The two biggest kids are chosen to be team captains. One by one, the captains choose kids for their teams. You stand there, waiting to hear one of them call your name, silently enduring the scrutiny of your potential teammates. Will you be chosen next? Last? At all?

Is that what it means to be called by God? To passively wait until either God or the devil chooses you for his team? Nope.

First, ever since sin entered the world, humanity is born on the devil's team. We are destined for the losing side of a conflict much more serious than kickball.

Second, God and the devil aren't on equal footing. God is all-powerful, all-knowing, and all-wise. The devil is wily, but he has his limits.

Lastly, in kickball, the team captain's goal is to pick people with inherent strengths that will help them win the competition. But in life, God doesn't pick the most handsome, the smartest, or the most well-spoken for His team. In fact, 1 Corinthians 1:27 (NIV) says, "God chose the foolish things of the world to shame the wise; God chose the weak things of the world to shame the strong."

Still, the call itself is what matters. God *has* chosen you for His team, and He will equip you to succeed. Now that you are on God's team, you can choose for yourself what kind of teammate you'll be. You can show the world you're on His team by the way you live out your faith.

What does 2 Peter 1:5–11 say about how to be a good teammate? How does it feel to be on God's team?

BE THE MAN WHO DOESN'T ENTERTAIN FEAR

"Don't be afraid, for I am with you. Don't be discouraged, for I am your God. I will strengthen you and help you. I will hold you up with my victorious right hand. See, all your angry enemies lie there, confused and humiliated. Anyone who opposes you will die and come to nothing. You will look in vain for those who tried to conquer you. Those who attack you will come to nothing. For I hold you by your right hand—I, the LORD your God. And I say to you, 'Don't be afraid. I am here to help you.'"
ISAIAH 41:10–13 NLT

Every father remembers a time when nightmares chased the sleep from his child. . .who in turn chased the sleep from Dad. The father undoubtedly lifted his kid into bed or walked her back to her room with a firm, gentle reassurance. *Maybe the rest of the night will be different*, Dad hoped. *Maybe sleep will return.*

It's important to remember that fear is a universal emotion—for small children but also for grown men. Dark nights and bad dreams can inspire it, but your imagination is the worst offender. Fear, however, is not entertained by courage—it's intimidated by it.

Fear is always trying to chase courage from the room. It shows up shouting and thumping its chest, but courage says, "I don't think so!" Suddenly, fear's punch seems like little more than the futile bragging of a bully.

Don't leave home without courage—it's your "fear shield." Don't back up when the only way out is straight ahead. You have a God who renders fear toothless.

Fear is the tail; courage is the head. Which one will you choose?

How can entertaining fear hurt your progress as a Christian?
How can courage be the antidote to the fear you encounter today?

BE THE MAN WHO PARTICIPATES IN GOD'S STORY

You are a letter from Christ showing the result of our ministry among you. This "letter" is written not with pen and ink, but with the Spirit of the living God. It is carved not on tablets of stone, but on human hearts. We are confident of all this because of our great trust in God through Christ.
2 CORINTHIANS 3:3–4 NLT

The greatest story you'll ever write will be in the lives of people you love and help. The good things that happen in the lives of these people show that your life was useful in strengthening someone who would have otherwise remained weak. The apostle Paul knew, wrote, and lived this truth.

On his missionary trips, Paul discovered that when God's Spirit led him to those who struggled, their story became part of his story. He met so many people and learned to love them deeply. He recognized that God was writing a story bigger than his own. This divine story was not only important but transformative.

By widening your sphere of influence, you gain confidence because you're no longer alone. God is working in you and others with the goal of bringing His children together to do a work that's greater than the sum of its parts.

A faithful man combines personal humility with the knowledge that he's part of God's bigger story. Serve with others, share in their story, and discover a bond among the faithful and forgiven.

Is it difficult for you to include others in your schedule? How can confidence in a shared goal provide a strength that you'd otherwise forfeit?

BE THE MAN WHO HAS A GOOD REPUTATION

A good name is better than precious ointment;
and the day of death than the day of one's birth.
ECCLESIASTES 7:1 KJV

What is the value of a reputation? In the Old Order Amish community of Lancaster County, Pennsylvania, reputations have financial ramifications.

In a 2008 interview with NPR's Adam Davidson, Bill O'Brien of Hometowne Heritage Bank in Pennsylvania explained how he approaches loans for a community without credit scores. "I'll find out who his dad was," he says. "I'm also interested in who his wife's father is. . . . It takes a team to make a farm go."

Even without credit scores and modern banking tools, Hometowne Heritage Bank has done well with vetting its clients by family reputations. "We've never lost any money on an Amish deal," says O'Brien.

Reputations are built over time, and their ramifications transcend finances. Proverbs 22:1 (KJV) says, "A good name is rather to be chosen than great riches, and loving favour rather than silver and gold."

Why is a good name so valuable? Because it helps people see God in us. First Peter 2:12 (NLT) says, "Be careful to live properly among your unbelieving neighbors. Then even if they accuse you of doing wrong, they will see your honorable behavior, and they will give honor to God when he judges the world."

Our reputations act as shields against unwarranted accusations, testifying to the life-changing effects of God's presence. For a faithful man to have a good reputation, his life must show a consistent pattern of God-honoring choices.

Famous basketball coach John Wooden once said, "Be more concerned with your character than your reputation, because your character is what you really are, while your reputation is merely what others think you are."

When we live intentionally for God's glory, we'll have both.

What are you known for? What is your reputation worth?

BE THE MAN WHO SEES THE IMAGE OF GOD IN OTHERS

"Whoever sheds human blood, by humans shall their blood be shed; for in the image of God has God made mankind."
GENESIS 9:6 NIV

Murder is a big deal. Ending someone's life prematurely cannot be undone, yet it goes even deeper than that. People are valuable not only because they are irreplaceable but because they are made in the image of God. Out of all God's creation, we are the closest thing to Him, so any assault on another person is like an assault on God Himself.

But it's not just murder that offends God so much. Jesus said in Matthew 5:21–22 (NIV), "You have heard that it was said to the people long ago, 'You shall not murder, and anyone who murders will be subject to judgment.' But I tell you that anyone who is angry with a brother or sister will be subject to judgment. Again, anyone who says to a brother or sister, 'Raca,' is answerable to the court. And anyone who says, 'You fool!' will be in danger of the fire of hell."

We are to recognize God's image in people so clearly that we don't even insult them—unless we want to insult their Creator as well. This applies to everyone. Those who don't look, act, or speak like you. Even those who don't value the things you value. To overlook God's image in someone invariably leads to treating that person as less than human.

Sins like human trafficking, slavery, racism, and murder simply wouldn't exist if people valued others as reflections of God Himself. Hating people with differing opinions becomes impossible once you realize they are loved by God.

Today, ask God to open your eyes to see people as He sees them—and to love them as He loves them too.

Have you ever overlooked God's image in another person? How might you treat someone you disagree with as God's image bearer?

BE THE MAN WHO WALKS IN ASSURANCE

Moses summoned Joshua and said to him in the presence of all Israel, "Be strong and courageous, for you must go with this people into the land that the LORD swore to their ancestors to give them, and you must divide it among them as their inheritance. The LORD himself goes before you and will be with you; he will never leave you nor forsake you. Do not be afraid; do not be discouraged."
DEUTERONOMY 31:7–8 NIV

The crowd eagerly awaits the entrance of a high official. But before this person arrives, men in black jackets and sunglasses walk in and "sweep the room," looking for anyone who might have a weapon. Once they leave, the VIP can enter the room without fear.

Wouldn't it be nice to have that level of protection? Well, you do! Because God protects His children, you can be courageous, knowing with absolute certainty that God has swept the room and taken care of any threats. You'll still encounter difficulty, but this protector walks with you inside the trouble zone. He "works for the good of those who love him, who have been called according to his purpose" (Romans 8:28 NIV).

You'll never have abandonment issues with God. He lives where you live, walks where you walk, and knows what you know. This knowledge should leave you with nothing to frighten or discourage you.

Today, walk forward with the confidence that God's plans will move you beyond any trouble you see. . .or simply imagine.

Do you ever worry that God somehow doesn't know about your troubles? How can you dispel this irrational fear and remember that God has already "swept the room"?

BE THE MAN WHO LIVES ASSURED

God also bound himself with an oath, so that those who received the
promise could be perfectly sure that he would never change his mind.
HEBREWS 6:17 NLT

The idea of being "perfectly sure" is impressive. It leaves no room for doubt and results in a growing faith. It implies a friendship that transforms worry and blocks anxiety. It's an invitation to witness a miraculous change. Assurance is just one more aspect of strength—and it doesn't come from you.

God made a promise to you, and He won't (and can't) change His mind. His love for you isn't based on your deeds, and it's never up for annual review.

How different the world would be if Christians truly internalized God's promises—if we were all perfectly sure they'll come true. Gone would be the second guessing, late-night wondering, and our petty comparison games. We'd live without doubt, walk with no fear, and honor God with gratitude.

God's promises are many. Not only can He make you a new creation—He *will*. Not only did He start your story—He'll *finish* it. Not only did He give you life—He's made it *abundant*. His generosity is legendary. His grace is more than enough. His mercies are delivered daily.

A faith-fueled man smiles with joy, lives with purpose, and presses on without hesitation. He celebrates good news and realizes that bad news isn't the final word. He believes the best about God and knows the worst in mankind can be transformed. He knows he's flawed, but he celebrates forgiveness.

These are just some of the things about which a faithful man is perfectly sure.

How does assurance of God's goodness translate into improved
spiritual strength? Why is it hard to be perfectly assured?
Is something preventing you from being certain about God?

BE THE MAN WHO DOES THE FIRST THINGS FIRST

*Put your outdoor work in order and get your
fields ready; after that, build your house.*
PROVERBS 24:27 NIV

If you are going to do something, do it right. This doesn't apply only to the level of craftsmanship you apply. It also means completing jobs in the right order, prioritizing some tasks over others, and finishing what you've started.

Being a faithful, purpose-driven man means having a plan. The best plans put each task in the right order. If you're grilling burgers and you want to top them with cheese and bacon, you need to cook some bacon and make sure the cheese is sliced before you fire up the grill. Otherwise, your burgers will get cold, the cheese won't melt properly, and no amount of bacon will rescue the taste.

The wise planner looks at each step of a job and determines its proper order. Which things can be done ahead of time? Which ones simultaneously? When must I start?

If prioritizing tasks isn't an issue for you, maybe procrastination is. There is a quote, often misattributed to Mark Twain, which says, "If the first thing you do each morning is to eat a live frog, you can go through the day with the satisfaction of knowing that that is probably the worst thing that is going to happen to you all day long."

When eating a live frog is on your to-do list, do it first and move on. Procrastination changes difficult tasks into insurmountable ones.

God wants us to be wise with our time because it's actually His time. Prioritizing tasks and avoiding procrastination allows us to use that time for God's purposes.

How well do you order your to-do list? How often do you procrastinate?

BE THE MAN WHO PERSEVERES UNDER TRIAL

*Blessed is the one who perseveres under trial because, having
stood the test, that person will receive the crown of life
that the Lord has promised to those who love him.*
JAMES 1:12 NIV

We live in dangerous days. Though sin and death have already been defeated, they have yet to be abolished. The devil knows his doom is near, but he's still free to twist the world's systems toward chaos and drag as many souls as possible toward his destiny. There's no chance he'll win, but he has nothing left to lose either.

One method to dampen Christians' effectiveness in spreading the gospel is to make life tough for them. But the danger (for Satan) is that these trials can cause Christians to tap into God's power, making them even more committed.

Another method is to make Christians apathetic about their faith. If they are suitably distracted by the entertainment and comforts of this world, they won't care about spreading the good news of Jesus.

Finally, cheap victories can sometimes make Christians ineffective. Some Christians are satisfied with "likes" on social media when they share a religious post. They unknowingly quote verses out of context because they get warm fuzzies for knowing the Bible—not for applying it accurately. They make it through tough days at the office and expect the crown of life, even though they never share the gospel. If they think they're being effective when they aren't, they'll never pose a risk.

Trials of the faith are different for each person. Persecution—active, apathetic, or sinister—must be met with perseverance. We shouldn't want just to make it through the day but rather to accomplish the mission for which we were born. The reason we persevere is to share Jesus. Are you actively working for that crown of life?

Which of Satan's strategies listed above would be most effective at keeping you from sharing the gospel? With whom might you share the good news today?

BE THE MAN WHO LEAVES HATE BEHIND

"I tell you the truth, I am the gate for the sheep. All who came before me were thieves and robbers. But the true sheep did not listen to them. Yes, I am the gate. Those who come in through me will be saved. They will come and go freely and will find good pastures. The thief's purpose is to steal and kill and destroy. My purpose is to give them a rich and satisfying life."
JOHN 10:10 NLT

People captured during wartime often have harrowing stories to tell. During World War II, people like Louis Zamperini (Olympic runner turned American bomber crew member) and Corrie ten Boom (a Dutch watchmaker who hid Jews in her home) experienced the horrors of Japanese and German prison camps, respectively.

When they were finally released, they had a choice to make: they could spend the rest of their lives hating their captors, or they could forgive and walk into a rich and satisfying life with God.

Satan wants to hold you captive in his own prison of anger and revenge while he destroys everything you love. He hopes you'll be so filled with anger and revenge that these emotions destroy your life.

God, however, chooses to redeem, repair, and restore. When Jesus died on a cross to rescue you, His final words were "Father, forgive them, for they don't know what they are doing" (Luke 23:34 NLT).

God wants an abundant life for you that rejects anger, retaliation, and anything else that's not conducive to new life. A faithful man will pass his worthless mass of hurt, anger, frustration, and pain to the God who knows what to do with it. And then he'll leave it in God's very capable hands.

Why do people tend to crave revenge as a form of fairness?
What would your life be like if God gave you what you deserved?

BE THE MAN WHO ESCAPES THE STENCH

So God has given both his promise and his oath. These two
things are unchangeable because it is impossible for God to lie.
Therefore, we who have fled to him for refuge can have great
confidence as we hold to the hope that lies before us.
HEBREWS 6:18 NLT

Imagine a world filled with uncertainty. Wait. . .you don't have to imagine that—you live in it every day. In this cesspool of uncertainty, the assurance you should celebrate doesn't seem to have room to grow.

But you don't have to live in the stench of this place. You don't have to exist in self-imposed exile. You don't have to fear every noise. God is both your refuge and your strength. Following Him provides all the reasons you need to back away from uncertainty, loneliness, and fear. Run to Him, leaving behind your trepidation. And never go back.

You've been given new life in the midst of old struggles. God's Word can replace the world's "spiritual junk food," causing you to look and act more like the God who brought you new life.

It might be tempting to stand tall and work things out on your own. But all that brings is self-inflicted loneliness. You'll have no one to help, no one to walk with you, and no one with whom to cooperate.

A faithful man will accept help and friendship. He doesn't exist to amass trophies, take home ribbons, and share stories of why he never needed God.

God has a future for you, so when you keep refusing His help, you're simply wasting time.

Have you ever tried to "go it alone" without God's help? What does
it take to trigger your willingness to ask God for help? Why?

BE THE MAN WHO STEPS OUT OF THE BOAT

Then Peter called to him, "Lord, if it's really you, tell me to come to you, walking on the water." "Yes, come," Jesus said. So Peter went over the side of the boat and walked on the water toward Jesus.

MATTHEW 14:28–29 NLT

Peter was a fisherman before becoming a disciple of Jesus. He knew how water typically works. You can't just traipse across the waves without something holding you up. That's why he and the other disciples had a boat. Boats are great for keeping people afloat.

After a full day of teaching crowds and miraculously feeding them with five loaves of bread and two fish, Jesus needed to recharge. Sending the disciples ahead of Him to the other side of the lake, Jesus went up in the hills to pray. But before the disciples reached the other side, Jesus caught up with them, walking on the water.

It wasn't calm water either. A storm was raging. Even though several disciples had seafaring backgrounds, they struggled to keep the boat from sinking. They had seen some incredible things, but seeing a figure approaching them on the water after a sleepless night was too much. They thought Jesus was a ghost.

Matthew 14:27 (NLT) says, "But Jesus spoke to them at once. 'Don't be afraid,' he said. 'Take courage. I am here!' "

Peter must have believed it was Jesus, even before calling back to Him. Why else would he offer to test the ghost's identity by stepping onto a stormy lake? Whatever the reason, Peter stepped out. After hours of trying to keep the boat afloat, Peter knew Jesus was an even safer bet for keeping him above water.

When troubles threaten to capsize your boat, look for Jesus. He's not a ghost waiting for you to fail. He's the Savior who will help you find your feet, even on the waves.

What things do you credit with keeping you afloat?
Do you have the faith needed to step out of the boat?

BE THE MAN WHO ACCOUNTS FOR HIS TIME

So then every one of us shall give account of himself to God.
ROMANS 14:12 KJV

According to a 2019 survey from the United States Bureau of Labor Statistics, on any given weekday, the average male over the age of fifteen spends: 9.13 hours on personal care (including sleep); 1.16 hours eating and drinking; 5.57 hours working and doing work-related activities; 4.86 hours on leisure and sports (including television and web surfing); 0.18 hours—around 11 minutes—on organizational, civic, and religious activities. (The other 3.1 hours on a mix of household activities, educational activities, buying things, talking on the phone, and answering emails.)

Take another look at the numbers for leisure and sports. Now compare them to the numbers for organizational, civic, and religious activities. We spend close to five hours each day entertaining ourselves and around eleven minutes working for our community and for God.

How we spend our time is important. Not only is time a nonrenewable resource that is unpredictable in length, it isn't even *ours*! In the same way that all our riches belong to God and should be used for His glory, our time is His too.

None of us know how much time we have on this earth. James 4:14 (NIV) says, "Why, you do not even know what will happen tomorrow. What is your life? You are a mist that appears for a little while and then vanishes."

Before it vanishes, we can choose whether we will spend our time on ourselves or on others, hiding behind screens or spreading the gospel. Ephesians 5:16 (NLT) reminds us, "Make the most of every opportunity in these evil days."

One day, we'll be called before God to account for how we spent the time He entrusted to us. Yesterday's over—we can't change how we spent it. But we can start spending today on God's priorities so that we can confidently say we made the most of every opportunity.

What would your statistics look like if you were to track your activities for a week? How might you better optimize your time usage for God?

BE THE MAN WHO IS CONTENT TO WAIT

You, therefore, have no excuse, you who pass judgment on someone else, for at whatever point you judge another, you are condemning yourself, because you who pass judgment do the same things. Now we know that God's judgment against those who do such things is based on truth. So when you, a mere human being, pass judgment on them and yet do the same things, do you think you will escape God's judgment? Or do you show contempt for the riches of his kindness, forbearance and patience, not realizing that God's kindness is intended to lead you to repentance?

ROMANS 2:1–4 NIV

Don't you wish that the violent and greedy were banished from modern society? *Why*, you might wonder, *doesn't God do something about it?* There is, after all, a standard of right and wrong—and so many people are clearly in the wrong. Yet the Bible states plainly that everyone (including you) will sin. Evil men as well as good men break His laws.

So when God shows mercy, you should rejoice! Don't get mad at God for showing other sinners the same kindness He's shown you.

Faithful men view God's kindness as a great equalizer. Some people are stubborn, and it's God's kindness (not vengeance) that softens the hardest heart. Ezekiel 36:26 (NIV) explains this process: "I will give you a new heart and put a new spirit in you; I will remove from you your heart of stone and give you a heart of flesh."

Embrace the courage to love imperfect people. Don't follow their example, but follow God's example by believing that anyone can be redeemed. God is still at work among hard men, and the outcome can't be rushed. You can rest assured that your patience will pay off and many men will come to Him.

That's today's good news.

How can you be patient and compassionate to "lost causes"?
What change has God's kindness made in you?

BE THE MAN WHO UNDERSTANDS ANCHORS AND CURTAINS

This hope is a strong and trustworthy anchor for our souls.
It leads us through the curtain into God's inner sanctuary.
HEBREWS 6:19 NLT

Most people don't know much about anchors. Sure, we all know that anchors are designed to keep boats in place. But did you know there are numerous types of anchors? Yes, these handy devices come in types like Danforth, Fluke, Fisherman, Grapnel, Delta, Plows, Bruce, Bügel, Bulwagga, Spade, and Rocna.

There's even a difference between temporary and permanent anchors. The first can hold you in place for a while, but it might come loose, causing a noticeable drift. A permanent anchor, however, is designed to securely keep your ship in place.

But despite their differences, all these anchors have one thing in common—they're heavy. You wouldn't want an anchor made from paper!

There's another word picture in today's verse: curtains. They are designed to be decorative, but they can also be designed to provide separation.

Okay, now back to the verse. The author of Hebrews says that your hope in God is like a permanent soul anchor. He won't let go, even when life's storms try to drive you off course. And this same hope that keeps you from drifting also welcomes you into God's presence. There is no more curtain. The No TRESPASSING sign has been removed, and a welcome mat has been put in its place.

A faithful man understands the value of God's anchor and the freedom in bypassing the curtain that once kept us from God. This hope comes from a perfect trust in a God who wants to spend time with you.

Does thinking of hope as an anchor inspire confidence in God? How can the idea of a removed curtain between you and God make you bold?

BE THE MAN WHO LISTENS BEFORE SPEAKING

To answer before listening—that is folly and shame.
PROVERBS 18:13 NIV

A baby boy is flexible enough to easily place his foot into his mouth. Some grow up to become men who never learn how to stop, figuratively speaking. Fortunately, there are two surefire ways to prevent yourself from saying something embarrassing. First, you can practice your flexibility and literally put your foot in your mouth so that no one can understand what you say. Alternatively, you can listen before speaking.

Listening is the most important part of communication, so how can we improve?

The first step is to focus. Limit anything which would call your attention away from the speaker. Turn off the television. Put down the cell phone. Turn to face the person and maintain eye contact as much as possible.

Second, ask questions based on the information you're hearing. Ask for clarification. Ask what happened next. Let the speaker know you are following the conversation.

Third—and this is the toughest one for men—listen to understand, not to fix. If the speaker asks for your help or opinion, give it. Otherwise, just listen, showing how much you care about what the speaker is saying.

Lastly, don't interrupt. Nothing will send the message that someone's words are unimportant like cutting that person off. Only when a person is finished talking should you respond.

Listening isn't just a polite thing to do. It will benefit every relationship in your life. And not only human relationships but your relationship with Christ too! What if the Lord is trying to speak to you, but you've been too distracted to listen?

How would you rate yourself as a listener?
Which aspect of listening will you work on today?

BE THE MAN WHO LEADS BY EXAMPLE

In everything I did, I showed you that by this kind of hard work
we must help the weak, remembering the words the Lord Jesus
himself said: "It is more blessed to give than to receive."
ACTS 20:35 NIV

If your boss assigned a big work project then took a half-day to work on his backswing, what would you think? You'd probably feel like hard work is useless for helping you get ahead. In fact, maybe you should start working on your golf swing too!

However, what if a manufacturing supervisor took language classes to better communicate with the company's nonnative employees? You'd probably think the company values communication. Maybe you'd even try to pick up a few phrases to better communicate with your colleagues too.

We are always leading by example. People are watching to see if our words line up with our actions and whether our attitudes support our mission. Leading a team—at home, at work, in sports, anywhere—means setting the example that others will *want* to follow.

In the passage where today's verse is found, Paul encouraged the leaders of the Ephesian church to follow his example in a variety of ways: (1) to serve the Lord with humility (verse 19); (2) to speak openly and honestly (verse 20); (3) to welcome all people with open arms, regardless of their background (verse 21); (4) to follow the Holy Spirit's leading, even when it means going through hardship (verses 22–23); (5) to spread the gospel (verse 24); (6) to work hard and give generously to those in need (verse 35)

The Ephesian church knew these qualities were important—not just because Paul said they were but because he lived them out. Are you following Paul's example in these areas of faith? How do your actions back up your words?

In what ways have you led a team by example? Based on the example you've set, what would others say your priorities are?

BE THE MAN WHO SEES STRUGGLE AS VALUABLE

The LORD is my light and my salvation; whom shall I fear? the LORD is the strength of my life; of whom shall I be afraid? When the wicked, even mine enemies and my foes, came upon me to eat up my flesh, they stumbled and fell. Though an host should encamp against me, my heart shall not fear: though war should rise against me, in this will I be confident.

PSALM 27:1–3 KJV

Reading Psalm 27, with its numerous examples of God's goodness, not only inspires courage but invites praise.

Here is a quick summary: There's no enemy that needs to be feared (verse 1). Communication with God is important (verse 4). You are protected by God (verse 5), so He's worthy of your praise (verse 6). When you need help, God hears and answers (verse 7). He can teach you how to withstand the enemy (verse 11). Courage comes when you believe in God's goodness (verse 13) and patiently wait on Him (verse 14).

God knows that blocking your struggles won't produce courage, but He does stand with you as they arrive. If we had nothing to overcome, no enemy to encounter, and no fear to eliminate, why would we ever need courage or the armor of God (see Ephesians 6:10–18)? Patience isn't necessary when everyone agrees with you, and there's no need for an endurance test when everything is perfect.

You should never place your courage in anything other than God— He is good, patient, and wise. You can rest assured that He's orchestrating good outcomes in each bad situation.

Why do you think God allows difficult circumstances to occur?
How can you incorporate Psalm 27 into a courageous life?

BE THE MAN WHO APPROACHES GOD

*This is the confidence we have in approaching God: that if
we ask anything according to his will, he hears us.*
1 JOHN 5:14 NIV

Let's take some time to focus on two words in today's verse: *approaching God.* To come near God, you must believe that He exists, that He can be found, and that He wants to be near you.

Approaching God carries with it the idea of walking with God. You aren't running away or making fun of Him. You see Him as a worthy companion, friend, and walking partner.

By approaching Him, you are proclaiming that you're not afraid of this God who continually expresses love for you. It means you know where to go for answers, whom you can trust with your secrets, and what kind of relationship you want with the God who made you.

Approaching God involves being confident that He wants the best for your life. When you want the same thing, it pleases Him greatly. The strength you'll find in a friendship with God isn't transferable. . .but it is sharable. Your words and actions should cause someone else to want to approach God too. This person might want to walk with Him, learn not to be afraid of Him, and embrace a new strength that frees them from a life of bad decisions.

You can walk with God as a friend. You can find Him and share Him. So why not start today?

Do you find it hard to be confident when praying to God? How can approaching
God bring an undeniable freedom to your friendship with Him?

BE THE MAN WHO GIVES THANKS

O give thanks unto the LORD; for he is good;
for his mercy endureth for ever.
1 CHRONICLES 16:34 KJV

Imagine giving a gift to a child. The child unwraps it, squeals with delight, and immediately starts using it. The child's parents look at you and say, "Awesome gift! Thanks for giving it to our kid."

What's wrong with this scenario?

The child should have been the one to thank you. The parents might be grateful on their kid's behalf, but they weren't the direct recipients. Even though that's not why you gave the gift, a bit of gratitude on the child's part would have made the gift-giving much more satisfying.

Like joy, gratitude is a choice, not just a feeling. It is the intentional recognition of being the recipient of something good. It would be sad indeed if we were to treat God as the child treated you in the above scenario.

What are some simple things to be thankful for? Life, breath, food, water, God's mercy, the freedom to make your own choices. These are all worthy of your gratitude, but if you want to go even further, try being thankful for hard things as well.

First Thessalonians 5:18 (NLT) says, "Be thankful in all circumstances, for this is God's will for you who belong to Christ Jesus."

When a relationship breaks down, thank God for never forsaking you. When you lose your income, thank God for His miraculous provision. When others reject you or mock you for your faith, thank God you can experience what Christ suffered on earth.

Gratefulness is a muscle that's strengthened through intentional use. Are you working it out daily?

What is a good thing you are thankful for?
What is a hard thing you can be thankful for?

BE THE MAN WHO PUBLICLY CALLS OUT SIN

Forgive me for shedding blood, O God who saves;
then I will joyfully sing of your forgiveness.
PSALM 51:14 NLT

Forgiveness is a strange thing to sing about. Most people would agree that receiving forgiveness after you've done wrong is a wonderful feeling, but few people publicly acknowledge what they were forgiven for. The feeling is public, but the sin that required forgiveness stays private.

Apparently, King David didn't get the memo. He wrote Psalm 51—an intensely personal prayer for forgiveness after his adulterous affair with Bathsheba led to the murder of a loyal friend—then had everyone sing it together.

How did David avoid crumbling under the guilt while a congregation sung his sins? How did he not think that joy would be forever out of his reach? Because he knew that God's forgiveness is always greater than our sin.

Instead of dwelling on the severity of the sin, believers should focus on the overwhelming depth of God's forgiveness. When a sin has been forgiven, it loses all power to affect your joy. Christians who are stuck regretting past sins and worrying they'll be found out have never experienced the relief that God's love provides.

Is it strange that David wrote his sins into a song? Maybe a little, but God's forgiveness is worth singing about. Are you holding onto regrets? Take a note from David's songbook and bring them into the light. Allow God's forgiveness to cleanse the old wounds, and then bask in the joy of His forgiveness. Will there be consequences for revealing past sins? Probably, but they can't compare to the feeling of being forgiven.

Are you still gripped with shame over past sins? If so,
how can you publicly "sing" about your forgiveness?

BE THE MAN WHO MAKES A BREAK WITH THE PAST

Moses told the people, "Don't be afraid. Just stand still and watch the LORD rescue you today. The Egyptians you see today will never be seen again."

EXODUS 14:13 NLT

The people of Israel had come to Egypt as guests when a famine struck their land. Over time, however, subsequent Pharaohs began treating the Hebrews as slaves and forbidding them to leave. So when God sent Moses to lead the people out, Pharaoh had no intention of complying.

The following ten plagues changed his mind. The Israelites were happy to leave, and the Egyptians were happy to see them go. But suddenly, once it occurred to Pharaoh that his country no longer had the support of the Israelites' forced labor, he sent troops to bring the slaves back.

The slaves needed courage. An uncrossable sea stretched in front of them, and an army of horses and chariots thundered behind. Moses consulted God, who then split the sea down the middle, leaving a dry path for hundreds of thousands of people to take.

Even after witnessing this miracle, however, the Hebrews would take a while to abandon their slave mentality.

You might feel this way sometimes. As you walk in the new life God gave you, your old life keeps calling you back. Sometimes, you might even start viewing your sinful past through the deceptive lens of nostalgia.

That's when you must stand still and pay attention. God has rescued you from slavery—why on earth would you return?

How often do you think about returning to your old lifestyle? Why does it take courage to wait on God to remove obstacles that seem too big?

BE THE MAN WHO KNOWS THE SOURCE OF CONFIDENCE

*"The hopes of the godless evaporate. Their confidence hangs by a thread.
They are leaning on a spider's web. They cling to their home for security,
but it won't last. They try to hold it tight, but it will not endure."*
JOB 8:13–15 NLT

Bildad was the wise friend of a very rich man named Job. When the latter fell on hard times, the former used his wisdom to make seemingly practical conclusions. In other circumstances, Bildad's statement might have been enshrined as a fresh proverb. Many may have admired the words that flowed from his tongue. But because Bildad left empathy behind, what was otherwise a sound bit of wisdom became a blunt object that Bildad used to accuse Job of wrongdoing.

If you read the first chapter of Job, you'll discover that God's adversary had wanted to harm Job because he was certain God was unfairly protecting him. Job was innocent. Bildad, however, found it impossible to believe that. So this man who called himself Job's friend started kicking him while he was down. He essentially told Job that he had no reason to hope, that his confidence was fleeting, and that his riches would dissolve.

His words, while true for those who are actually godless, didn't bear the mark of a true friend. Bildad spoke without learning the backstory.

Don't let confidence come from what you know. . .but rather from *whom* you know. Love others, walk with them, and trust that God is working in their lives in ways you can't understand. You won't have to know their backstory to walk with them in the presence of your confidence-giving God.

How is confidence in God different from self-confidence? Have you ever allowed the second kind of confidence to replace the first?

BE THE MAN WHO NUMBERS HIS DAYS

*So teach us to number our days, that we
may apply our hearts unto wisdom.*
PSALM 90:12 KJV

With a couple of notable exceptions (see Genesis 5:23–24 and 2 Kings 2:11), everyone dies. Our days are numbered, whether we realize it or not. Psalm 90 opens with the stark difference between God's infinite glory and man's brief lifespan:

"A thousand years in your sight are like a day that has just gone by, or like a watch in the night. Yet you sweep people away in the sleep of death—they are like the new grass of the morning: In the morning it springs up new, but by evening it is dry and withered" (verses 4–6 NIV).

While a bit morbid, the Latin phrase *memento mori*—which means "Remember you will die"—is actually a reminder to live. If death were not a concern, we wouldn't worry about how we spend our time any more than a billionaire worries about clipping coupons.

Sadly, many of us treat time like an unlimited resource. According to a 2018 Neilsen survey, "American adults spend over *eleven hours per day* listening to, watching, reading or generally interacting with media." Our time is valuable, at least to the advertisers paying to show us their products, but how much do *we* value it?

How we spend our time is important. When we waste our lives in front of a screen, we miss opportunities to glorify God, spread the gospel, and pray. Our activities are self-serving rather than God-honoring.

Psalm 90 ends with an appeal for God to imbue our lives with significance. "May the favor of the Lord our God rest on us; establish the work of our hands for us—yes, establish the work of our hands" (verse 17 NIV).

Your days are numbered, and your time is valuable. How will you choose to spend it?

Have you ever measured your average daily screen time?
How could your time be put to better use?

BE THE MAN WHO GIVES HONEST FEEDBACK

A lying tongue hates those it hurts, and a flattering mouth works ruin.
PROVERBS 26:28 NIV

Giving feedback is complicated. What if you don't have many positive things to say? How do you speak the truth without coming off as judgmental? What if the person who requests feedback only wants to hear praise and encouragement instead of constructive criticism? One thing is for sure: you must be honest. Lying will always result in ruin.

If it is your responsibility to provide feedback, there are ways to be both honest and helpful:

- Let your listeners know you care about them as people. A bit of empathy—understanding who they are, where they came from, and what concerns they have—will go a long way toward helping them hear your honest thoughts.
- Understand what people are looking for before you start offering your thoughts. If someone is just looking for encouragement rather than advice, your conversation will look very different. If you don't know what someone wants, just ask.
- Be timely. If you have thoughts to share with someone, don't wait. That person might forget the original incident, and you'll look petty for bringing up mistakes from the distant past.
- Don't forget the good stuff. If all your feedback fixates on stuff that went wrong instead of pointing out the stuff that went well, people will stop listening.

When you are known for being open and honest, your words—both complimentary and constructive—will mean more to whomever you're talking to. But if you lie while giving feedback, your credibility drops. Then the next time something goes seriously wrong, no one will listen even if you present a good way to fix it.

What kind of feedback do you like to hear the most?
Are there any methods above that you could use some work on?

BE THE MAN WHO KNOWS
THE VALUE OF A KIND WORD

*Anxiety weighs down the heart, but a kind word cheers
it up. The righteous choose their friends carefully,
but the way of the wicked leads them astray.*
PROVERBS 12:25–26 NIV

Dale—an elderly, retired man—had a mission in life: helping children learn to swim. Every afternoon, he stood in the waist-deep section of the local pool as children swarmed to visit him. He always brought a waterproof bag filled with coins that he would scatter across the pool's floor, encouraging the children to practice swimming underwater to retrieve them. Along the way, he offered plenty of guidance and praise.

His dedication did not go unnoticed: eventually, this municipal pool was renamed after Dale.

Would parents have felt as kindly about Dale if he had asked their children to swim with weights around their ankles? That would have restricted their freedom of movement, making it hard to stay afloat and leaving them at an obvious disadvantage.

For grown-up guys, "swimming" in a sea of jobs, relationships, and societal craziness, anxiety can attach weights to your ankles. . .and toss you into the deep end. Stress and fear can leave you gasping for air, lungs on fire. God, however, uses Dale's strategy: He offers encouraging words that inspire you to step out in faith, swimming beyond your comfort zone in search of His blessings.

What kind of encouraging words? How about "God demonstrates his own love for us in this: While we were still sinners, Christ died for us" (Romans 5:8 NIV). Or Jesus' promise in John 16:33 (NIV): "I have told you these things, so that in me you may have peace. In this world you will have trouble. But take heart! I have overcome the world."

Does anything routinely weigh you down? How has recognizing
and accepting God's kindness brought freedom to your spirit?

BE THE MAN WHO'S UNDER THE INFLUENCE

The wise fear the LORD and shun evil,
but a fool is hotheaded and yet feels secure.
PROVERBS 14:16 NIV

When you hear someone say an individual is "under the influence," nothing good usually comes to mind. To be under the influence suggests that a man is making very out-of-character (and usually very poor) decisions. Certain substances can induce this altered frame of mind, causing the guy to forget his own choices.

But did you know there are other "influences" that have the same effect?

You can be under the influence of bad advice and make similar poor choices. You could be under the influence of various forms of media, and it might alter how you view the world. You can even be under the influence of an untrue view of yourself, which will cause you to act in ways that don't reflect an accurate assessment of your character or purpose. This is especially obvious with pride, which can wrongly convince you that you're better than most or even cause you to rejoice in the suffering of others.

God wants you to be under the influence of His Word and His plan for your life. He wants you to reject self-assurance—and the harmful choices that often accompany it—for the certainty that He provides.

A faithful man stands in awe of God and resists evil. So today, embrace the confidence that comes solely from His hand. Accept God's strength and stand firmly under His influence.

Has self-confidence ever left you under the wrong influence?
How can you change what influences you?

BE THE MAN WHO IS A CLEAN VESSEL

In a large house there are articles not only of gold and silver, but also of wood and clay; some are for special purposes and some for common use. Those who cleanse themselves from the latter will be instruments for special purposes, made holy, useful to the Master and prepared to do any good work.
2 TIMOTHY 2:20–21 NIV

According to a 2020 report from the National Coffee Association, 62 percent of Americans drink coffee daily, and the number of people surveyed who reported drinking coffee within the past day has risen by 5 percent since 2015. Whether at home, in a restaurant, or at the office, there's one thing all coffee drinkers prefer: a clean cup.

We may differ over light roast or dark roast and whether coffee should be enjoyed black or with cream and sugar, but no one argues for drinking from a filthy mug. We don't stop there though: most people have a favorite mug. According to researchers, nearly 60 percent of us have an "emotional attachment" to our favorite mug, and 38 percent would consider hiding it so others couldn't use it.

Now imagine the roof starts leaking over your desk. Ideally, you'd grab a bucket to catch the water, but your favorite coffee mug is already beside you. Or imagine needing a place to put a bunch of flowers. A vase would be your first choice, but what if the mug were closer? In either case, the next time you wanted coffee, you'd definitely make sure your mug was cleaned out before pouring in some java again.

In 2 Timothy, Paul compares us to household vessels. Some are made of gold and others from clay. But it doesn't matter what we're made of; if we are clean and willing, we'll be set aside and "made holy, useful to the Master and prepared to do any good work" (2:21 NIV).

Want to be God's favorite mug? Start by asking Him to cleanse you. Then be willing to do whatever He asks.

How are you like your favorite mug? What might God need to cleanse in you before you are willing to be used?

BE THE MAN WHO KNOWS UNMEASURABLE LOVE

So that Christ may dwell in your hearts through faith. And I pray that you, being rooted and established in love, may have power, together with all the Lord's holy people, to grasp how wide and long and high and deep is the love of Christ, and to know this love that surpasses knowledge—that you may be filled to the measure of all the fullness of God.

EPHESIANS 3:17–19 NIV

The road to God's strength isn't paved with peace and prosperity—it's a rugged ride headlong into the wind of God's great adventure. You'll face opposition, you'll become weary, and you'll start wondering if the troubles are worth it after all.

But you'll also witness something that far outweighs these difficulties. You'll get to experience a love that can't be measured or understood. You'll get to learn that God remains with you, even when others run away.

If life were perpetually easy, what use would you have for God's strength? If work came without effort, how would you ever overcome the temptation of weariness? If there were no bad days, why would God ever need to encourage you?

There's nothing bigger than God, stronger than His love, or richer than His mercy. Because trouble is a promise, so too is your access to the strength that helps you overcome this trouble.

Gain strength from knowing there's no place you can go where God's love won't follow you. There's nothing you can do that will cause God to turn His love away. Never mistake trouble for a lack of love—consider it an opportunity for God to show you how much He cares.

When was the last time you sought strength in the fact that God loves you? How can God's love strengthen your spiritual spine?

BE THE MAN WHO KNOWS GOD COUNTS HAIRS

Are not two sparrows sold for a farthing? and one of them shall not fall on the ground without your Father. But the very hairs of your head are all numbered. Fear ye not therefore, ye are of more value than many sparrows. Whosoever therefore shall confess me before men, him will I confess also before my Father which is in heaven.
MATTHEW 10:29–32 KJV

A quick search on your computer, phone, or tablet will reveal that the average number of hairs on a human head is one hundred thousand. However, only God knows the exact amount—nobody else has the time to count.

Similarly, if you look online for the price of birds, you might be surprised to find some figures meandering into the thousands. But those are for the colorful and exotic species from around the world. There's one bird that these websites likely won't mention: sparrows. They are so common that they're easy to overlook.

God, however, made the whole world the sparrows' cage—and He provides an abundance of food for them in the grass, the dirt, and the cracks in the sidewalks. And if God's care extends to both hair counts and the ubiquitous sparrows, how much more extensive must be His care for His human family members?

Today, be the man who's convinced that God loves His own children most.

Have you ever considered that God cares for even the smallest things? How can this information bolster your courage?

BE THE MAN WHO TAKES THE COURSE CORRECTION

The LORD's justice will dwell in the desert, his righteousness live in the fertile field. The fruit of that righteousness will be peace; its effect will be quietness and confidence forever. My people will live in peaceful dwelling places, in secure homes, in undisturbed places of rest.
ISAIAH 32:16–18 NIV

Isaiah seems like a book of doom mixed equally with gloom, with a liberal dash of despair for bad measure. This book tells the story of a people who rejected God and ignored His warnings. Maybe they thought He would never actually correct their behavior. After all, they'd been living in the wild embrace of sin for a very long time. They probably felt they were getting away with it. They might have felt God was too weak to mount a challenge to their lawbreaking ways.

They were wrong.

When the promised exile happened, it probably looked like chaos. . . but it was a promised alteration that would eventually lead them to newly discovered obedience.

God reinstated the high bar of righteousness for a people who had long forgotten what it looked like. He brought justice to facilitate His course correction. But then came His great and profound promise— peace, quietness, and confidence. Soon, this out-of-control crowd would finally obey. And when that happened, they would have security and rest. A national sigh of spiritual relief was just ahead.

What God wants to give us is exactly what we should want. It's certainly what we need. A faithful man is wise enough to trade chaos for peace, restlessness for rest, and uncertainty for confidence.

Do you need a course correction in your friendship with God? Are you willing to make that happen? How might you begin today?

BE THE MAN WHO KNOWS HOW TO BE GENTLE

*Always be humble and gentle. Be patient with each other,
making allowance for each other's faults because of your love.*
EPHESIANS 4:2 NLT

Relative to their size, jaguars have the strongest bite force—about 1,500 pounds per square inch (psi)—of any of the world's big cats. For comparison, humans bite with a force between 150–200 psi. Jaguars, unlike other big cats which go for the throat, kill by crushing the skulls of their prey. Even so, jaguars also use their jaws to carefully carry their young.

As cubs, jaguars are born with their eyelids sealed shut, and they can't open them for about two weeks. They don't start learning to hunt or fend for themselves until they're about six months old. Until then, they are completely vulnerable and require their mother's constant attention.

Weakness is like a newborn jaguar cub, while gentleness is like a jaguar mother caring for that cub. Mistaking one for the other could be fatal. Being gentle implies the restraining—not deficiency—of strength.

Likewise, humility is not the absence of greatness. It is the decision not to brag when the world thinks we could.

For the faithful man, this behavior is the natural response to God's gentleness and humility toward us. Colossians 3:12 (NLT) says, "Since God chose you to be the holy people he loves, you must clothe yourselves with tenderhearted mercy, kindness, humility, gentleness, and patience."

If God has chosen you to be His child, you can choose to restrain your strength while dealing with others and remain silent when you feel like bragging. Only then will others see Him in you.

Have you ever confused weakness with gentleness? How can you
better restrain your strength so that others can see God in you?

DAY 354

BE THE MAN WHO IS KNOWN BY HIS LOVE

*Beloved, let us love one another: for love is of God; and every
one that loveth is born of God, and knoweth God. He
that loveth not knoweth not God; for God is love.*
1 JOHN 4:7–8 KJV

Some guys are known for certain things. Sean Connery was known for his accent (*ack-shent*, in Connery-ese). John Wayne was known for his ability to play the quintessential cowboy. Abraham Lincoln was known for his honesty (and for holding the Union together, but he'll always be remembered as "Honest Abe"). Christians are to be known for their love.

In John 13:35 (KJV), Jesus says, "By this shall all men know that ye are my disciples, if ye have love one to another."

There are two solid ways to ensure that you're known for something. The first: get caught doing something so distinctive that it ingrains itself into everyone's memory. Imagine seeing a guy who's knuckle deep up his nostril when you first meet him. You'd think of him as "the nose picker" from then on.

The other is to consistently do a thing (speak with a unique accent, act multiple times in a distinctive role, or be honest) for long enough that people come to associate you with that thing.

For us Christians to be known for our love, both methods are effective. We should strive to be caught showing love to others in practical ways as often as possible, and then we are to reinforce that perception by consistently loving people over a long period of time.

The long-term goal is that no other characteristic will "outdistinguish" your love. If you are fifteen feet tall, people should still know you as a loving Christian first and as a tall guy second. Why? Because you use your incredible height in the service of the gospel.

May you employ every characteristic in your identity to spread God's love and let others know you love Him.

Whose first impression has stuck with you the longest? What's the
next way you can be caught showing God's love to someone?

BE THE MAN WHO HAS A PLACE RESERVED

*[Jesus said,] "Don't let your hearts be troubled. Trust in God,
and trust also in me. There is more than enough room in
my Father's home. If this were not so, would I have told
you that I am going to prepare a place for you?"*
JOHN 14:1–2 NLT

The story of Christmas is probably familiar to you. Jesus wasn't born in
the local palace or in the presence of kings. No, He was born in a Beth-
lehem stable because there was "no lodging available" (Luke 2:7 NLT).
While every child is a miracle, Jesus was, to most, just one more in a sea
of babies.

Jesus, however, knew things would be this way. His plan was bigger
than the notions of the spiritual elite. Because His plan didn't conform
to their best guesses, Jesus became an outcast to the very men who'd been
looking for His arrival their entire lives. He was not welcome here, but
His lack of acceptance did not derail His mission or stop Him from welcoming sinners. He spoke honestly, loved completely, and forgave those
who took His life.

Long before our planet was created, God began preparing a place
for His family. There's more than enough room, and faithful men long
to be there.

Refuse to let doubt turn into disbelief. Ask God questions, not as a
skeptic but as an eager student who's willing to learn. God won't hang out
a NO VACANCY sign—His Son has left a light on just for you.

He wants you to find Him.

How can you convert any doubts you entertain into trust? Why did
Jesus make room for you even before you became part of His family?

BE THE MAN WHO CHOOSES FIRM STEPS

[God] lifted me out of the slimy pit, out of the mud and mire;
he set my feet on a rock and gave me a firm place to stand.
PSALM 40:2 NIV

We've all experienced setbacks that have left us sitting in a filthy pit of despair, wondering how we'll ever get out of this mess. We live on the fringes of this pit every day. One false move, and we're stuck and in need of help. But Psalm 40:2 offers some great news: we have a flashlight! Every day, we can access the wisdom of God's Word so that we can confidently know where to step.

Sometimes, spiritual failure is the most effective way to learn wisdom. But this route is never mandatory or even advisable. Intentionally breaking God's law to gain a better testimony should never be your goal.

You'll never gain God's strength by disregarding His guidance or walking with the wrong company. When you refuse strength that only God can give, you're declaring that you have every intention of remaining weak. Does that sound like a good admission to you?

You can—and should—possess strength. You can be weak all by yourself, but strength is a gift that's sourced in God. Allow Him to release your feet from the "sin mud" that keeps you a prisoner to bad choices.

Then. . .watch your step!

Where have your spiritual feet led you lately?
How often do you let God know you want to be strong?

BE THE MAN WHO STAYS COOL

*Have no fear of sudden disaster or of the ruin that
overtakes the wicked, for the LORD will be at your
side and will keep your foot from being snared.*
PROVERBS 3:25–26 NIV

Insurance salesmen love to pitch their products as peace of mind for people entering risky situations. Homes and vehicles, unexpected medical costs, and even the death of a loved one are all covered by various types of insurance. One London-based insurance firm has even sold more than thirty thousand alien abduction insurance policies throughout Europe, provided its policyholders have physical proof of their abduction.

Insurance companies thrive on the fear of uncontrollable circumstances. And while getting coverage for our belongings, health, and lives is important, we as God's children shouldn't fear the uncontrollable—since we know God controls everything.

Bad things happen, but we're not to react to them as the world does. When earthquakes and wildfires strike, we can trust God. When people turn against us or enemies attack, we know God still fights for us and encourages us to react with love.

In Matthew 5:43–45 (NIV), Jesus says, "You have heard that it was said, 'Love your neighbor and hate your enemy.' But I tell you, love your enemies and pray for those who persecute you, that you may be children of your Father in heaven. He causes his sun to rise on the evil and the good, and sends rain on the righteous and the unrighteous."

Insurance doesn't hold a candle to the peace of mind God gives. Even if our physical belongings or bodies are destroyed, nothing can separate us from God's love (see Romans 8:38–39). He has not insured our lives against trouble—He has insured our souls against harm.

Do you stay cool as the world around you burns? How can your eternal
insurance help you navigate life when you experience trouble?

BE THE MAN WHO DOESN'T SEEK REVENGE

*Do not repay anyone evil for evil. Be careful
to do what is right in the eyes of everyone.*
ROMANS 12:17 NIV

In ancient times (as in certain areas in the world today) people lived in a culture of honor. Things like reputation determined a person's worth. If someone threatened you with violence, you'd escalate the violence to maintain your social image. If someone injured you, you'd strike back with murder. The stakes would keep rising until no one dared challenge the winner.

Therefore, the Old Testament's nonescalated form of justice (see Exodus 21:23–25) represented a huge cultural step forward. Revenge was now governed by authorities, and victims could appeal to a common standard for their wrongs.

By the time Jesus came on the scene, culture had shifted again—this time toward recognizing personal dignity. Citizens were able to appeal to an established system of laws and have a certain amount of trust that the government would enforce those laws. An eye for an eye was no longer the aspirational standard because Jesus wanted people to see that true justice could be found only in the person and timing of God Himself.

That's why Matthew 5:39 (NIV)—"I tell you, do not resist an evil person. If anyone slaps you on the right cheek, turn to them the other cheek also"—sounds so unlike the Old Testament law.

If revenge had a place in antiquity, its goal was to provide a man with a strong reputation and relative safety. In serving God, our reputations are to be kept pure in different ways, and our strength is found in our reliance on Him. Any vengeance we might take on our attackers cannot stand up to the justice God has already secured.

Today, a faithful man of honor—as opposed to a culture of honor—recognizes God's image in others and treats them with His love.

Do you feel the need to get even with others? Can you think of a time in
which you—or even someone you hurt—turned the other cheek?

BE THE MAN WHO'S WILLING TO REORGANIZE PRIORITIES

The LORD is my shepherd; I shall not want. He maketh me to lie down in green pastures: he leadeth me beside the still waters. He restoreth my soul: he leadeth me in the paths of righteousness for his name's sake. Yea, though I walk through the valley of the shadow of death, I will fear no evil: for thou art with me; thy rod and thy staff they comfort me. Thou preparest a table before me in the presence of mine enemies: thou anointest my head with oil; my cup runneth over. Surely goodness and mercy shall follow me all the days of my life: and I will dwell in the house of the LORD for ever.

PSALM 23:1–6 KJV

Young people focus on everything they want to accomplish in a career. They have dreams, aspirations, and ideas they want to explore. During this invigorating time in life, it's hard to accept that anything is impossible. By middle age, however, doubts start creeping in about the importance of everything you sought to achieve. As you continue to mature, your priorities begin to shift. You started bold, but your boldness is gradually turning to *courage*. Eventually, your long-term goals lead to a different place entirely.

If you've been paying attention, then you've seen the fingerprints of God's mercy scattered throughout your life. He's been there in job loss, health crises, and the death of a loved one. When trouble comes, things you thought were important take a back seat, and the truly vital things become job one. Your new, eternal life with God overshadows any of your past achievements.

Today, what will you pay attention to—temporal possessions or God's infinitely better promises?

Have your priorities changed with the passing of time? If so, how have these changes impacted your willingness to follow God?

BE THE MAN WHO EMBRACES MANHOOD

*When I was a child, I spake as a child, I understood as a child, I thought
as a child: but when I became a man, I put away childish things.*
1 CORINTHIANS 13:11 KJV

We'll never become faithful men if we aren't willing to grow up. We must
put away childish things, growing into our identities as men of God.

When other men chase after the things of this world, our priorities
should be different. First Timothy 6:11 (NIV) says, "But you, man of God,
flee from all this, and pursue righteousness, godliness, faith, love, endurance and gentleness."

Righteousness and godliness were made possible for us through
Christ's sacrifice. Second Corinthians 5:21 (NIV) says, "God made him
who had no sin to be sin for us, so that in him we might become the
righteousness of God."

Our example will put us at odds with the world. Second Timothy
3:12–13 (NIV) says "In fact, everyone who wants to live a godly life in
Christ Jesus will be persecuted, while evildoers and impostors will go
from bad to worse, deceiving and being deceived."

Even in persecution, though, we know we're on the right side.

As men, we must have faith stronger than doubt, love stronger than
hate, endurance stronger than temptation, and gentleness stronger than
anger. For all this, we need God's help.

Being a man doesn't mean going solo against the world. It means
partnering with the one who has overcome the world, inviting Him into
every area of our lives and freely admitting our need for His grace, mercy,
strength, and peace.

When we embrace our purpose as men, we can share in Paul's joy
and confidence "that he who began a good work in you will carry it on to
completion until the day of Christ Jesus" (Philippians 1:6 NIV).

Are you maturing in your faith? In what areas can you pray for God's assistance?

BE THE MAN WHO SHOWS NO PARTIALITY

My dear brothers and sisters, how can you claim to have faith in our glorious Lord Jesus Christ if you favor some people over others?
JAMES 2:1 NLT

Celebrities live in a different world than common folk. They are recognized in public, often surrounded by bodyguards, and harassed by the paparazzi's constant attempts to take embarrassing photos of them. The challenges of fame do come with some unique benefits, however.

An investigation by NBC Los Angeles reported the story of Yolanda Baskin, who was in the midst of a sixteen-month battle with cancer but forced to wait for emergency treatment. Why? Because rapper Kanye West had supposedly been admitted to the same hospital on the same day for exhaustion. Yolanda's husband, Robert Baskin, said, "There was obviously a greater security presence then what there typically was. It definitely impacted our getting to the hospital, it definitely impacted the time of getting her in there."

In an interview about the preferential medical treatment given to celebrities, Robert Pedowitz, former chairman of UCLA's orthopedic surgery department, said, "The ethics of it would suggest that every person who's at the medical center deserves the same access, the same treatment and the same protocols, so it is not fair."

It isn't fair to treat those with fame and power differently, especially when lives are on the line. But how often does this happen in churches, where eternal lives are at stake? Churches justify special treatment because wealthy people can afford to give greater gifts to the church. Or maybe they don't even realize they're treating people differently.

Remember, the only wealth that matters is your connection to God and your ability to connect others to Him. How can you use that wealth to make the world a healthier place?

Have you ever been unjustly treated because someone was richer than you? What does showing partiality in church say to those who are not wealthy or powerful?

BE THE MAN WHO PRAYS FOR COURAGE—FOR HIMSELF AND FOR OTHERS

*And pray in the Spirit on all occasions with all kinds of prayers
and requests. With this in mind, be alert and always keep on
praying for all the Lord's people. Pray also for me, that whenever
I speak, words may be given me so that I will fearlessly make
known the mystery of the gospel, for which I am an ambassador
in chains. Pray that I may declare it fearlessly, as I should.*
EPHESIANS 6:18–20 NIV

When you ask people to pray for you, do you ask them to pray that God takes your trouble away or that He enables you to endure it?

Both are good prayer policies. The apostle Paul struggled tremendously as he followed Jesus. He even asked God three times to remove "a thorn in the flesh" (see 2 Corinthians 12:7 KJV; nobody knows exactly what the "thorn" was). However, in Ephesians 6, Paul also asked people to pray for him so that he could courageously say, "There's no price I'm unwilling to pay to keep sharing the truth."

Paul called himself an ambassador because he represented Christ to the world. Sometimes his audience responded with skepticism, hostility, and even violence. Not everyone who heard good news accepted it as such.

You can (and should) pray for God's comfort and relief from the things that are too difficult for you, but don't forget also to pray for the ability to withstand them. Sometimes, God will answer the second prayer before He answers the first.

> If you could choose between asking for relief or asking
> for endurance, which option would you take? Why?

BE THE MAN WHO IS WARY OF FALSE MARKETING

Woe unto them that call evil good, and good evil;
that put darkness for light, and light for darkness;
that put bitter for sweet, and sweet for bitter!
ISAIAH 5:20 KJV

Companies love making money. If they didn't, they wouldn't stay in business. Problems arise, however, when companies use deceptive marketing tactics—also known as lies—to convince people to buy their products. When a company gets caught lying to its customers, it runs afoul of the Federal Trade Commission.

In 2014 Red Bull, the energy drink company, got into trouble with a group of consumers for its slogan "Red Bull gives you wings." Although consumers probably didn't expect the drink to transform them into angelic beings, the slogan ran alongside statements that suggested the drink could improve someone's concentration and reflexes. That's where things went awry. Red Bull settled the lawsuit out of court and gave out ten dollars to every US consumer who had bought the drink since 2002.

Whenever a company claims a product will do something amazing—increase focus, provide instant weight loss, make you smarter, and so on—it's wise to seek supporting evidence. Whenever someone offers you big rewards for low efforts, look for what you're not being told.

The forces of evil have a history of using lies to get humans into trouble. Remember Eden? That was a masterful bit of false marketing! Just make sure you don't fall for the same schemes. The only great deal out there is salvation, but even that cost Jesus His life—and it will cost you your devotion.

Do you scrutinize situations that seem too good to be true?
What questions could you ask about an offer to see if it is legit?

BE THE MAN WHO ACCEPTS A COMMISSION

Jesus came and told his disciples, "I have been given all authority in heaven and on earth. Therefore, go and make disciples of all the nations, baptizing them in the name of the Father and the Son and the Holy Spirit. Teach these new disciples to obey all the commands I have given you. And be sure of this: I am with you always, even to the end of the age."
MATTHEW 28:18–20 NLT

You need direction—everyone does. You need an assignment—God gives them to His followers. You may not recognize your mission at first due to its seeming simplicity. It could be holding the door open for someone or politely waving at a grumpy neighbor. These random acts of kindness often make the most impact and can affect a person's life much longer than you might think.

God commissions ambassadors like you to be faithful men of courage who recruit by sharing the truth about the Christian life. You will do everyone a disservice if you declare that Christians never struggle or make mistakes. If you're honest, you'll easily admit that you have struggles. . .but also that you don't face them alone.

Courage is vital to your commission. You'll go places you wouldn't normally go and talk to people you've never noticed before. God wants to make it clear that He is with you today, tomorrow, and the rest of your existence.

When your struggles come, they will also go. When trouble finds you, God will eventually show it the door. When pain appears, your promised future will one day banish it forever.

Faithful men share this wonderful news to everyone who needs to know.

How can the idea that God has commissioned you motivate you to share your faith? How can you use your struggles to connect with others when talking about God?

BE THE MAN WHO WEARS ONE FACE

With the tongue we praise our Lord and Father, and with it we curse human beings, who have been made in God's likeness. Out of the same mouth come praise and cursing. My brothers and sisters, this should not be. Can both fresh water and salt water flow from the same spring? My brothers and sisters, can a fig tree bear olives, or a grapevine bear figs? Neither can a salt spring produce fresh water.

JAMES 3:9–12 NIV

There's a famous anecdote about Abraham Lincoln from one of his political debates with Stephen Douglas. During the debate, Douglas accused Lincoln of being two-faced, to which the self-effacing Lincoln replied, "If I had two faces, would I be wearing this one?"

Today's passage outlines how everyone can present two faces to the world. We praise God then treat His image bearers like dirt. As James states, this should not be.

Being an honorable, faithful man means showing only one face to the world, no matter how homely it is. It means using our words to tell the world how God's Spirit dwells within us. It means recognizing others as made in His image, and thus inherently deserving of dignity and respect.

When our words flip-flop depending on our audience—if we act holy on Sunday morning and wholly selfish the rest of the week—our ability to show others the life-changing power of Jesus is diminished. Or perhaps we haven't experienced it in the first place.

Unfortunately, those who put on a faithful act make it extremely difficult for the world to take seriously those who truly are faithful to God. It isn't the imperfect but honest man who messes things up for Christians; it's the two-faced man who wants the assurance of heaven while roasting marshmallows over the flames of hell.

Today, listen while you speak to hear whether your words line up with the Spirit inside you. Watch and see how your actions are spreading God's love. Look in the mirror and see if you notice two faces looking back.

Why is a two-faced Christian a greater threat to the faith than an unbeliever? Are there any ways you can be more genuine in expressing your faith?

SCRIPTURE INDEX

OLD TESTAMENT

NEW TESTAMENT

DEVOTIONS FOR GUYS WHO LOVE GOD'S CREATION

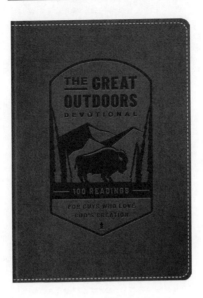

The earth. . .the animals and plants. . .the sun and stars. . .all tell of God if we'll simply listen. This 100-entry devotional draws parallels between your Christian faith and those fascinating features of the great outdoors. Plus, you'll enjoy questions for further thought and the prayer starters with each reading.

Flexible DiCarta / ISBN 978-1-63609-878-4